Appraisal, Feedback and Development

Performance appraisal is an almost universal feature of organisational life. Most organisations operate systems for monitoring and developing staff performance, but few develop these systems to their maximum potential. In this fully revised and updated edition of his ground-breaking book on performance appraisal, Clive Fletcher explores the key elements of the appraisal process, and through best practice examples explains how such processes can motivate and develop staff, fostering commitment and positivity, and ultimately improving an organisation's performance.

Drawing on the wider critical literature on performance management and organisational psychology, and based firmly on evidence-based analysis and organisational experience, the book stresses the vital role of performance appraisal in the identification, development and retention of talent. It includes comprehensive discussions of key topics such as:

- Designing appraisal schemes
- Appraisal as an ingredient of performance management
- Multi-level, multi-source ('360 degree') feedback
- Identifying and assessing potential
- Implementing appraisal with professional groups
- The international and cultural adaptation of appraisal systems

Exploring both public and private sector contexts, this is essential reading for all students of human resource management and business psychology, and for any manager or HRM professional looking to develop more effective performance appraisal systems.

Clive Fletcher is Emeritus Professor of Occupational Psychology at Goldsmiths College, University of London and Honorary Professor at Warwick Business School. He is also Managing Director of Personnel Assessment Limited, has been involved in research on appraisal and development for over 25 years and is a consultant to a wide range of organisations.

Appraisal, Feedback and Development

Clive Fletcher

Routledge
Taylor & Francis Group

LONDON AND NEW YORK

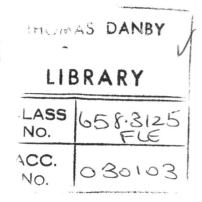
First published 2008 by Routledge
2 Park Square, Milton Park, Abingdon, Oxon, OX14 4RN

Simultaneously published in the USA and Canada
by Routledge
270 Madison Avenue, New York, NY 10016

Routledge is an imprint of the Taylor & Francis Group, an informa business

Transferred to Digital Printing 2010

Typeset in Sabon by Graphicraft Limited, Hong Kong

British Library Cataloguing in Publication Data
A catalogue record for this book is available from the British Library

Library of Congress Cataloging in Publication Data
Fletcher, Clive
Appraisal, feedback and development / Clive Fletcher.
p. cm.
Rev. ed. of: Appraisal and feedback, 3rd edn. 2004
Includes bibliographical references and index.
1. Employees—Rating of   2. Performance standards.
I. Title.
HF5549.5.R3F557 2007
658.3'125—dc22   2007027078

ISBN10: 0-415-44690-2 hbk
ISBN10: 0-415-44691-0 pbk

ISBN13: 978-0-415-44690-7 hbk
ISBN13: 978-0-415-44691-4 pbk

Contents

Preface and acknowledgements

This is a new version of a book that has been in print for about 15 years now, so I suppose I must have been doing something right! However, it might still be helpful to explain some of the rationale behind the way the material is presented and the changes made for this edition. Perhaps the biggest shift has been to make the book more suitable for students. Although originally conceived of as a book mainly for HR practitioners or Occupational Psychologists, it has been widely recommended for various courses and professional qualification programmes. In view of this, the present edition incorporates summaries and students' questions or discussion points, as well as being more heavily referenced. There is always the danger that the last mentioned can break up the flow of the text, but most of the additional referencing is kept to areas where there has been a good deal of research output in recent times, so I hope that it combines the academic and the practical without detracting from the overall ease of comprehension. There is always a danger of falling between two stools in trying to meet the needs of student and practitioner audiences, but in this instance I have not so much fallen as deliberately dived between them – because I strongly believe in evidence-based practice, and also that students who are studying topics in this area should be given a good grasp of the practical realities and not just the theory.

In terms of other changes for this edition, apart from general updating, three areas stand out. The first is the ever-greater use of multi-source, or 360-degree, feedback. The two chapters devoted to this have been expanded to reflect that growth and the increasing knowledge base about what such feedback processes achieve and the factors that impact on their effectiveness. The second is a lengthening of the chapter on assessing and developing potential – something that organisations have become more focused on in recent years as they have increasingly recognised the need to nurture the talent they already have rather than simply seek fresh transfusions from outside. This chapter does range in some depth over a number of subjects – assessment centres, psychometrics, interviewing – which might at first glance seem outside the scope of a book on performance appraisal, but in view of the development of appraisal as a series of interrelated processes, it is important for anyone working in this field to have a good understanding of them. The third main change relates to a fuller treatment of the influence of cultural differences on performance appraisal; cultural diversity is a subject of growing significance for many organisations with the internationalisation of business and the freer movement of labour, and a chapter of the book is devoted specifically to looking at some of the possible ramifications for appraisal practices.

In many instances, I have presented examples of particular organisations' practices to illustrate points. Whilst some of these are not new examples, others are – however, even amongst the latter – given the rate that organisations change – these may have been superseded by different approaches in the organisations concerned. The important thing, though, is that they still communicate a flavour of what organisations actually do. Turning to another aspect of content, despite the considerable increase in the amount of citations and references to be found in the pages that follow, I have still laced the book with some of my own experiences and anecdotes. Whilst this may reflect a degree of indulgence on my part, I hope it makes the book a little more personal and perhaps adds a little colour in places – anyway, the feedback has been positive! Talking of feedback, I would like to thank Dr Jenny King (Edgecumbe Consulting Group), Richard Williams (Home Office and Birkbeck College) and Lynne Spencer for their helpful comments and suggestions on the content of the book. Finally, my thanks as ever are due to my family, and in particular my wife Linda and my sons Daniel and Jed, not least for leaving me alone in my study to get on with writing it (relatively) undisturbed.

Disclaimer

The publishers have made every effort to contact authors/copyright holders of works reprinted in this new edition of *Appraisal, Feedback and Development*. This has not been possible in every case, however, and we would welcome correspondence from those individuals/companies whom we have been unable to trace.

Chapter 1

Appraisal today

This is intended to be a book on appraisal that gives the reader both a sound grasp of the academic theory and research base that underpins the ever widening concept of performance appraisal and also of the practical issues that arise in assessing and developing performance in the workplace. As such, it is aimed both at those on formal courses and programmes which include or specifically focus on the subject of appraisal, and at personnel professionals, consultants and line managers who have the responsibility for setting up appraisal systems or revising existing ones. The vast majority of organisations already have some kind of appraisal arrangements in place, so most readers in the latter categories are probably seeking to build on previous appraisal work in their organisation. It would be nice to think that this new building will be on sound foundations rather than on the ruins of an appraisal system that has become discredited, but experience suggests that this is not always going to be the case (see, for example, Catano *et al.*, 2007). There are few more persistent topics of dissatisfaction in organisations than the appraisal scheme. A study by Hirsh (2006) found that only a third of HR professionals felt appraisal achieved its objectives and that most appraisees could not think of more than one or two appraisal discussions that had helped improve their performance. It is scarcely more popular amongst those who have to make it work, the appraisers; in one survey of managers in the US, 15 per cent of them said they would prefer a visit to the dentist than carrying out an appraisal!

Indeed, appraisal has become an emotive word. This is partly because it tends to be done rather poorly and partly because organisations persist in ignoring the clear messages academic research provides about what will and won't work, and why. Perhaps as a result of this unpopularity, many organisations have displayed considerable ingenuity in thinking up alternative titles for what is often much the same process: 'Performance Reviews', 'Work Planning and Review' and the like. The drift of these changes has been to emphasise the more forward-looking aspects of appraisal, and to play down the retrospective assessment element. But it takes more than a change of name to shift people's perceptions, and staff still usually refer to it as 'the appraisal' irrespective of any new label it has been given.

No matter how hard it is to devise a satisfactory performance appraisal scheme, there is no real alternative to turn to. Appraisal will take place in an unstructured and perhaps highly subjective form wherever and whenever people work together. They will automatically form judgments about their own abilities and performance and that of their colleagues. To try to deny this is foolish. Have you ever talked to employees who had no opinions about their bosses, their peers, their subordinates, or themselves? Organisations that try to avoid the issue by not having an appraisal scheme will simply end up having the same processes occurring without them being open to scrutiny or to control, with all the potential for bias and unfairness that this holds.

So, appraisal is here to stay. But the wider context in which it is set has changed. The advent of performance management, with its more strategic and holistic approach to organisational and individual performance, gives performance appraisal a central role in a more integrated and dynamic set of HR systems. Potentially, as is explained more fully in Chapter 4, this offers an opportunity for performance appraisal to achieve more than it could do alone in the past. It also brings with it some more problems, too. Performance-related pay (PRP) is often a part of performance management – though it is by no means essential to that approach – and has become more widespread in the UK. Inevitably, PRP tends to have some links with appraisal, and both research and experience indicate that this can create many pitfalls in constructing an effective appraisal scheme (see Chapter 4). Fortunately, there has been a balancing trend in recent years which has emphasised the developmental aspects of appraisal, and its role in identifying staff with potential to move onward and upward. The greater attention given to this more forward-looking approach is reflected in Chapter 10.

Another major change has been appraisal's wider application. Within the public sector, appraisal has been used in the UK Civil Service for many years, but now it has been introduced into schools, universities, healthcare settings and local government. These widely differing organisations present a fresh challenge for appraisal to demonstrate its relevance to such diverse needs and groups. However, the increased range of application does not simply cover types of organisation. There has been a steady trend towards covering more staff levels, too. Where once it was the case that just middle and senior managerial groups were appraised, we now find that top management, scientific and professional staff, secretarial and clerical staff and operatives are often included, although the nature of their appraisal may be somewhat different. And with the increasing internationalisation of business, appraisal now takes in staff from more varied cultural and ethnic backgrounds (Bailey and Fletcher, 2007). Managing diversity is very much part of what appraisal is about – though there is precious little written about the impact of culture in the appraisal literature (see Chapter 12).

Finally, in terms of changes, many organisations have undergone quite radical restructuring throughout the last ten years. They have become more organic and less mechanistic, with fewer management levels and more flexible modes of operating. Managers have to build and manage teams that cross organisational – and sometimes international – boundaries and may exist only for the duration of the immediate task. They also have to deal with more information and take on a wider range of responsibilities. The kinds of staff they manage are changing, too, with more of them being knowledge workers. The role and perspective of the personnel practitioner have shifted with the new approaches to managing and structuring organisations. These developments have far-reaching implications for appraisal practice, and have fuelled the application and impact of multi-source, multi-level approaches to assessment. So significant have '360-degree feedback systems' become that they have attracted a considerable body of research, and this is reflected in the chapters devoted specifically to them here (Chapters 6 and 7)

This, then, is the backdrop against which performance appraisal has to be viewed and studied. All of the changes outlined, and their impact on appraisal, will be dealt with in some detail in the pages that follow. Because of them, writing a book on performance appraisal is not as straightforward as it might sound. Although there is an expanding and promising research base to give general guidance (Fletcher, 2001), it does not always tell us quite enough about a specific organisational situation or context; what is practical and appropriate in one organisation is quite impracticable and unsuitable in another, and even within the same organisation the requirements of the various groups and levels can differ. As will be seen in the chapters that follow, we are witnessing the demise of the 'one-size-fits-all' monolithic appraisal system. Doubtless the idea of a universally applied, standard procedure that stays rigidly in place for years (perhaps kept there by the weight of its own paperwork) will lumber on in some quarters for a while yet, but its days are certainly numbered. In keeping with that, the reader will *not* find in these pages copies of umpteen varieties of appraisal forms and documentation. This is not a book that places great emphasis on this aspect of appraisal, chiefly because there is little reason to believe that the forms themselves are all that important. Rather, the book will present a series of key issues in developing and implementing appraisal, review the relevant theory, give a description of some of the ways taken in dealing with them and, where possible, offer an evaluation of these approaches based on research. And as that research shows, performance appraisal *can* be highly effective in generating positive attitudes, fostering commitment and impacting on organisational performance (Fletcher and Williams, 1996; Patterson *et al.*, 1998; see final section, Chapter 13).

Such is the remit of performance appraisal that a book on it has to cover a very wide range of complex topics and techniques – job analysis, management competencies, assessment centres, and so on. Many of these merit a book in themselves, so wherever relevant the reader will be given references to more specialised texts. The evaluation of the varying approaches to appraisal looked at here will be based on organisational experience and on research findings. It would be less than honest to pretend that such an evaluation could be totally objective, any more than appraisal itself. The author's own views and preferences, and personal experience, will be clear enough from time to time. Arising out of the material reviewed, the lessons for good practice will be identified which will, hopefully, help students and practitioners to build future performance appraisal schemes better suited to the needs of both their organisations and the people working in them.

Chapter 2

Deciding on the aims of appraisal

The organisational perspective

The most fundamental question facing an organisation that is setting up appraisal is what the aim of the exercise is to be. Get this bit wrong, and you can bet that whatever else follows, the appraisal system will not run smoothly – if it runs at all. To be sure, it is not hard to think up a number of aims that appraisal may serve, but the main problem is setting up a realistic and achievable agenda.

Let us look at some of the aims that appraisal is commonly supposed to meet. One of the most frequently cited purposes of appraisal is to enable some kind of assessment to be made of the appraisee. This may be against some pre-set objectives, or it may be in terms of ratings on job competencies, or the like. But assessment, whilst constituting a core element of appraisal, is not in itself one of its fundamental objectives – assessment done for its own sake is of little value. What it provides is a basis for several key aims of appraisal, especially:

- *Making reward decisions.* The notion is that if you are to engage in any kind of equitable distribution of rewards, be they pay, promotion or whatever, then some method of comparing people is necessary. If an assessment of performance is made annually, it can be used to direct rewards to those most deserving of them.
- *Improving performance through facilitating learning.* One of the basic principles of human learning is that to improve performance, people need to have some knowledge of the results they are already achieving. Making an assessment and conveying it should enable this and help enhance performance. An accurate assessment of performance is also likely to bring to light training and development needs, and so improve performance through this, too.
- *Motivating staff.* There are three ways that appraisal seeks to motivate employees:

1   Since the earliest appraisal schemes, it has been an article of faith that giving feedback, quite apart from assisting in task performance, is something that motivates people (Kluger and DeNisi, 1996). And there is some justification for this, as employees in all types of organisation frequently express a desire for more feedback. The assessment made in appraisal provides the basis for such feedback, and thus *in theory* contributes to motivation.

2   Assessment increases motivation by facilitating the fair distribution of rewards. The importance of perceived fairness in how people respond to appraisal can hardly be overstated. For example, Taylor *et al.* (1995) found that making explicit the performance standards, applying them consistently and giving people a fair hearing all impacted on atttudes to appraisal.

3   Setting targets that improve on previous performance is a further motivating device (Donovan, 2001).

- *Succession planning and identifying potential.* By identifying good and poor performers, the appraisal assessment can enable the organisation to focus succession planning and resources on the individuals who are most likely to respond positively and effectively to it.

- *Promoting manager–subordinate dialogue.* This is not always stated explicitly as one of the aims of appraisal. However, providing a formal occasion for the two parties to discuss performance is a way of encouraging more contact between them.

- *Formal assessment of unsatisfactory performance.* In its most negative (and fortunately most infrequent) garb, appraisal can be part of the process whereby unsatisfactory performance is documented and used in evidence in disciplinary or dismissal proceedings.

These are some of the purposes that, in theory at least, can be served through having an appraisal scheme that includes some element of assessment. On the face of it, they seem entirely justifiable. Unfortunately, although each one in itself is indeed reasonable, together, they most certainly are not. All the above points reflect things very much from the perspective of the organisation and its needs. If managers and subordinates had exactly the same needs, all would be fine. Alas, they do not. The result is that the various aims of appraisal are very difficult to reconcile with each other in real life, a fact that was pointed out long ago (Maier, 1958) and has been echoed since in the findings of Strebler *et al.* (2001) that aligning appraisal systems too closely with organisational goals detracts from the feedback and counselling aims of appraisal.

The participants' perspective

If performance appraisal is to be constructive and useful, there has to be something in it for the participants – both the appraisers and appraisees (Fletcher, 2002). They, after all, are the people who have to make it work. What does the appraisal situation look like from their viewpoint?

Taking the appraisees first, they often do want feedback, are interested in improving performance, have training needs and do want to have a chance for constructive dialogue with their bosses. They also usually believe in fair distribution of rewards. Although this might sound like a perfect match with the organisation's needs, it is all conditional on:

> their perceiving the assessment as accurate and fair
> the quality of their existing relationship with the appraiser
> the impact of the assessment on their rewards and well-being.

The first of these is a condition that often does not appear to be met. Perhaps it is because of all the biases that can creep into judgments about others, or the imperfections of memory, or lack of contact between appraisers and the appraised, but there is a lot of evidence that appraisees do not readily accept the more unfavourable aspects of their assessment (Fletcher, 2002). Even when there is sound evidence of poor performance, there can be a reluctance to accept it. Although some people are more objective about themselves than others, and some are more resilient and able to take criticism without feeling wounded, in general, the capacity to take negative feedback without experiencing any threat to self-esteem is fairly low. When people do face threats to their self-esteem, the most frequent reaction is mentally to rubbish the message and/or the source.

This is not to say that it is impossible to have any meaningful discussion of performance in the appraisal, but it does indicate that such discussion has to be handled with the greatest care and that it may lead to defensiveness rather than to increased motivation. The chances of defensiveness are increased greatly if pay or promotion are affected by the assessment. It takes a remarkably dispassionate, honest and self-denying individual to remain completely objective when faced with an assessment that may have adverse financial consequences. If, on top of all this, the existing relationship with the appraiser is not a good one, then it is extremely unlikely that the assessment will be seen as fair and acceptable. The main purpose of the appraisal, for the appraisee, becomes one of fighting a defensive action. As Hirsh (2006) remarks, appraisals marked by ratings and pay linked to performance shift the discussion between manager and subordinate on to 'a more nervous and adversarial footing'.

The appraisers' agenda for appraisal is also often far removed from what the organisation would like it to be (Fletcher, 2002). As already suggested, the person appraised will not always agree with the appraiser's views, irrespective of the objectivity and accuracy of the latter. The appraisers are all too aware of this; in addition, the more insightful of them realise that assessing others is a tricky business, and that either they may lack the information and evidence necessary to make a fair judgment, or they may have biases that affect the way they interpret the information they do have. So they have ample reason to feel apprehensive about the situation and the likely reaction they may get from appraisees – particularly if they have had rather limited contact with them on a day-to-day basis. The appraisal interaction has to be seen for what it is in the eyes of most appraisers – one isolated event in the year. It might not be so tricky to deal with if the effects could be contained within that one event, but the truth for many managers is that any adverse reactions from the person appraised can make working relationships more problematic for a long while afterwards. Small wonder, then, that managers are prone to avoid carrying out appraisals if they can, and where they cannot, they tend to give overly favourable ratings (Arvey and Murphy, 1998). Even this tactic – being generous in the assessment – is not without problems, as it not surprisingly generates unrealistic expectations about future rewards on the part of the appraisee and so simply stores up trouble for a later date.

In the case of genuinely high-performing subordinates, one might expect the appraiser to be only too happy to sit down and have the pleasure of passing on their satisfaction. After all, the appraisee's reaction will be no cause for concern, apart from their reasonable expectation that the appraiser will be able to accompany the words with some tangible reward (which is not always possible). Unfortunately, it is not unknown for managers to be reluctant to identify high performers to the personnel department, because they fear that they will lose them through promotion or transfer. On top of all this, developing subordinates has seldom ranked high in organisations' priorities, or been something that is rewarded. Indeed, the evidence indicates quite the opposite – that managers who are good at staff development are less likely to make rapid career progress. The message is further reinforced in some organisations by the lack of central action in response to recommendations that come out of appraisals, and the lack of response to failure to carry out appraisals at all.

For all these reasons, the annual appraisal is, for many managers, a high-risk activity with little immediate positive outcome or reward. Organisations typically set up appraisal with a mix of short, medium and long-term objectives. But in present times, immediate results rather than uncertain longer-term benefits are what most managers are expected to produce. In a series of research studies, Longenecker and his colleagues (e.g.

Longenecker and Gioia, 1988; Gioia and Longenecker, 1994) have specifically focused on what they call the politics of appraisal. Amongst other
things, this research identified the following reasons why managers inflate
their ratings of subordinates:

1   believing that accurate ratings would have a damaging effect on
    subordinate motivation and performance
2   desire to improve the subordinate's chances of getting a pay rise
3   a wish to avoid others outside the department seeing evidence of
    internal problems and conflicts
4   preventing a permanent written record of poor performance com-
    ing into being which might have longer-term implications for the
    subordinate
5   need to protect subordinates whose performance had suffered from the
    effects of personal problems
6   wanting to reward subordinates who had put in a lot of effort even if
    the end result was not so good
7   avoiding confrontation and potential conflict with 'difficult'
    subordinates
8   aiming to promote out of the department subordinates who were
    disliked or problem performers.

Though less frequently reported, some reasons for deliberately mani-
pulating performance assessments in a downward direction were also
uncovered:

1   scaring people into performing better
2   punishing difficult or non-compliant subordinates
3   encouraging unwanted subordinates to leave
4   minimising the merit pay award(s)
5   complying with organisational restrictions on the number of higher
    ratings given.

The general observation from this research is that managers frequently
allow their appraisal of staff to be influenced by non-performance issues.
Indeed, Cleveland and Murphy (1992) suggest that arriving at an objective
and accurate assessment of performance is usually not the highest priority
for the appraiser.

Setting realistic aims for appraisal

If there is so much potential conflict between the different aims of appraisal,
and if the participants frequently have differing objectives, what can we

reasonably expect of the appraisal process? The answer is – quite a lot, though not perhaps as much as has traditionally been demanded. The failure to realise that appraisal cannot do all that has been asked of it, and that there has to be something in the process that will be seen to be of benefit to the participants, has probably been the root cause of the lack of success of so many appraisal systems.

The question becomes one of priorities: what are the essential purposes of the appraisal system, and how are they to be identified? The most common way of determining this is for the HR director and/or the HR department to dream the whole thing up themselves. Sometimes (and increasingly of late) top management take a direct interest, too. The likely outcome is an appraisal system that is all about the organisation's needs, with scant attention paid to the perspectives of the appraisers and appraisees. To avoid such an undesirable and, ultimately, unworkable result, it is necessary at the outset to involve representatives of managers and staff. Some examples of this and the mechanisms for it will be given in Chapter 4.

Wider participation in the design of appraisal does not automatically make the process easier. There will be differing needs and perceptions which have to be reconciled through negotiation. The end product should represent something for everyone – a not impossible objective if the parties accept from the start that this is a joint venture that must have everyone's commitment if it is to be successful and worthwhile. The most usual divide is between top management, who want a primarily assessment-driven appraisal (but which in theory fulfils all the other goals as well), and appraisers and appraisees, who want the appraisal to be primarily oriented towards development and motivation. This schism is not easily bridged.

As will be seen in the course of this book, research and experience suggest that the best option is to define the function of appraisal in terms of development and motivation. There are several reasons for this:

- This is acceptable and welcome both to appraisees and most appraisers.
- It represents what is generally the highest priority for the organisation – a strategy for improving performance.
- The effectiveness of appraisal as a device for assessing individuals relative to their peers is often rather doubtful.

Some of the rationale for this last point, on assessment, will be given in the next chapter. However, some organisations' needs or perceptions are such that they will focus appraisal more on the assessment function. This book will therefore try to provide guidance on setting up appraisal schemes of either complexion. This is necessary because the aims of appraisal crucially affect the nature and content of the appraisal scheme. If the aim is primarily one of assessment, with a view to making comparisons between people, then the appraisal is centred on common dimensions or aspects of performance that all staff within a particular group can reasonably be assessed on. For a more motivationally oriented scheme, there is no requirement for common dimension ratings or the like, and the emphasis instead is on improving skills and setting personal targets. The nature of the various approaches to appraisal will be described in detail in the next chapter, along with the strengths and weaknesses associated with them.

In summary

The first and crucial question in designing an appraisal scheme is deciding and prioritising what its primary aims are. Typically, these revolve around providing a basis for reward decisions, enhancing motivation and improving performance, identifying potential and generally improving communications and problem solving. However, the needs of those involved – the organisation, the appraiser and the person appraised – do not always coincide, and indeed may conflict. Understanding these differing perspectives is essential to establishing an effective appraisal system – one which sets realistic and achieveable goals that offer something of value to all parties.

Discussion points and questions

If your performance was to be appraised tomorrow, what would you be aiming to get out of the appraisal session? How would you be feeling about it?

In what ways can we use performance appraisal to motivate people? What are the pros and cons of using appraisal as a way of assessing performance?

Write down either the aims of the existing appraisal scheme in your organisation, or what the aims of a new appraisal scheme should be.

Key references

Donovan, J. J. (2001) Work motivation. In N. Anderson, D. Ones, H. Sinangil and C. Viswesvaran (eds) *International Handbook of Industrial, Work and Organizational Psychology*. Sage: London.

Fletcher, C. (2002) Appraisal – an individual psychological analysis. In S. Sonnentag (ed.) *The Psychological Management of Individual Performance: A Handbook in the Psychology of Management in Organisations*. Wiley: Chichester.

Strebler, M., Robinson, D. and Bevan, S. (2001) *Performance Review: Balancing Objectives and Content*. Institute for Empoyment Studies: Sussex.

Chapter 3

The content of appraisal

Within the broad distinction of appraisal for assessment and comparison on the one hand, and appraisal for development and motivation on the other, lie a number of methods and techniques that form the content of appraisal in each case. The main ones are reviewed here.

Appraising for assessment and comparison

Appraisal of personality

This strikes a somewhat historical note, as you would be hard put to find any current UK appraisal schemes that focused overtly on personality attributes. In the 1950s, however, it was a different story, with many appraisal forms listing what were essentially personality traits. This gradually died out due to its extreme unpopularity with appraisers and appraisees, although Holdsworth (1991) mentions a British retailing organisation that included the assessment of 'moral courage' in its appraisal scheme as late as the early 1970s.

Whilst appraising personality is not in vogue, it would be a mistake to think that it has gone away altogether. There are certainly remnants of it to be found in more ambiguous form. So, for example, 'drive' (or one of its synonyms) might well feature as one of the job-related attributes that an individual is assessed on. The idea, of course, is to try to keep away from direct comment on personality, as this is an area of great sensitivity and any criticism on these grounds is likely to elicit defensiveness and even outright hostility. Also, it is hard enough for people to deliberately change their personalities over a protracted period, let alone to do it more or less over-night at the instigation of the appraiser.

Does this move away from appraising personality mean that personality is now viewed as irrelevant to work performance? Far from it, as the very considerable and sustained growth in the use of personality questionnaires

(Shackleton and Newell, 1997) indicates. It is perhaps not entirely by chance that the decline in personality-linked appraisal was followed by the rise in the popularity of such questionnaires. They are chiefly used in selection, promotion assessment and individual development (see Chapter 10), which clearly demonstrates that organisations *do* feel personality to be important in determining performance. It is just that they have found another, more indirect but possibly more objective, manner of bringing personality into the picture in making basic personnel decisions.

Appraising job-related abilities

A sensible approach is to try to keep appraisal firmly locked on to the job and the abilities needed to perform it effectively. This represents a more detached, less personal way of discussing performance, and one which in theory is less likely to be threatening to the appraisees' self-esteem. It also tackles skills and abilities that should be amenable to training, development and improvement. However, as with appraisal focused on personality attributes, the basic intention is usually to compare the individual with other people at the same level and in similar work roles.

The first question that arises here is: which of a legion of possible job-related abilities – e.g. planning and organising, numeracy, ability to communicate clearly, capacity for coping with pressure – should be appraised? The aim is to identify those abilities that are central to good performance and can discriminate between staff with varying levels of effectiveness. There are a number of ways of going about this. The least successful, and also (alas) the most widely used, is to get together a committee or working group, usually consisting of personnel representatives and top management, to decide what the most important abilities are. This is a largely unsystematic procedure, which tends to be heavily influenced by the seniority of the group members. The fact that what it produces does not rest on any observable and quantifiable data can have unfortunate legal consequences.

Fortunately, more appropriate job analysis techniques are available (see Bartram, 2007; and Brannick *et al.*, 2007 for a wider discussion of the topic). These include diary methods, direct observation, questionnaires and interviews. A further method, called the Rep Grid, will be described later when we talk about competencies. All these yield relevant information, though not always of the same kind:

- As their name implies, diary methods require the job holder to keep an hour-by-hour record of their activities over a set period. This should provide a clear account of how time is spent on the job, and what it involves. It does, however, rely on the conscientious completion of the diary and on the decision of the job holder as to what to record.

- Direct observation of people doing the job in question can be very useful in getting a feel for the job, and has the virtue of providing an external and perhaps more objective view. However, it is often difficult to arrange, is time-consuming and the presence of an observer is sometimes a distorting factor (people may behave differently when they are being 'watched').

- Questionnaire methods of job analysis generally present the incumbent with a series of job components or elements that they tick or rate in terms of their relevance to the job. A well-known example of this approach is the Position Analysis Questionnaire (see Box 3.1). Questionnaire methods are very good at providing quantitative information on what the job entails.

- Interviews with the job holders are useful for throwing light on the more social and psychological aspects of the work, as well as giving a more all-round perspective when bosses, peers and even subordinates of the job holder are included in the interview process.

- A special variation on the interview method is known as the Critical Incidents interview. This is a fairly variable approach which typically involves the job incumbents and/or their bosses being asked to recall incidents when the job seemed to go particularly well – when they performed at a high level and felt satisfied with their efforts – and ones when it had gone much less well. Having thought of a group of such incidents, the respondents are asked to talk them through, describing what happened, the nature of the situation, what they had done, and the consequences. The idea is that by collecting such information and analysing it (though little clear guidance is available on just how to do this), you can build up a picture of the important attributes that determine success and failure in the job.

These approaches to job analysis will not necessarily always identify the abilities needed to do the job, but they will supply the information from which the latter can be inferred with a high degree of accuracy. Any one of them is likely to be superior to the so-called committee method. However, the best bet is often to combine two or more job analysis methods to gain a more comprehensive and accurate description of the job.

Rating scales

Having identified the abilities necessary for effective performance in the job (though what follows applies also to the personality based approach to

Box 3.1: the questionnaire method of job analysis

The *Position Analysis Questionnaire* (PAQ) was developed principally by an American psychologist called McCormick, with his colleagues Jeanneret and Meacham. The PAQ analyses job elements and relates them to the basic human behaviours involved, regardless of specific technological areas or functions. It consists of 187 items relating to job activities or the work environment. The job analyst interviews the incumbent and rates each of the job elements in terms of importance, frequency and so on. These elements cluster into six broad areas to give a picture of the job structure:

- Information Input: where and how does the individual get the necessary information?
- Mental Processes: what reasoning, planning, etc. activities are involved in doing the job?
- Work Output: what physical activities are performed and with what equipment?
- Relationships with Others: what does the job entail in terms of relating to other people?
- Job Context: what is the physical and social job context?
- Other Characteristics: any other activities or conditions that are relevant to performance.

The PAQ can be scored manually or by computer, and because it has been around for some time it is backed up by considerable research literature and a large database.

appraisal), the next step is to form them into some kind of rating scales. There are numerous ways of presenting rating scales, and the main ones are illustrated in Box 3.2. Whichever one is chosen, a good deal of research suggests that people have difficulty in making meaningful distinctions if they are asked to handle more than seven categories. So rating scales should not have more than seven points. Some organisations feel that the advantage of having an even number is that there is no middle category, which thus forces the rater to make an assessment that points clearly to the upper or lower half of the scale.

There are many advantages to using rating scales: they are easily understood; they offer a lot of flexibility; they encourage a more analytical view of performance by asking appraisers to think about the different aspects

Box 3.2: some rating scale formats

Four types of rating scale format are presented here. The first two are far more widely used than the second two.

1 *Scales with verbally described intervals:* These can be illustrated by the following:

Overall performance:

Outstanding   Very   Good   Fair   Not quite   Unsatisfactory
              good   adequate

2 *Numerical (or alphabetical) ratings:* The individual is rated on a number of criteria using a scale ranging from best to worst, with a number or letter given to each interval point. For example:

Effectiveness with people   High   1_2_3_4_5_6_ Low

3 *Graphic rating scales:* These generally dispense with formal interval points apart from the two extremes and the middle, but define in some detail the behaviour associated with the quality being rated. For example:

Dependability is evidenced by the following behaviours
(1) follows instructions (2) completes work on time (3) is punctual and regular in attendance (4) does not require excessive supervision.

High *----------------------------------*-----------------------------------* Low

4 *Comparative scales:* The individual is rated on some quality in terms of his standing relative to others of his level. For example:

Initiative
   A   Not as good as the great majority
   B   OK, but many I have known have been better
   C   Typical of the middle group
   D   Better than most, though I have known better
   E   One of the best I have known

of the job; and of course they facilitate comparisons between people – which is usually their *raison d'être*. But there are also a number of problems and pitfalls associated with the use of rating scales, and it is worth outlining them here.

Ratings are essentially subjective, which leads to a variety of distortions and biases creeping in. The most frequent one is the halo effect – one strongly positive attribute is allowed to colour the assessment of all the person's other attributes (see Box 8.2, page 104 for a fuller outline of sources of bias). This leads to a lack of effective discrimination. Subjectivity can also leave its mark in the way scale titles are interpreted – for example, 'drive' means different things to different people.

Appraisers are not very good at spreading their ratings across the full width of the scales. The most common findings are either a strong central tendency (nearly everyone is marked as average) or a positively skewed distribution (nearly everyone is rated highly). The reasons for this lie mainly in the problems appraisal poses for managers which were outlined in the last chapter.

The effect of these limitations is to undermine the fundamental purpose of having rating scales – to compare people. If assessments are subject to bias, if raters interpret the meaning of the same scales differently, if they fail to spread their assessments across the scale, then the appraisal does not provide the basis for fair and accurate discrimination between people of varying performance levels. Can anything be done to avoid these typical failings in the use of ratings?

Improving rating scales

There are four basic approaches to achieving more effective use of the rating method. They are:

- *Training.* Rating scales are, as already stated, easily understood – almost too easily. It is tempting to give impressionistic judgments without reviewing the evidence on which they are supposed to be based. The best defence against this is good training of appraisers at the outset. We will look at this subject in detail in Chapter 8.
- *Forced distributions.* If appraisers, when left to their own devices, do not distribute their ratings effectively, then they can be pressed by the HR department to adhere to a set distribution. For example, 10 per cent get the top rating, 20 per cent the next to top, 40 per cent the middle, 20 per cent the one below the middle, and 10 per cent the lowest rating. In practice, the use of forced distributions is usually found in connection with overall ratings of performance, rather than on individual performance characteristics. It serves the purpose of making appraisers differentiate between appraisees, but at a cost. They may feel alienated by a system that so proscribes what they do.

They and the appraisees may perceive some unfairness, and maybe justifiably, if some divisions have genuinely higher-performing staff yet have to apply the same distribution as lower-performing divisions. For these and other reasons, the use of rigid forced distributions is relatively uncommon now. However, many organisations do in effect manage to impose some control over the spread of assessment markings by more indirect means, as we will see when Performance Related Pay is discussed later in the book (Chapter 4).

- *Increasing the number of raters.* If subjectivity is a problem, then one way of overcoming it is to involve more people in the rating process, on the principle that the combined judgments of several raters are likely to be nearer the truth than any one of them alone. The most frequently encountered versions of this are the combination of self-appraisal and superior-appraisal, and/or the use of more than one superior in the process (often the immediate boss and his or her own superior), but there are examples of schemes that have attempted to integrate superior, peer and self-appraisal; see Chapters 6 and 7 for a discussion of multiple source appraisal.
- *Behaviourally based rating scales.* This represents the most sophisticated approach to improving the problems inherent in rating scale use. Essentially, it tries to put the appraiser into the role of an objective observer of behaviour rather than a judge, and seeks to minimise the scope for subjectivity. There are a number of variations on the theme:

  - BARS: Behaviourally Anchored Rating Scales (Smith and Kendall, 1963)
  - BES: Behavioural Expectation Scales (Zedeck and Baker, 1972)
  - BOS: Behavioural Observation Scales (Dunnette *et al.*, 1968).

The first and third of these, the most frequently used examples, are explained and illustrated in Box 3.3. These methods are undoubtedly time-consuming to devise, which deters many organisations from using them, and various problems do arise. For example, managers are not always able to identify where on the scale they should place the behaviours they see; the anchors, after all, are only indicative, not comprehensive, behavioural descriptions. In addition, research evidence shows mixed results with BARS and their early promise of being technically superior has not always been borne out, though there are certainly success stories too (e.g. Catano *et al.*, 2007). Because they are behaviourally specific, perhaps the value of these kinds of approach lies more in their potential to direct development than in their acting as superior assessment methods as such.

The use of training, multiple appraisers and BARS can lead to a substantial improvement in the effectiveness of rating scales as a way of assessing and comparing people. These refinements all take time and resources to implement, but without them research and experience strongly suggest that the rating method will fail to discriminate fairly and accurately between people.

Box 3.3: behaviourally based rating scales

The basic concept and methodology for all these approaches stems from BARS. The development of BARS goes through five stages:

(1)   Examples of behaviours reflecting effective and ineffective job performance are obtained from people who are knowledgeable about the job to be rated.

(2)   The examples are grouped into a series of separate performance dimensions by these experts.

(3)   Another expert group repeats the second stage, allocating the examples to dimensions. They provide an independent check on the relevance of the behavioural examples to their dimensions. Any which are allocated differently by the two groups are probably too ambiguous and should be discarded. Also as a result of this, the dimensions should be quite independent of each other.

(4)   Taking each dimension separately, the examples relating to it are rated by the experts in terms of effectiveness on a numerical scale. Where an example does not get rated similarly by different judges, then it will be deleted; a high level of agreement on how an example is rated on that dimension is required.

(5)   The resulting dimensions are each expressed as a scale, the points of which are anchored by the behavioural descriptions arrived at through the preceding stages. The number of dimensions can vary according to the job; anything from six to nine would be quite typical.

A variation on this method is offered by the use of BOS. Here, again, the end result is a series of performance dimensions linked to behavioural descriptions. The way the rating task is structured is rather different, though. Each behavioural example relating to the dimension is given a separate rating, and the overall dimension rating is the sum or average of these. Illustrations of BOS and BARS are given below.

BOS example: teamwork dimension

Teamwork
(a) Tolerant to others and shows patience with them
Almost Always 1 2 3 4 5 Almost Never

(b) Consistently seeks to offer help and support
Almost Always 1 2 3 4 5 Almost Never
(c) Plays full and balanced role in team discussions
Almost Always 1 2 3 4 5 Almost Never
(d) Keeps colleagues informed where necessary
Almost Always 1 2 3 4 5 Almost Never
(e) Volunteers for fair share of less popular duties
Almost Always 1 2 3 4 5 Almost Never
(f) Willing to change own plans to cooperate with others
Almost Always 1 2 3 4 5 Almost Never

Here is the same kind of dimension, this time expressed in BARS format:

BARS example: teamwork dimension

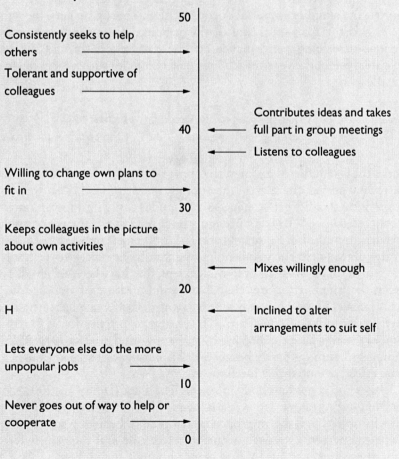

Appraising to motivate and develop

Results-oriented appraisal

The origin of results-oriented appraisal can be found in the Management-by-Objectives (MBO) movement that emerged in the 1950s, although results-oriented appraisal is less systematic and comprehensive than MBO schemes tended to be. Essentially, the notion is that the appraisal session is one where manager and subordinate jointly review the latter's achievements against objectives or targets in the last six or twelve months, and then set objectives for the next period. As far as possible, the objectives are stated in quantified, time-limited terms, and in this they differ from aims, which are general statements of intent that are usually not specific in either timing or content.

One immediate effect of basing appraisal on results in this way is to shorten and simplify appraisal documentation. There is no need for rating scales and the like – the core of the appraisal form simply comprises sections describing performance against past objectives and the new objectives set for the year ahead. A set of headings for such a form can look like this:

Key Objectives	Priority Ranking	Action Needed: Who and When	Extent to Which Objectives Achieved

Under the last of these headings, the appraiser would record, at the end of the review period, the success the appraisee had attained. This approach to appraisal steadily gathered popularity and is easily the most frequently encountered now. Why has it been so attractive? The advantages of results-oriented appraisal are quite substantial, and chief amongst them is its greater objectivity. The whole point of quantifiable objectives is that it is easy to determine whether, or to what extent, they have been achieved. This means that there is a more reliable and valid measure of an individual's performance. This is obviously worth having in itself, but it has further and very significant knock-on effects. The greater objectivity serves to reduce some of the appraisees' concerns about the appraisal process, as well as the appraisers'. Perhaps partly because of this, results-oriented appraisal is a more effective motivating mechanism.

A large and consistent body of research findings (Donovan, 2001) confirm that setting targets is a powerful way of increasing motivation. Apart from its objectivity, this approach is supposed to be highly participative, giving the person appraised a much greater role and thus engendering a more positive attitude. When people commit themselves publicly to achieving goals they have some responsibility for defining, their self-esteem is bound up in the successful attainment of those goals.

In addition to its motivational qualities, result-oriented appraisal is by nature job-related, and therefore legally more defensible in terms of any personnel decisions taken as a result of it. It also involves some examination of the appraisees' priorities, which is a useful exercise that can avoid many misunderstandings that might otherwise arise. So, with all these advantages – objectivity, motivational power, participative nature, job-relatedness and so on – it is perhaps difficult to understand why results-oriented appraisal is not the only approach taken, let alone the dominant one. There are, however, some inherent limitations to going down this route.

The fundamental problem with appraisal centred on objective-setting is that it is difficult to make comparative assessments between people. Unless you have two or more people doing the same job in the same conditions and being set exactly the same objectives each year – circumstances that seldom, if ever, arise – then there is no common basis for comparison of the kind provided by rating scales. The reality of results-oriented appraisal is that differing goals will be set according to past achievements, present priorities and the appraisees' particular circumstances. If the objectives differ, it is difficult to compare the achievements of different individuals. It is not impossible to do so, but unless the comparison is in very general terms (exceeded target, attained target, fell short of target) and is made on the assumption that all targets are of equal difficulty (an assumption that will be discussed in a moment), a great deal of subjectivity will begin to enter the judgment.

The fact is that all targets are not, and should not be, equal in difficulty. They have to take account of the appraisees' capabilities. There is little point in pitching them so high that they are unlikely to be achieved, or making them so easy that they present no challenge. But then how do you compare the performance of these two hypothetical cases doing a similar job?

Appraisee A has reached the quite modest performance targets asked of him. Although they are modest, they nonetheless represent a considerable achievement in view of his experience and abilities.

Appraisee B has exceeded the objectives set. However, she has ample experience and ability, and the achievement has to be viewed in this context.

In other words, are we evaluating just the quantifiable attainment, or what that represents in terms of the individual's effort and ability? The answer is probably both, which is what makes results-oriented appraisal more difficult to use as a comparison mechanism. The picture is further complicated by the way appraisers and appraisees may collude to set objectives that make life easy for both of them – a little too easy for the appraisee to attain, so avoiding any need to discuss a short-fall in achievement.

There are some other drawbacks to results-oriented appraisal. One objection often raised is that not all jobs are amenable to framing in terms of objectives. There is an element of truth in this, though not as much as some would have you believe. I remember one senior university academic, who had presided over a faculty with a particularly abysmal research record, vehemently opposing the concept of objective-setting on the grounds that this was a nasty industrial concept of no relevance to academic work – how could you talk about enriching young minds in terms of objectives, etc. It had to be pointed out to him that there were really rather a lot of relevant quantifiable objectives to consider, such as research output (e.g. number of articles published), course drop-out rates, and so on. There is a point here, though. Whilst much – given a little thought and imagination – can be specified in terms of objectives, not *everything* that is important in a job is necessarily appropriately described in this way. There are dangers to evaluating performance exclusively in terms of ends rather than means. The examples of asking police officers to be assessed purely in terms of arrest rate (or surgeons to be assessed on numbers of operations) should be enough to give pause for thought. Indeed, on the day this is being written, *The Times* newspaper is running a story that, according to their union, police officers are being driven to making 'ludicrous' arrests for trivial incidents to meet targets set for them.

Results alone are not enough to go on. External constraints also have to be considered: the individual's capacity to determine the targets achieved in the light of the resources available, the limitations imposed by circumstances, and so on. Any assessment has to take account of such factors. Partly because of this, the objectives set have to be reviewed at regular intervals to see if they are still appropriate or if they need modifying in the light of changes that have taken place.

So results-oriented appraisal is not as straightforward as it may first appear. It is certainly not an approach that automatically lends itself to assessing and comparing people against a common standard. But it does have some very powerful arguments in its favour, not least of which is its potential for motivating individuals and improving performance – at least, in terms of end results. However, that is perhaps also its main limitation. As indicated earlier, there is a danger in over-emphasising ends at the expense of means. An example of this is provided by a business services organisation, where staff complained that managers were much more likely to be rewarded for achieving set financial targets than for being good at managing and developing staff. Not only does focusing exclusively on results direct attention away from the manner in which the results were achieved, but it may also leave a gap as regards developing individuals. It offers little in the way of a framework for analysing the skills and abilities the appraisee has acquired or needs to enhance. Mainly because of this, a number of organisations now try to combine the results-oriented approach with a competency-based appraisal system.

Competency-based appraisal

The notion of 'competency' must stand a good chance of winning any competition for the most over-worked concept in HR management in recent times. It is defined in myriad ways, which understandably leads to some confusion. Boyatzis (1982), whose work in the US created much of the interest in this area, defines a competency as 'an under-lying characteristic of a person', which could be 'a motive, trait, skill, aspect of one's self-image or social role, or a body of knowledge which he or she uses'. This is a very broad definition, and others adopt more succinct descriptions of what constitutes a competency, such as 'an observable skill or ability to complete a managerial task successfully' or 'behavioural dimensions that affect job performance' (Woodruffe, 2007) – either of which will suit the purpose of our current discussion. Another distinction can be drawn between individual- and organisational-level competences. Box 3.4 presents a summary of the characteristics and differences between these two levels of analysis, as described by Sparrow (1996).

There is actually very little that differentiates competencies from the assessment dimensions used in many assessment centres for years. But competencies are applied more widely now in setting performance standards for managers. Some examples of competencies that have been used in major companies are given in Box 3.5. They illustrate the way the key competencies associated with high performance in an organisation can be incorporated into selection, training and development processes. Clearly, if they are being used in this manner, then they should have some place in appraisal. It makes sense for people to be appraised on the competencies that have been singled out as the most important for success.

There is a newer and slightly different perspective on competencies that should be mentioned here. Hall (Hall and Moss, 1998; Briscoe and Hall, 1999) puts forward the notion of 'metacompetencies', which are competencies so powerful that they affect an individual's ability to acquire other competencies (see Table 6). Hall's work, in turn, is influenced by McCall (Spreitzer et al., 1997), who pointed out that the skills needed tomorrow may not exactly be the same as those needed today, and that the ability to

Box 3.4: three concepts of individual and organisation competences and competencies

Element of definition	What are management competencies?	What are behavioural competencies?	What are organisational competencies?
Describe	Knowledge, skills and attitudes (and a few personal behaviours)	Behavioural repertoires that people bring to a job, role or organisation context	Resources and capabilities of the organisation linked with business performance
Identified through	Functional analysis of job roles and responsibilities	Behavioural event investigation techniques	Market analysis methods, strategic and business planning evaluation
Which focus on	Task-centred analysis of jobs which reflect expectations of workplace performance	Person-centred analysis of jobs that reflect effectiveness	Internal resources (such as tangible technical or capital assets as well as strategic management skills)
And indicate	Areas of competence (fields of knowledge) which a person must demonstrate effectively	What people need to bring to a role to perform to the required level	What makes the organisation more successful than others – i.e. long-term and fixed sources of competitive advantage
Performance criterion based on	Entry (threshold) standards – i.e. wide reach into a broad range of management jobs	Characteristics of superior (excellent) individual performance – i.e. senior management levels	Superior records of innovation, learning, quality and other long-term business criteria
Applied to	Generic vocational education and training standards across organisations and occupations – i.e. common denominators	Tailored excellent behaviours to integrate all areas of HRM – i.e. reinforce distinguishing characteristics	Marketing and product strategies, selection of best economic rent-generating activities, underlying business process

Level of analysis	Occupation- and sector-based on sample of key jobs	Job level, or across the management hierarchy	Organisation level and underlying business process
Ownership	Competence owned by national institutions and organisations and granted to individuals	Competency held by the individual and brought to the organisation	Competence held by the organisation and jointly developed by individuals
Assessment onus	Accreditation of past activities to grant professional status	Identification of potential to ensure best internal resourcing decisions	Articulation of key success factors and unique proprietary know-how
Rewards motivation	Externally transferable achievement and qualification	Internally rewardable achievement and recognition	Organisationally sustainable employment and security

From Sparrow (1996)

Box 3.5: examples of competencies used in major UK companies

(a) The first example is provided by Cadbury Schweppes. They identified nine major dimensions of management competence:

Strategy:	vision, critical thinking, innovation, environmental awareness, business sense.
Drive:	self-motivation, initiative, tenacity, energy, independence, risk taking, resilience.
Relationships:	sociability, impact, acceptability, awareness.
Persuasion:	oral communication, written communication, flexibility, negotiation.
Leadership:	delegation, subordinates' development.
Followership:	followership, teamwork.
Analysis:	problem analysis, numerical analysis, listening, creativity, judgment, intuition.
Implementation:	planning and organising, decisiveness, organising sensitivity, management control, work standards, detail handling, compliance, stress tolerance, adaptability, commitment.

Personal factors: integrity, management identification, career ambition, learning ability, professional/technical.

These are only partial descriptions of each competency. To show what a complete competency description looks like, the one for Analysis is given here; it breaks down into six components:

Problem analysis: seeking pertinent data, recognising what is important, identifying possible causes, recommending action.

Numerical analysis: analysing, organising and presenting numerical data to support research and recommendations.

Listening: drawing out information in face-to-face discussion.

Creativity: introducing fresh ideas and insights, seeing new angles.

Judgment: evaluating data and courses of action without bias or prejudice and reaching logical conclusions.

Intuition: using hunch, feel and sixth sense to identify issues and possible solutions.

(Glaze, 1989)

****

In BP, the competencies fell into four groups:

Achievement orientation: personal drive, organisational drive, impact, communication.

People orientation: awareness of others, team management, persuasiveness.

Judgment: analytical power, strategic thinking, commercial judgment.

Situational flexibility: adaptive orientation.

Again, to go into a little more detail, two of the competencies are described more fully.

Personal drive: Self-confident and assertive drive to win, with decisiveness and resilience

Decisive even under pressure, assertive and tough-minded in arguing his/her case, very self-confident, shrugs off setbacks	Will commit him/herself to definite opinions, determined to be heard, can come back strongly if attacked	May reserve judgment where uncertain, but stands firm on important points, aims for compromise, fairly resilient	Avoids taking rapid decisions, takes an impartial co-ordinator role rather than pushing own ideas	Doesn't pursue his/her points, goes along with the group, allows criticism or setbacks to deter him/her

+ Indicators

    tough-minded driving style/pushes to get own way

    persistent in arguing points

    concerned to get solution he/she owns

    can confront others where important

    makes clear decisions when required

    commits self to definite opinions

    resilient to setbacks

    enjoys challenge, can accept mistakes

    maintains confidence

− Indicators

    rather soft or 'nice'

    doesn't pursue his/her points

    doesn't like confronting others

    inclined to give way if attacked

    lets others make the decisions

    backs off from giving definite view

    reacts emotionally to setbacks

    anxious, worried about mistakes

    lacking confidence, appears uncertain

Team management: Ability to stimulate a productive team climate. Able to manage interaction of people with different perspectives, conflicting views

Provides process leadership to promote team spirit and enthusiasm, builds others', commitment to achieve super-ordinate goals	Encourages others to contribute, will act as a facilitator for the group, builds alliances between people and groups	Balanced approach, will suggest methods and procedures for how to tackle the task	Tends to overstate the importance and value of one's own contribution, will reluctantly involve self in group	Prefers individualistic, self-centred approach, will tend to be indifferent to others and will do nothing about it

+ Indicators

    uses humour to reduce tension

    tries to get agreement on principles

    behaves as a member of team and can get others to contribute

− Indicators

    attacks others, raises tension

    individualistic, not interested in group approach

behaves unilaterally e.g. as the decision-maker

draws out quieter members

directs discussion by carefully-timed interventions

encourages an open flow of communication between members

process-oriented, facilitative

ignores quieter members

impulsive in his/her interventions

becomes impatient with openness between members

task-fascinated

(Greatrex and Phillips, 1989)

It can be seen from these two company examples that although there are clear areas of overlap, the competencies also reflect idiosyncratic aspects of the individual organisations' needs and cultures at the time.

learn from experience may be more important than existing competency levels. Thus, the basic idea behind Hall's metacompetencies is that they describe the characteristics underpinning the ability to both acquire experience and to learn from it, which is the key to development generally. Some competency frameworks include elements of this thinking, but many do not. One positive example of a metacompetency is found in a Civil Service competency framework (see Box 3.6)

Box 3.6: metacompetencies

Hall (Briscoe and Hall, 1999) proposes two metacompetencies – Identity and Adaptability.

The learning behaviours associated with Identity include –

- Accurate self-assessment
- Seeking, hearing and acting on feedback
- Exploring, communicating and acting on personal values
- Being open to diverse people and ideas
- Engaging in personal development activity
- Being able to modify one's self-perception as one's attributes change

The learning behaviours associated with Adaptability include –

* Being able to identify for oneself the qualities that are critical for future performance and being able to make the changes needed to develop them
* Eagerness to accept new challenges
* Exploration of new territory
* Comfort with turbulent change

These concepts have echoes in some of the work on self-awareness (Fletcher, 1997) – see Chapters 6 and 7 – and on emotional intelligence (Higgs and Dulewicz, 1999).

A UK Senior Civil Service competency framework included 'Learning and Improving' as one of six key competencies (Cabinet Office, 2001), and this clearly exemplifies the ideas behind learning competencies. Here are some of the associated behavioural indicators for this competency –

* Aware of own strengths, weaknesses and motivations
* Applies learning from own and others' experience
* Understands, values and incorporates different perspectives
* Seeks new or different opportunities to learn
* Readily shares idea or information with others
* Encourages experimentation and tries innovative ways of working.

A further example of elements of this thinking is provided by the financial services group, UBS – their *Developing Self (Learning)* competency was defined thus:

Is concerned to continuously expand their own skill set and specific knowledge of business. Remains abreast of developments in own area, creates and pursues own development plan and finds opportunities to achieve own objectives.

Level 1 Curious and interested in topics related to their work, open to development opportunities as they arise, accepts feedback from others.

Level 2 Is systematic and deliberate about pursuing their own self-development, seeks feedback from others.

Level 3 Actively encourages feedback from others, creates development opportunities to support own progression.

Level 4 Identifies and considers a wide range of opportunities and plans own development.

Before looking at the operation of competency-based appraisal in more detail, the question of how to go about identifying the relevant competencies has to be addressed. This can be done by using most of the traditional job analysis techniques described earlier as a basis, but one method in particular has been used in many cases. This is known as the Rep Grid and was originally devised by a psychologist, George Kelly, as part of his Personal Construct theory of personality. Since then, it has been adapted to a wide range of other purposes, including a way of identifying – in behavioural terms – the broad dimensions or competencies that differentiate good from poor performance in a job or group of jobs. It is described in Box 3.7. Another method that has been used successfully is the generic competency questionnaire, which lists a wide range of competencies and their behavioural descriptions and asks respondents to rate each one in terms of its importance for effective performance in the company (Dulewicz and Herbert, 1992).

Whatever method is used to derive the competencies, one of the most important points to bear in mind is that the organisation cannot afford simply to observe the status quo. Framing the question in terms of what constitutes the main dimensions of effective performance now does not tell you what those dimensions will be in the future. Competencies are forward-looking, and should have within them elements that are anticipated as being the key attributes in five or ten years' time. Thus, some generic competency questionnaires ask respondents to rate competencies in terms of their importance now and, separately, five years ahead.

Having established what the key competencies are, they can be built into the appraisal system. Does this mean that they are to be part of what is essentially an *assessment* process, with people being rated and compared on their levels of competence? It is true that they could be used in this way, but that would rob them of much of their value. Competencies should not be equated with ratings of single job-related abilities. They are much broader and more complex than that. An individual may have mastered some aspects of a competency but not others. Ideally, the competencies used in appraisal would be represented in the kind of behavioural detail exemplified by the BP approach shown in Box 3.5. This allows for progression and development over time. Moreover, the competencies appraised might change as an individual's career progresses. It is unlikely that, say, a graduate entrant at the time of initial selection has had the opportunity to acquire and display all the skills and abilities that will be needed for success in an organisation. Some will only come after a fair amount of work experience. So while there will be some competencies that can be appraised from the outset, others will only come into the picture later.

Competency-based appraisal does allow some scope for comparing people, but its real strength is in analysing the progress of the individual and in directing attention to those areas where skills can be improved. It is developmentally oriented, and as such is likely to be motivating for the person appraised. The emphasis is on both parties in the appraisal working together to chart the levels of competence attained by the appraisee and decide the appropriate training and experience needed to make further progress. Because it is behaviourally based, it is more objective and less likely to generate disagreement or conflict – although it cannot be said that disagreements never occur. It does not deal with results achieved in any direct way, and is more concerned with the medium and longer term than with just the next six to twelve months. However, all the potential advantages of competency-based appraisal can quickly be nullified if, as seems to be the intention of quite a few companies, rewards are directly linked to competency assessment (Sparrow, 1996).

Box 3.7: the Rep Grid

The great advantage of the Rep Grid is that it allows the individuals interviewed to identify what they think is important in their own words; it does not force them into using some preconceived dimensions that the investigator has in mind. Taking its use in identifying competencies (so flexible is the technique that it can be applied to all sorts of other problems too), the steps in the process are given below. This is not the only way of doing it, though; there are many variations on the theme. The procedure is followed on a one-to-one basis with a manager one or two levels up from the job(s) being looked at, though job incumbents can also be included.

I   Ask the individual to think of six managers in the level or role under consideration. They need to be people the respondent has known well, who have worked in the organisation for two or three years, and who differ in effectiveness. Ideally, three would be above average or outstanding performers, while three would be below average or poor performers. The respondent does not have to name these people to the interviewer, but to facilitate remembering who they are the respondent is asked to write down some way of identifying each one of them (e.g. their initials) on a set of six cards. The better performers can be designated A, B, C and the other three as D, E and F.

2   The individual is asked to focus on cards/people A, C and E and to say – with their work behaviour in mind – which two seem more alike and different from

the third. They are then asked to specify one aspect of work behaviour that reflects this. It is important that they (a) keep this to one aspect of behaviour, and (b) that their description has a verb in it – in other words, it is behavioural and not just a vague adjectival description. When they have done that, they also have to describe how the behaviour of the third person differs in this respect. The responses are recorded by the interviewer, who will ask follow up questions to probe the replies in order to refine and clarify the nature of the behaviour being described. In Rep Grid terminology, the dimension so elicited is called a Construct.

3   The procedure is repeated, this time with another triad – B, D and F. The same questions are posed, with the request that this should cover a different aspect of behaviour than for the first triad.

4   This is continued with further combinations of the six cases, making sure that none are repeated. It may be that the respondent will not be able to go through all the permutations without running out of new behavioural differentiations.

5   The interviewer may record the responses on a sheet as the session progresses, something like this:

'Pair Alike: A, E – These two plan ahead; they take time to prepare in some detail.
Single Different: C – Always leaves things to the last minute. Does not think ahead – everything comes as a surprise to him'.

The dimension here looks as if it centres on planning, but the exact nature of it does not matter too much at this stage, as the interviewer will want to administer the grid to several more respondents to get a good-sized and representative sample of views.

6   The grid can be analysed in a number of ways, and it is at this point that expertise and experience with the method is most needed. The simplest way is to label the dimensions that have come out in each respondent's grid, and then to go through them all, weeding out the ones that have not consistently been perceived as differentiating between high and low performers. Also, some of those dimensions that look a little different from one another (either within one person's grid or comparing across grids) will, on closer inspection, turn out to be the same thing in slightly different words.

Alternatively, and much more ambitiously, each triad differentiation can be put on a separate sheet of paper, and all of them mixed up so that they are no longer 'attached' to the respondent they were elicited from. Then the interviewer reads through all of them, sorting them into piles, each one of which is made up of replies that seem to reflect the same kind of dimension. When this is done, each group of statements is looked at again, and the precise nature of the dimension and the behaviours relating to it are defined.

From the above description, it will be appreciated that this method is far from quick. It can also run into problems in terms of managers not being able to think of enough cases of good and poor performers, or having such simple views on the world that they have only two or three constructs they use to differentiate people. But it does yield rich behavioural descriptions that, with further scrutiny, can form the basis of the competencies used by an organisation.

You can try it for yourself! Either you can think of people you work with, or just with friends, family or acquaintences

In summary

In earlier years, appraisal tended to focus on personality attributes and then, later, on job related abilities – the latter were particularly associated with the use of rating scales, of which there are many varieties and perhaps even more problems. Placing greater emphasis on performance improvement rather than on assessment per se lead to an emphasis on results-oriented appraisal, and this, along with the assessment of competencies, underpins the content of most appraisal schemes today. All the different approaches have their advantages and disadvantages, and achieve different things. Putting together results-oriented appraisal with competency-based appraisal is a combination that can work well. It allows the more immediate and legitimate concern for achieving performance targets to co-exist with a focus on developing the appraisee – which in turn is related to the future performance of the organisation. It combines the two most motivational elements of appraisal, namely goal-setting and personal development. To maximise motivation and performance improvement, this would seem to be the most promising way forward.

Discussion points and questions

Outline the various approaches to job analysis, and assess their strengths and weaknesses.

What are the main problems with performance ratings – and how can we make ratings more accurate?

How do competencies help us in describing and assessing performance? What do they give us that assessing people against objectives does not?

Key references

Brannick, M. T., Levine, E. L. and Morqueson, F. P. (2007) *Job and Work Analysis*. Sage: Thousand Oaks, CA.

Catano, V. M., Darr, W. and Campbell, C. A. (2007) Performance appraisal of behavior-based competencies: A reliable and valid procedure. *Personnel Psychology*, 60, pp. 201–230.

Sparrow, P. (1996) Too good to be true? *People Management*, 5 December, pp. 22–29.

Chapter 4

Appraisal as an element in performance management

Performance management has emerged from the 1990s onwards as an approach not only to HR policies but to running the business as a whole. For many organisations, the term 'performance management' is synonymous with performance appraisal, or with performance-related pay (PRP). But performance management is much more than either or both of these. There is no single, universally accepted definition; indeed, it is perhaps better to think of it more as a philosophy than as a clearly defined process or set of policies. The most prevalent notion of performance management is that of creating a shared vision of the purpose and aims of the organisation, helping each individual employee to understand and recognise their part in contributing to them, and thereby managing and enhancing the performance of both individuals and the organisation (Williams, 2002).

The main building blocks of such an approach are:

1 the development of the organisation's mission statement and objectives
2 associated with this, the development of a business plan (business being interpreted in the broadest sense of the word)
3 enhancing communications within the organisation, so that employees are not only aware of the objectives and the business plan, but can contribute to their formulation
4 clarifying individual responsibilities and accountabilities (which means, amongst other things, having job descriptions, clear role definitions, and so on, and being willing to be held accountable)
5 defining and measuring individual performance (with the emphasis on being measured against one's own objectives rather than being compared with others)
6 implementing appropriate reward strategies
7 developing staff to improve performance further, and their career progression, in the future.

There are other elements to performance management that one could identify in various places – Total Quality Management (TQM) (Kanji and Asher, 1996) is perhaps the most obvious – but these seem to be the main ones. From the above list it can be seen that performance appraisal and possibly (but not necessarily) PRP may be part of performance management, but integrated into a much broader approach. However, there are some underlying principles that are not necessarily obvious from a simple list of elements of this sort, and which make performance management more than the sum of its parts. They are:

- Performance management is supposed to be owned and driven by line management, and not by the HR department or one or two directors – in marked contrast to many appraisal systems.
- There is an emphasis on shared corporate goals and values.
- Performance management is not a package solution, it is something that has to be developed specifically and individually for the particular organisation concerned.

You could add to these that performance management is something that applies to all staff, not just a part of the managerial group. This is certainly the case in some organisations, but by no means all.

If the performance management approach is successful, then it should result in more than just an improvement in the bottom line or the delivery of services:

- The culture of the organisation should be clearer and more readily identified with by those working in it.
- It should lead to higher levels of job satisfaction, job involvement and organisational commitment.
- It might be expected to have a positive impact on recruitment and retention, on quality issues, and on general human resources policy.

In fact, successful performance management should affect all aspects of the organisation's functioning; it is a holistic phenomenon. Encouragingly, research indicates that performance management systems (PMSs) indeed bring real benefits. Fletcher and Williams (1996) found from their study in nine UK organisations that elements of performance management were related to organisational commitment and, in particular, job satisfaction. The Audit Commission, in their major study of people, pay and performance in local government also found a strong link between effective PMSs and positive employee attitudes (Audit Commission, 1995a, b, c). Not surprisingly, performance management has become the centre of an immense amount of interest and activity in both public- and private-sector organisations.

How appraisal fits in

Performance appraisal has a central role to play in PMSs. It is the usual vehicle by which the organisational goals and objectives are translated into individual objectives. It also remains the chief means of discussing and acting on the development of the individual. The difference is that, within the context of a PMS, appraisal is now much more closely linked with the broader business context. This is illustrated in Box 4.1 by the case of a manufacturing company who operate an advanced PMS. There are, though, a number of issues that arise or which gain greater prominence when appraisal operates within the framework of PMS. These are discussed below.

Box 4.1: performance management and appraisal: an example from a manufacturing company

In this large, research-based manufacturing organisation, the cycle starts with strategic company objectives being set by the board. These are then broken down and put into measurable terms for other management groups. They are discussed at team level and the members of the team may set their targets for the team as a whole. Individual managers have their role and job description agreed in the performance planning session, and agree their own targets in the light of the team targets. The importance of balancing team and individual achievement is highlighted in the appraisal training, as the company does not want to promote counter-productive competitiveness.

An individual's targets are reviewed when necessary, but at least quarterly, and on each occasion the person's development needs are also reviewed – with the emphasis on those with particular relevance to achieving the targets. There is an end-of-year review of success against those targets, which feeds into the reward system. Significantly, the single-sheet discussion record is held only by the person appraised, and there are no performance rating scales. The company has, however, invested considerable time and effort in identifying a set of key competencies that are used as a development tool. When development needs are agreed with the individual, it is up to the line manager to work with the individual to decide upon the appropriate means of meeting them – exemplifying the PMS approach of giving responsibility to the line manager rather than simply passing action on to the personnel department.

Individual versus team achievement

One of the potential problems of creating a performance culture – which is what many organisations are seeking to do through adopting a PMS – is that there is a risk of encouraging individual achievement at the expense of team effort and cohesion. This risk can be overstated, but it is important that when objectives are set in the appraisal, they reflect the priorities of the unit and not solely the narrower focus of the individual. This suggests that there has to be a clear understanding of the team goals, and that it would be helpful for some sort of group review and discussion to take place to facilitate this, before individual appraisals are carried out.

Line-driven appraisal

The emphasis on line management driving PMSs has implications for how appraisal operates. In terms of the purposes of appraisal, it accords with the views expressed in Chapter 2 on the importance of finding a formula for appraisal that meets the needs of the participants as well as the requirements of the organisation. It is essential that line management have a major input in determining the nature of the appraisal system; we will look at some detailed examples of this in Chapter 5. The line influence can go beyond simply saying what some of the aims of appraisal might be and extend to actually designing the forms and deciding on the way the system will operate. Part of the rationale for this is that line input will be sensitive to local needs and requirements, and will develop appraisal to suit these better than any centrally imposed scheme is likely to.

While this level of line management involvement is laudable and welcome, and should raise commitment to the whole process of appraisal, it can create some problems. A company in the business services field found that when their line managers, as part of a PMS, took on the design of appraisal schemes, the results were very mixed indeed. Different parts of the company adopted different approaches according to their needs. Some of these were sensible and worked well, but some were poorly designed and were ultimately failures. This hands-off approach by the HR department perhaps went too far. The example provided by a large local authority is probably a better model. Here, the HR department – after a consultative process – defined a core appraisal scheme, which the line management could add to and (up to a point) adapt to meet their departmental needs.

Appraisal as part of a feedback loop

Another aspect of PMSs that has an impact on the role of appraisal is the operation of a feedback loop. If a PMS is to work effectively, it cannot be an exclusively top-down process. There has to be some mechanism whereby the strategic goals of the organisation and their implications at lower levels can be influenced and modified by the line. Without it, the chances of gaining commitment to the aims of the organisation are reduced. To some extent, this is covered by the emphasis on team discussion and the framing of team targets mentioned earlier. Such a mechanism necessitates an interim stage in the process, before individual targets are set in the appraisal, and should act as an opportunity to feed reactions to strategic objectives back to senior management. The appraisal itself also has some capacity to act as a feedback mechanism. Appraisees should be in a position to agree realistic and important targets rather than simply accepting those imposed on them.

The consequences of not allowing appraisal to operate in this way are illustrated by a major UK bank. Although a PMS was set up through careful consultation and line management involvement, when it was implemented it was seen as a wholly top-down process. Managers complained that they were unable to negotiate their objectives, with the result that they felt little ownership of the PMS and saw it as being driven by the HR department – despite the HR department having a fairly low-key facilitating role in the enterprise.

Excessive bottom-line emphasis

The main thrust of PMSs in many organisations is about bottom-line or service-delivery issues. This is understandable, but it can be taken too far. It brings back, in a slightly different form, the problem of excessive emphasis on ends rather than means. The concern becomes one of achieving short-term results at the expense of the longer-term aims – not least of which may be the development of the individual. Where it is part of PMSs, appraisal may become so focused on the individual's targets and their achievement that the developmental aspect is neglected. If this happens, the appraisal process will fail to generate as much commitment from those appraised and will suffer in effectiveness. Worse still, excessive bottom-line emphasis in PMSs can induce high stress levels that detract from employee well-being (Fletcher and Williams, 1992a).

To some extent, the twin aims of achieving improved performance and developing individuals can go hand-in-hand, as illustrated earlier in Box 4.1. However, it may be the case that, in the context of PMSs, holding development reviews separate from – but not unrelated to – the objective-setting and review process makes good sense. This kind of separation of appraisal functions into different occasions and sessions has long been advocated (e.g. Meyer et al., 1965), though more often driven by the need to take pay discussion out of the appraisal arena. With the emerging popularity of PMSs, the merit of such an approach is increasingly evident.

Appraisal and pay

Performance management does not, of itself, have to embrace the concept of performance-related pay. However, PRP is more often than not a part of a PMS, even in public-sector organisations (Bevan and Thompson in CIPD, 1992). The first thing to recognise is the importance of payment systems to organisations. The payroll takes up about 40 per cent of the total costs of the average manufacturing company, and in the case of public-sector organisations this proportion can rise to around 75–80 per cent. Clearly, any changes to the basis for payment can have profound implications for the organisation as a whole. This is not a book about PRP, but it is so often linked to appraisal in people's minds and in practice, that it is crucial to devote some time to considering it in detail.

Merit pay

There are lots of way of relating performance to payment, but the one most frequently encountered in PMSs is merit pay. This is where part (conceivably, all) of the basic salary increase is determined solely by the individual's performance. It is usually given annually, sometimes along with a cost of living rise, sometimes not. It generally falls within the range of 3–10 per cent of salary, though it can be more than this.

Survey findings repeatedly show support for the principle of merit pay amongst employees across a wide range of jobs and organisations. There is a strong and widely shared belief in the idea that those who perform well should gain greater benefits, and that allocating rewards this way is the fairest principle to follow. Thus, when a local authority offered staff the chance to transfer to PRP or to stay on the existing incremental system, they found that less then 3 per cent of the staff opted for the latter.

When we look a little deeper into this subject, however, we begin to see that the basis of the support for PRP is rather more questionable. It is neatly illustrated by a simple exercise carried out some years ago by an occupational psychologist (Meyer, 1980) who asked all staff in a major company how they felt they were performing compared to their peers. He found that *on average*, people thought they were performing better than 75 per cent of their peers! And the higher you went in the company, the greater this proportion became. The implication of this is that people think PRP is fine chiefly because they assume that they are going to benefit from it. No doubt this is behind the example given by Wright (1991) of a financial services company where 75 per cent of the staff were in favour of PRP, but more than 70 per cent of them were rated as superior on their appraisals.

To some extent, then, the popularity of the idea of PRP may be based on widespread overly-positive self-appraisal, and an anticipation of the direct benefits PRP will bring to the individual. Consequently, there is a substantial problem of dealing with people's expectations when PRP is introduced – the majority are going to find they are getting less than they expected, and in some cases, a lot less. If money is to be attached to appraisal assessments, organisations cannot afford to go on permitting very positively skewed distributions of ratings, as it would have a serious impact on their financial viability. They have to make sure that the assessments follow a more normal distribution. Not surprisingly, this sometimes has adverse effects. For example, Taylor and Pierce (1999) found that high level performers showed substantial downturns in their ratings of satisfaction and cooperation with their bosses following the appraisal and associated pay decision. These staff, having been expecting a higher performance rating, made external attributions, blaming their boss, the organisation or the performance management scheme. In my own research on performance management, I found staff who described getting the average assessment and pay award as a 'kick in the teeth'. Potentially, PRP has just as much power to de-motivate as to motivate.

There are other problems too. What do you do about employees who have performed well when the organisation as a whole has done very badly, and is in no position to award pay rises? How can adequate allowances be made for all the factors beyond the control of the individual in deciding whether their performance merits increased pay? And so on. The research evidence does not show that adoption of PRP is associated with high levels of organisational performance (Bevan and Thompson, 1991) or of individual performance (Hirsh, 2006). In itself, this is hardly surprising, any more than is the absence of a direct relationship between job satisfaction and performance. In both cases, one has to understand that performance on both the individual and the organisational level is determined by a multiplicity of factors.

It would be foolish to suggest that neither job satisfaction nor financial reward are important; there is certainly some relationship with overall satisfaction with pay and organisational performance measures (Currall et al., 2005). But the simple-minded way in which pay is trotted out as the answer to motivating people at work flies in the face of all the evidence and theory. Certainly, financial reward can be a motivator for some people, some of the time (Rynes et al., 2005). However, its effect is likely to vary hugely. Even within one person, the power of money as a motivator is likely to change radically depending on what life and career stage the individual is at. As long ago as the 1960s, research (Nealy, 1964) demonstrated that employees of different ages had very different reward preferences, and that the application of one incentive system to all employees in a particular job group did not make sense in motivational terms. We will return to this theme later.

By now it will be evident to the reader that there are many criticisms of the concept of merit pay and the way it tends to be used. None the less, it is often linked to appraisal in varying ways, and it is certainly not devoid of virtue, so it is important to examine the relationship in some detail.

Direct and indirect links with merit pay

Performance appraisal systems that are geared primarily towards assessment for comparison purposes usually have the most direct link with pay decisions. Such appraisal systems typically use rating scales, and have an overall rating of performance that in some cases is the principal or only determinant of the PRP award. Here there is no ambiguity – a basic purpose of appraisal is to help establish an equitable basis for reward decisions. Employees who get the highest overall ratings are those who get the highest pay increases (or perhaps the only pay increases).

As we have noted earlier, in Chapter 2, the down-side of this approach tends to be its poor record as a motivating or performance improvement mechanism, which is rather ironic, given that one of the main reasons for adopting PRP is to drive performance. Because of the repeated problems experienced in tying appraisal too closely to pay, the majority of organisations have opted for a more distant link. Some of them still have overall ratings and are oriented towards making and conveying an assessment in the course of an appraisal. But they make the PRP decisions on a separate occasion and at a later date, allowing factors other than just the performance ratings to determine the outcome. This takes some of the heat out of the appraisal discussion, as no reward decision is immediately pending and the appraisee is not given the impression that the overall rating is the sole arbiter of what follows. However, the appraisal is still centred on reward-linked assessment, with some of the associated difficulties.

What happens when the appraisal scheme falls into the development and motivation category? Does this preclude having any links with pay and rewards? No, it does not. But the pay decisions are made on a different basis and usually by a different method. Instead of resting on an overall rating, they will relate to achievement against targets and/or increases in competence – though linking rewards to the latter, as Sparrow (1996) points out, may not be a good idea at all. And they are likely to be related to other broader factors, such as unit performance, individual circumstances and experience levels. In some organisations, the approach of getting groups of managers together to discuss intended PRP awards has been adopted. Such meetings, often presided over by a member of top management or by the HR department, have the purpose of ensuring that similar standards are being applied across the organisation, and that an individual manager's reward decisions are justifiable and accountable to peers.

There is clearly still a link between appraisal and reward in this approach, but it is a broader-based and less clear-cut one. It may be carried out at a different time to the appraisal – although difficulties can then arise over sequencing. It makes sense, in PMSs, for the appraisal cycle to be tied-in with the business cycle. If strategic business goals are to be reflected at the level of team and individual target setting, then the latter have to follow the former in fairly short order. The review of achievement against targets logically takes place at or near the end of the next business year, and it is only at this point that the organisation knows what sums will be available (if any) for distribution in the form of PRP. This has the effect of bringing the pay decision back closer in time to the appraisal process, not in itself a very desirable thing. One of the ways around this evolved by some organisations is to have a separate development review (as opposed to the target review and setting session) a little while before the end of the cycle. This ensures that a constructive discussion can take place without the distraction of reward issues.

Appraisal and wider reward policies

Besides merit pay, there is a whole host of financial inducements of varying kinds (Rynes *et al.*, 2005), as well as a potentially vast array of non-financial rewards. Performance appraisal can live alongside some of these other reward strategies rather more easily than it can with merit pay, especially when they are can reflect the individual differences in needs mentioned earlier. The CIPD Reward Management Surveys (e.g., CIPD, 2003) show that organisations seem to be moving more towards flexible benefit packages that allow staff to make some choices that suit their personal circumstances and preferences. However, they still tend not to consult the individuals who have to implement reward strategy – the line managers – in developing it in the first place, and still less so those who are on the receiving end, the employees.

A positive development is that the use of one-off, unconsolidated bonus payments for exceptional performance, which might include such things as continuing to perform under especially difficult circumstances (e.g. short handed through staff illness) as well as achieving exceptional target performance, is becoming more popular (CIPD, 2003). Such bonus payments does not cause too many problems for appraisal, as very few people qualify for such awards, and they are more likely to be widely recognised as deserving them since it is not simply a case of being above average, the category so many people like to identify themselves with. The fact that they do not lead to permanent pay differentials is another factor that makes them acceptable, whilst still being motivating to the individuals receiving them. Other financial rewards operating at a team or organisational level (such as profit sharing) also present less problems for appraisal. Because of their wider basis, they make less impact on the individual in the appraisal situation.

The use of non-financial rewards still seems to be under-developed, though getting more recognition; Rose (2001) points out that non-cash recognition schemes can be a cost effective way of increasing staff commitment and performance. The point was made earlier that there are substantial individual differences in what motivates people, not only between individuals but within the same person at different life and career stages. Performance appraisal lends itself to the use of non-financial rewards that are tailored to the needs and preferences of the appraisee. Here are some examples of the kinds of reward that can be used:

office decoration (prints, flowers, etc.)
greater responsibility
praise and positive feedback
recognition from more senior/external sources
greater exposure to more senior management
enhanced job title
conference attendance
improved office and/or equipment
assignments involving overseas travel
sabbaticals.

Non-financial rewards do not, of course, automatically mean no-cost awards, but the first six items listed above, for example, have little or no expense attached to them.

Effective use of non-financial rewards in the appraisal process assumes two things. The first is that the scheme is set up to allow for it in the first place (though even if it is not, a manager with any initiative will still be able to get round this, up to a point). The second – and more difficult – is that the manager doing the appraisal knows what rewards to apply and when. This means possessing enough knowledge and understanding of the appraisee to be aware of what rewards that individual will appreciate at that time.

This is not commonly an element in appraisal training, but perhaps it should be. Nearly all appraisal schemes, even those that are essentially focused on assessment, purport to increase motivation, yet very few ever address this issue directly in training. Instead, they concentrate on the mechanics of the scheme and on the conduct of the appraisal interview. We will return to this subject when considering training in Chapter 8.

Giving non-financial rewards in appraisal does not usually generate the kind of problems associated with merit pay and some other forms of PRP. Perhaps this is because they are more individual and do not invite direct comparison, and because they often do not lead to permanent differentials. They are not valued the less for this, though. Many of them have the distinct advantage of being closer to intrinsic motivation than to extrinsic motivation. In other words, giving greater recognition, more responsibility, higher exposure to senior management and the like are all rewards that tap into the individual's pride in their work and achievement. Simply seeking to motivate with money sends the message that the reason for performing at a high level is personal financial reward. The question then arises: what happens to motivation and performance if (for various reasons, like economic recession) the money is not there any more?

In summary

Performance management is a more integrated and wholistic approach to human resource management that aligns it with the wider business goals. It sets some challenges for appraisal, not least the tendency to further increase linkages with reward policies. Performance related pay has a logical appeal on the surface, but experience and evidence suggests that its motivating qualities are doubtful, and that having a direct relationship between appraisal and financial rewards is likely to be counterproductive. In other respects, though, performance management – with its emphasis on greater involvement in and ownership of the objectives of the business, its focus on the development of a performance culture, and its concern with increasing motivation and development – has the potential to make appraisal practices far more effective than they ever were when they operated more or less in a vacuum. Performance appraisal is the pivotal mechanism of a good PMS, and within such a framework it can – perhaps for the first time – achieve the high expectations that organisations have set for it.

Discussion points and questions

What would you expect to find in a Performance Management system – and where would appraisal fit in to it?

What motivates *you*? How do you think the answer to this question might change over the various ages and stages of your life?

Is it (a) fair (b) effective to link people's pay with their performance?

Think of additions to the list of non-financial rewards given above on page 46 that you would value or which you think could be applied in your organisation.

Key references

Fletcher, C. and Williams, R. (1996) Performance management, job satisfaction and organisational commitment. *British Journal of Management*, 7, pp. 169–179.
Rynes, S. L., Gerhart, B. and Parks, L. (2005) Performance evaluation and pay for performance. *Annual Review of Psychology*, 56, pp. 571–600.
Williams, R. (2002) *Managing Employee Performance: Design and Implementation in Organizations*. Thomson Learning (Psychology@Work Series): London.

Chapter 5

Designing appraisal systems, and the use of IT

The first four chapters of this book have mainly addressed what might be thought of as the more theoretical and conceptual issues surrounding appraisal. Now it is time to face some severely practical matters, starting with the process of designing the appraisal system. Much of what has been said so far is a necessary precursor to this – not least the discussion of the aims of appraisal and where it fits in with the broader performance management picture. Many of the problems of appraisal systems can be identified as arising out of the design process. Get it wrong here and it is likely to stay wrong. Design needs careful thought and consideration of a number of issues. This chapter will go through them one by one though, in practice, organisations seldom have that luxury – they have to be dealt with almost simultaneously and often rather quickly. But a little thought at this stage can save a lot of wasted time and effort later.

Aims (1): The organisational perspective

The very first step in designing appraisal schemes is deciding on their aims; as was said in Chapter 2, if you get this wrong pretty much everything else will go wrong too. There is a slightly different starting-point for organisations that already have appraisal compared with those that do not. The ones that do have their reasons for changing their approach, and these often determine what the aims of the appraisal will be. The mistake is usually to try to carry on with much the same aims for appraisal and simply to adjust some of the administration and paperwork associated with it. If the scheme is to be reviewed, it is worth looking again at the purposes it is being put to. In today's fast-changing organisational environment, it is unlikely that any appraisal scheme will be fully relevant to the needs and situation of the organisation for more than a few years; after that, it will need a thorough overhaul – which, apart from anything else, will serve the purpose of keeping appraisal in the front of people's minds and ensure that it does not lapse into becoming part of the bureaucratic history of the place.

The method of determining what the aims of appraisal should be, whether reviewing an existing scheme or starting from scratch, has tended not to vary much. The usual device has been a working party dominated by the HR department, with some top management input (the latter has increased in recent years). The agenda for appraisal has thus been set to reflect the needs of those concerned – collecting information for personnel decision-making and distributing rewards in many cases. Little attempt has been made to relate the appraisal process to the wider and longer-term needs of the business and the people driving it. To achieve the latter, a more strategically oriented approach is necessary. It might involve taking some very senior managers (including HR managers) away for a series of seminar-type events that encourage them to focus on the future direction of the organisation, what that implies for the kind of staff that will be needed, and how they will be developed. Such events may need some external facilitating agent, generally a consultant, and take time. Sometimes, quantitative information, from attitude surveys, Rep Grid exercises or other employee audit methods, is fed in to act as a basis for the discussion.

An increasing number of public- and private-sector organisations are using this kind of approach to think through not only the problems already facing them but anticipating those they will face a few years hence. The aims and functioning of appraisal are appropriately raised in this arena, and where they are so considered the resulting appraisal scheme is likely to look a lot more relevant and realistic in its intent than where it has just been the product of a working party set up for the purpose. None the less, these 'away-day' discussions can provide only part of the picture; they should be just one element in a wider consultation process.

Aims (2): The consultation process

We considered the perspectives of the different parties to appraisal in Chapter 2; the point was made then and has been since that ownership of the appraisal process is not something that should reside entirely with top management or the HR department: there has to be some kind of consultation process. The needs of top management, of the HR department, and of the appraisers and the appraisees should all be reflected in determining the purpose and form of appraisal. While this means that the appraisal seeks to offer something to all involved, it also means that it is unlikely to give everyone everything they might want. In other words, the consultation process implies a degree of compromise in the pursuit of wider ownership of, and commitment to, the appraisal system. It requires negotiation of the aims of appraisal.

What does such a consultation process look like? There are various approaches. One large retailing company got more than half their senior appraising managers to participate in group discussions in which they were presented with some initial proposals on a new appraisal system. These were subsequently modified as a result of the feedback given. A more comprehensive consultation process is described in Box 5.1. This example illustrates another point about consultation. The author visited the organisation concerned in the early 1990s, by which time the company had

---

Box 5.1: an example of consultation and participation in the design of a company appraisal scheme

A motor manufacturer set up its own systems company, which decided to establish a new appraisal scheme to reflect its particular needs and circumstances. The principal consideration was to involve as many staff as possible in the design stage, not only to gain commitment but to draw upon their extensive experience of appraisal in the past.

A series of discussion groups, each consisting of 12 employees representing a cross-section of staff from differing divisions, organisational levels and occupational groups, was set up. Each group considered the need for an appraisal system and how present practices could be improved. Amongst the conclusions of these discussions were:

- performance should be measured against agreed objectives
- elements of self-appraisal should be included
- the overall performance rating should be dropped
- the employee development element of the system should be kept separate from the appraisal of performance element.

The next stage was to draft an appraisal form and procedure that conformed to the groups' requirements. The personnel department, which had taken the lead in facilitating the consultation process, then presented the provisional scheme to senior management and staff unions as the basis for appraisal over a trial period. Despite some reservations, this was agreed. The four-month trial took place, and all appraised under the new system were asked for their views through questionnaires and interviews. The reactions were very favourable, though there were some suggestions for changes (in relation to details rather than the overall approach) that were incorporated in the final version of the scheme. This was accepted by senior management and staff unions and put into operation (Scott, 1983). It ran successfully for many years after that.

changed hands and was – not surprisingly – rather different. The turnover in employees over such a long period had brought about a situation in which few staff had been there when the appraisal scheme was devised. Consequently there was no longer a perception of ownership of the appraisal system – it was thought of as something that had come from the personnel department. This demonstrates one aspect of a general principle of appraisal, namely that any scheme has a limited 'shelf-life'. Ownership lasts only as long as the participants and their memories of the consultation process; it needs to be revived in some form as part of the review mechanism of how appraisal is functioning.

As a result of the consideration of the aims of performance appraisal by the HR department and top management, and of the consultation with potential appraisers and appraisees, the general nature of the scheme – and maybe some of its specifics – will be set. These in turn will determine which of the various appraisal methods looked at in Chapters 2 and 3 will be required. Precisely how these are put into action, though, depends on other factors, described in the following sections.

Organisational structure and culture

The structure and the culture of organisations are dynamically interrelated, and both need to be considered in drawing up plans for an appraisal scheme. Is the company a highly structured, bureaucratic one in which there is a great emphasis placed on formal observance of rules and procedures, and in which power is vested in individuals largely as a result of their position in the hierarchy? If so, then the appraisal scheme will probably need to be a rather formal process too, with clear guidelines, a fixed timetable, and the appraiser firmly in control of the process, and so on. It might be argued that in circumstances like these, the appraisal should be an important vehicle in organisational development, helping change the organisation in the direction of greater flexibility. While this may indeed be the case, there is a danger that if it departs too quickly and radically from the existing culture, it will be rejected. An example of how appraisal was designed and, over time, gradually modified to suit the culture, is given in Box 5.2.

With the numerous changes and pressures of recent times, many organisations have shifted to a style and structure that a few years ago would only have been found in advanced technology and computing companies. The delayering process has removed several levels of management; greater autonomy and profit/loss accountability has been given to the individual operating units; the demand for speed in responding to market changes has increased (often necessitating changes in staffing and organisation, with more use of matrix management), and so on. Partly as a result of this, the power base of managers has changed and now often stems from their demonstrated expertise and competence as opposed to being legitimised simply by their rank in the hierarchy.

In circumstances such as these, a flexible and adaptable approach to appraisal is necessary, with a greater degree of local control over content and administration – much as was described in the context of performance management in the last chapter. This usually fits in well with appraisal that is primarily geared to motivation and development and has a high level of appraisee participation. But where assessment and comparison comes into

---

Box 5.2: evolving appraisal practices to match changes in the civil service culture

When a comprehensive performance appraisal scheme was introduced for the first time into the UK Civil Service in the early 1970s, the approach taken was carefully suited to the culture. It was a closed scheme, where the general standing of the appraisee as regards performance and potential could be discussed in the interview, but the actual ratings were not disclosed; in fact, none of the lengthy written report, apart from the agreed job description, was seen by the appraisee. The emphasis was on discussing performance in the light of detailed ratings of job-relevant qualities. The appraisee was invited to complete a preparation form before the appraisal interview, but this was not part of the record of the event.

In retrospect, this appears to be a rather formal and even paternalistic way of going about appraisal. However, in the context of the time and the stage of development of the organisation, it represented a significant move forward that did not shift too far away from the existing culture. It broke new ground by implementing a standard approach to appraisal, based on training the appraisers, that led to face-to-face job discussions between managers and subordinates. Given that such discussions had seldom if ever taken place previously, it would have been asking too much too quickly for appraisers to be required to take on a more open form of appraisal, incorporating elements of self-appraisal and objective-setting.

Once started, however, the appraisal system – along with other changes – paved the way for a rather more contemporary style of management and a different approach to appraisal. Over the years, the Civil Service appraisal system has become a more open, participative and flexible one. Looking at it now, it would be difficult to see any traces of the original scheme. With the introduction of objective-setting and (more recently) PRP, it looks more like the kind of appraisal scheme found in many business organisations, and as such is perhaps an indicator of how the Civil Service culture itself has changed.

the picture as the focus for appraisal, difficulties arise. The use of standard report formats and rating scales, completed at fixed times by the nominated appraising manager to facilitate cross-company comparison, does not sit comfortably within the framework of organisations geared to flexibility and quick reaction.

Even within a single organisation there can be marked variations in culture and attitude, however. An example of this will be found in quite a few local authorities, where the response of the social services department and of the highways department to what is ostensibly the same appraisal scheme frequently differ in ways that reflect aspects of the staff groups involved. The former has a strong social work ethos, with considerable emphasis on interpersonal issues, and so handling the appraisal interview process in an open but sensitive way becomes paramount. The latter department, whose staff are often professionally qualified engineers and the like, tend to have quite a different attitude. They are inclined to concentrate more on any quantitative elements in the scheme (which are usually to be found in the paperwork) and are usually stronger on directness than on subtlety in the communication process. Other departments that differ in terms of functions and staff make-up could just as easily exhibit these and other variations of response to appraisal. No doubt much the same is also true in some divisions of private-sector organisations.

How can these cultural differences be allowed for when devising the appraisal scheme? Again, the use of a core appraisal scheme with additional elements added locally to meet specific needs and to increase its relevance is one option. Any good consultation process should bring to light what variations are needed. However, it is not always the case that the scheme itself has to be modified. In the example given above of the social work and highways departments, the problem is perhaps more one of orienting the training and presentation of the scheme to address the likely differences in attitudes, reactions and skills. There are, of course, other cultural variations of a rather different nature that are found within organisations. The ethnic and national mix of employees is becoming more heterogeneous, and the concept of managing diversity has growing significance for performance appraisal. Again, however, this subject relates at least as much to training as to design, and cultural influences will be discussed later in both Chapters 8 and 12.

One of the effects of delayering has been to produce flatter management hierarchies. Some organisations have had this kind of structure for years anyway, and it does bring with it a problem for conventional appraisal systems. The norm has been for the individual's immediate boss to do the appraisal, with some input from the 'grandparent' – the boss two levels up. This becomes a less practicable arrangement when the structure of the management hierarchy means that each manager has many direct reports. The precise number that any one appraiser can manage is a favourite topic for taxing the minds of those trying to design and implement appraisal systems. There is of course no definitive answer to this question, and much depends on the timing – are all the appraisals to be done in a rather limited period, or can they be spread through the year? Assuming a restricted time limit and the requirement that the appraisals be done properly, a rough guide is one per week, with a maximum of, say twelve in eight weeks. That said, though, the situation often found now means that working to those figures would leave a lot of appraisals not done.

The problem is further compounded in many instances by the geographical spread of the organisation. With fewer management levels, and greater internationalisation of businesses, the appraisee's immediate boss can increasingly be based in another part of the country, or in another country altogether. It thus becomes very difficult for a manager in this position to be in full command of the facts about his or her subordinates' performance and development needs. All this leads to the next crucial question to be considered in designing appraisal schemes – who is the appraiser?

Who should appraise?

The rationale advanced for the traditional, one-up appraisal is that the immediate boss is in the best position to assess and guide subordinates, because of the amount of contact and greater experience. However, as we have seen, the contact argument does not always hold good. Moreover, the concerns about the appraisers' objectivity and fairness in assessment have made this model problematic. One of the ways in which appraisal has been modified over recent years is the introduction of people other than the immediate boss into the process. The various alternatives that have been tried are outlined below.

Self-appraisal

Over the last 30 years there has been a pervasive increase in the degree to which appraisal systems have been structured to allow and encourage participation by the appraisee. Initially, it was limited to giving the individual a form to assist in preparing for the appraisal, listing headings that formed an agenda for the appraisal interview and inviting the person to think about them beforehand. This moved on to including sections on the report form for the appraisee to add their own comments on the appraisal, and to register any disagreement if necessary. Eventually, some organisations adopted an appraisal process that involved both appraiser and appraisee completing nearly identical appraisal forms, discussing them in an interview, and filing a single agreed report on the basis of this. In addition, self-assessment is usually an integral element in 360-degree feedback.

There are numerous advantages to incorporating self-appraisal into the appraisal process. It is said to engender more commitment on the part of the person appraised, because of its participative nature. It reduces defensiveness by encouraging the appraisees to take the lead in reviewing their own performance, rather than having an assessment imposed on them. It encourages appraisees to think about their own performance and development needs in a focused way. And by giving the perspective of two people – the appraiser and the appraisee – it should lead to more objective assessment than if it rested on either one alone.

It is not surprising, then, that self-appraisal has become so popular. But there are some problems that inhibit its use. Possibly the greatest of these is the danger of inflated or excessively lenient self-assessments (Jones and Fletcher, 2002). This can certainly happen, sometimes through a fundamental lack of objectivity on the part of the appraisee, sometimes because the situation is not one that motivates the individual to be accurate, and sometimes because the nature of the exercise does not facilitate accurate self-assessment. Research (Mabe and West, 1982) suggests that while there are individual differences in self-assessment objectivity, on average people have the capacity to be reasonably accurate in reporting on their own behaviour. Whether they will deploy that capacity is another matter, though. If the motivational context of the situation is such that immediate decisions on rewards depend on it, then it is likely to strain anyone's objectivity and honesty, and people will be more inclined to be lenient in their self-assessments. Finally, if the invitation to self-assess is not framed appropriately, then it can promote inaccuracy (Jones and Fletcher, 2004). The latter is likely to arise when people are asked to compare themselves with others, especially if the others concerned are not all that familiar to them. It is often the case that people simply don't have the information to gauge their effectiveness against that of colleagues and peers and asking someone to make this kind of comparison is giving them a task they are likely not to be able to do very well.

All this serves to suggest that self-appraisal will do best where:

- the immediate boss does not see enough of the appraisee to be left as the only source of the appraisal data
- there are no reward decisions based solely on the outcome of the appraisal process
- the nature of the self-assessment is such that appraisees compare themselves against their own personal standards, and not against other people's.

This last point needs some elucidation. One of the most effective ways of using self-appraisal is to ask the person appraised to assess their performance against what they see as their own 'norm'. Thus, they might be invited to say what they feel they have done best and least well over the last year, or – in a more specific form – which of various listed attributes or competencies they feel themselves to be strongest on and weakest on. For example, an individual may rate him- or herself high on information collection and handling but low on delegating to subordinates, but the high rating does not imply that this person is better than average in the department, nor does the low rating imply being worse than average – they both reflect variations against that appraisee's notional individual standard. Used in this way, self-appraisal has been found to be more discriminating and less subject to halo effect than appraisal done by others (Williams, 1989). An example of a scheme incorporating a strong element of this approach to self-appraisal is given in Appendix A.

Self-appraisal probably has the greatest potential in an appraisal system geared primarily to motivation and development. None the less, it is likely to be important in any type of appraisal system, since the individual's self-assessment will be on the agenda implicitly, if not explicitly, and it is better that it is overtly brought into play in some fashion as part of the process. Self-appraisal, like most things, can probably be taken too far, though. There is no more value in basing appraisal exclusively on the appraisees' views than there is on the appraisers', so it is unlikely that schemes that seek to do this will be very effective. The author came across one such appraisal scheme in an airline company, and found that the output from the appraisal process appeared to be ignored in all personnel decision-making – a sure sign that it was not taken seriously.

Appraisal by peers

The involvement of peers in the appraisal process is something that has only recently become popular, largely in the context of 360-degree feedback systems, of which more later. It has a longer history, and greater appeal, in academic and teaching institutions, where there is often a dislike of formal hierarchical management structures. In universities it is commonly an important input to promotion decisions, external assessors being asked to comment on the candidates' work and its impact on the field. In theory, appraisal by peers should have a lot to offer, because peers may be in a position to give a unique insight into an individual's team contribution – no small concern when the pressure on people to achieve might sometimes lead them to put their own concerns ahead of the team effort. In fact, though, peer rating in general is not all that accurate or unbiased, judging from some of the research evidence (Antonioni and Park, 2001). However, because it takes place largely within the context of multi-source, multi-level feedback systems, it will be dealt with in the next chapter; it will also be mentioned in connection with the appraisal of professional groups (Chapter 11).

Multi-level, multi-source appraisal

This consists of assessments made on an individual (the 'focal manager') by subordinates, peers and bosses plus, in some cases, clients. Usually it also requires the person appraised to do a self-rating. Because this has become a major approach to appraisal and development in the last few years (under the banner of 360-degree feedback) it is examined separately and in depth in the next two chapters.

Appraisal by superiors

This heading does not refer to the traditional one-up appraisal process, but to the situation in which several bosses may contribute to the appraisal. It is, like peer appraisal, multi-source, but it is not multi-level appraisal; and it is becoming increasingly common. The reason for its growing popularity is that with the changes in organisational structure mentioned earlier, matrix management has become more prevalent. Where an individual works on a series of different projects over a year, serially or simultane-ously, each with different project leaders, it becomes very difficult to identify any one person who should be the appraiser. The two approaches that most often find favour here are either to have a series of separate, project-specific appraisals or to have one appraisal at the end of the review period to which all those who have managed the individual contribute. The former has some merit, but it does suffer from the lack of an overall view; it is quite likely that an individual will vary in performance (or, more accurately, be seen to) from one project to another, not least because of the different team make-up and the relationships that result. The alternative method has more to recommend it: a manager is nominated to collect the appraisal information from all the individual's team/project leaders through the year, and to base the appraisal on that. If there are reward implications, then again it is easier to deal with them on an overview basis. There is, of course, nothing to prevent there being informal review sessions with individual managers at the end of each project as well.

Appraisal by subordinates

Finally, and on a rather different note, there is the possibility of subordin-ates appraising their bosses – upward appraisal. This is not so much a question of 'who should appraise' as 'who should appraise whom'. Appraisal by subordinates is most often encountered in multi-level/source appraisal schemes, dealt with in the next chapter, though there it is slightly diluted by being just one of several sources of feedback. While it is possible to have upward appraisal without having a 360-degree feedback scheme, the issues and problems are much the same in each case, and so will be left to Chapter 6.

In conclusion

Although the practice of having appraisals done by the employees' immediate boss is still the norm, it is not likely to remain so. All the influences identified earlier dictate that appraisal will become a more diversified process, quite possibly with different arrangements as to who appraises for different people in the organisation, according to their circumstances. This in turn has implications for training in appraisal: the necessary skills may need to be spread more widely within an organisation, and conveyed earlier in an individual's career than they are now.

Who should be appraised?

One of the trends over recent years is that the coverage, in terms of staff groups, of appraisal schemes has grown (Industrial Society, 2001). Many organisations now include directors in their appraisal schemes, and this trend will show a marked increase following the Higgs report (Higgs, 2003) and its adoption by the Financial Reporting Council. Higgs' review of non-financial directors and of board functioning recommended that *all* directors be subject to performance review at least once per year, and that the company's annual report should state whether and how the reviews have taken place. At the other end of the scale, so to speak, clerical, secretarial, skilled and semi-skilled workers are increasingly being drawn into the appraisal arrangements. So the answer to the question of who should be appraised is, in the view of many organisations – everybody.

The extension of appraisal schemes to take in more categories and levels of employees does not imply that it is the same scheme for all. There is some virtue in uniformity, but not a lot. An example of how the desire for bureaucratic convenience and similarity of assessment can be taken to extremes is provided by an appraisal report form used in many government departments in the early 1970s. This form required all staff – from nuclear physicists to clerical officers, from first level supervisors to senior managers – to be rated on the same set of dimensions. The notion that the same attributes were relevant to such a wide range of jobs is quite ludicrous. The same *elements* of appraisal may be present in the appraisal scheme at different levels, in the sense that there may be some objective-setting and assessment of some job-related abilities, but the form and content of them should certainly vary to suit the circumstances. For instance, in jobs which allow for little personal discretion in determining work style and output, there may be limited scope for setting personal targets, in which case the results-oriented aspect of the appraisal would be diminished. For some unskilled and routine tasks, the purpose of the appraisal may be limited to simply acknowledging the part played by the individual and listening to any problems, views or ideas they want to raise. In the case of younger and more inexperienced staff, self-appraisal may be less helpful and appropriate as a method as they may have difficulty in judging their own performance at this stage.

So, performance appraisal has something to offer for all categories and levels of staff, but it is not the same in every case. The implication is that the organisation needs not one, but two or three schemes that share some common thinking and components and which are tailored to the needs of the level or group concerned. It is important, though, to try to ensure that no staff group end up feeling they they are being treated as second-class citizens on the basis of different appraisal processes. A medium-sized county council found that when it had PRP for senior levels and not for the management grades immediately beneath, the latter felt that they were missing out in some way, and that they were earning their bosses' pay rises.

The administration of appraisal

There are three main aspects to this that will be discussed here: frequency, documentation and timing. A fourth one, the monitoring and maintenance of appraisal schemes, will be looked at in Chapter 9.

Frequency

With the predominance of results-oriented appraisal, what was formerly the most usual practice of holding appraisals annually makes less sense. The problem is that objectives are so susceptible to changing circumstances, and progress against them needs to be reviewed more frequently than just once a year. Consequently, many organisations have a formal review and objective-setting session annually, but encourage the appraisers to hold interim reviews either quarterly or half-yearly. Apart from checking that objectives are still relevant, these also provide the opportunity to take remedial action if the appraisee is having difficulties. No additional paperwork need be involved in interim reviews, though any changes may have to be added to the original statement of agreed objectives.

The periodicity of appraisals may vary for other reasons, too. For *some* older staff nearing retirement, it may be that appraisals – or some elements of them – are less meaningful. They might be given the choice of opting out for a year, though not more than that. On the other hand, with younger staff who are new to the job or to the organisation, there is arguably a need for an appraisal session within the next six months and two in the first year.

Documentation

The one golden rule is to keep it to a minimum. The success of appraisal lies not in the paperwork but in the aims and attitudes of the participants. Like most things, this can be taken too far. There is a need for adequate background documentation to explain the scheme when it is launched, and for a sufficient formal record of the appraisal discussion and outcomes. The former will be dealt with when appraisal training is covered in Chapter 8. As far as the rest is concerned, the nature of the forms obviously depends on the scheme itself, but having something for the appraisee to work from, an agenda at very least (if no other self-appraisal is involved), is usually found to be necessary for a constructive session. The record of the appraisal has to be enough to give a clear picture of the main objectives and action points agreed when it is looked at in a year's time. What it does not have to do is to try to give a blow-by-blow account of the discussion, or to go into much detail. This kind of appraisal record usually generates more trouble than it is worth, and often reduces the appraisal to a kind of tortuous drafting session, with more emphasis on the formal record than on the substance of the discussion.

Who should actually hold copies of the appraisal forms also depends on the nature of the scheme. If the appraisal data is to be part of the process of determining pay and promotion, then usually it has to be made available to the personnel department. For appraisal where the focus is rather more on objective-setting and review, there may only be a need for the appraiser and appraisee to keep copies, though it is useful for there to be some notification to HR that the event has taken place. Also, the manager two levels up should perhaps have a sight of the appraisal report to keep in touch with what is going on – though sometimes the sheer volume of appraisees militates against this. In general, the principle of restricting access to appraisal data to those who have an immediate need to see it is the one usually followed.

Turning to a very different aspect of the paperwork, there is no law that states that appraisal forms must be designed to look about as visually appealing as an income tax return. Given the need for brevity – nobody wants to see six-page blockbusters landing on the desk waiting to be completed on each appraisee – it is probably worth getting some professional help in the actual lay-out and presentation of the form. This should facilitate the development of appraisal paperwork that is professional in appearance (i.e. visually pleasing without being distracting), economical in its use of space, and effective in generating the information required.

Appraisal is increasingly software-based, the forms and supporting documentation presented on a PC. This brings with it various issues which will be discussed below. Whether appraisals are paper-bound or PC-driven, to leave nothing to chance it is important to pilot all the appraisal documentation on some appraisers and appraisees. The aim is not to check whether the system will work – piloting the system as a whole is a nice idea, but is seldom viewed as feasible – but just to ensure that what is said is understandable by the participants and can be used as intended by them.

Timing

When appraisals should take place is not always easy to decide. The preferred pattern has been for them all to be done within a limited period, partly for administrative reasons; all the forms can be sent out together, all the information sought by HR can be collected at once. The disadvantage of this is that the load on appraisers is concentrated over just a few weeks, leaving them little time for anything else and probably feeling a bit jaded by the end of the process, too. It also does not necessarily match well with varying individual circumstances; an appraisee may have started the job only a few weeks before, or it may be that the appraiser is new to the position. For these reasons, some organisations have chosen to ask for appraisals to be done on the anniversary of the appointment to the current post, or have staggered them through the year on some other basis.

The balance, however, has swung towards the set-period approach. The reason for this is the tying-in of appraisal with other aspects of performance management. If the objectives set in appraisal are to link with the wider team and organisational objectives, if they are to relate to the business plan as a whole, then inevitably the appraisal process has to occur at a time that coordinates with these. The implication is that objective-setting will take place fairly soon after the business plan for the year has been laid down, and – where PRP is a feature of the situation – that the review of people's progress against objectives and the reward decisions arising out of it are made at a point when the results for the previous year are known (because the reward decisions generally rest on the amount of funds available for distribution in this form). If the organisation holds a separate appraisal session to focus on development needs, this can be timed with rather more flexibility.

Using Information Technology in designing and implementing appraisal

Reference has already been made to using software-based packages but the role of Information Technology (IT) in appraisal may go far beyond that in the future. Some of the developments in technology are not exclusively about IT but in one way or another all depend on IT to some extent. One aspect of the increasing role of computers in this context is in relation to the electronic monitoring of performance, which affords the ability to record a huge amount of data on multiple dimensions of work performance (Stanton, 2000). This facilitates a more continuous and detailed collection of performance data in some jobs – e.g. call centres – and has the capacity to do so in non-obvious, even covert manner. Another use of IT is in the feedback process; many software packages are available to record and aggregate performance ratings and written observations, and to make the information available online. The use of IT in these ways potentially helps in making the appraisal process more manageable, especially where multiple rating sources are involved. However, it also raises many questions about appraisees' reactions and possible effects on PA outcomes. How do people feel about being monitored in this way – are there shades of 'Big Brother' about it? Do they perceive the feedback so delivered to be credible? Do they attend to it, or switch off? Does it have the same impact as face-to-face feedback? At present, only limited research and experience is available to try to answer such questions (Fletcher, 2001), and in some cases the evidence is rather indirect. Nonetheless, it is worth looking at what we know so far, if only because commercial organisations promoting software based solutions will become more rather than less prevalent, making it important for HR practitioners to understand some of the issues.

Do people welcome feedback from electronic sources? Is computer-based appraisal too 'impersonal'?

The findings here are broadly positive. There is some reason to believe that feedback is *more* likely to be sought through electronic mail than through face-to-face meeting. A possible reason for this is that there may be less apprehension about the assessment and less emotion in getting feedback from a computer, and perhaps with good reason if a computer-based system helps focus the appraiser's attention on job-relevant behaviours and reduced the influence of potentially biasing interpersonal factors (Fletcher and Perry, 2001). Supporting this, one study (Weisband and Atwater, 1999) found that the potentially biasing effects of the appraiser's personal liking for the appraisee on their ratings were less where the ratings were made electronically. These findings perhaps illustrate that the more impersonal nature of entering and communicating assessments via a computer might lead to greater objectivity – which is clearly desirable in appraisal. Maybe as a consequence of this, individuals seem to trust feedback that they obtain on the computer more than feedback provided directly by their supervisor, which is important for actually taking it on board; of course, there is a certain irony in this if the feedback comes from the same source (the supervisor) in the first place. There is also evidence that feedback provided by computer results in better work performance and learning than when the same feedback is provided by a human (Fletcher and Perry, 2001). But, on the downside – is the cost of this impersonal approach also a loss of sensitivity? Will it lead to less tact in handling the feedback situation – because apart from anything else, there is no chance to directly observe the reactions of those on the receiving end? So, although performance feedback conveyed online may reduce face-to-face confrontation and be less emotionally laden, it may still lead to disagreement and resentment if individuals tend to be less polite and show less concern for others when communicating it.

Will more and quicker feedback be better feedback?

One of the benefits of computer monitoring of performance is that it has the potential to make more information available and faster, without the need to wait for a scheduled appraisal review to receive it. A basic psychological principle is that quicker feedback is more effective, so rapid feedback mediated by IT should enhance learning and be beneficial. The question of the value of *more* feedback is less clear cut. There is the possibility of habituation effects – people getting so much feedback that they cease to give it much attention.

At the present time the verdict has to remain open on the impact on-going feedback from monitoring will have on the appraisal session. One potential consequence, though, stems from the fact that many of the jobs most susceptible to this kind of performance monitoring are often not covered by formal PA schemes at present; it may be that the availability of such quantitative performance measures begins to bring the staff in these roles within formal organisational PA arrangements. Certainly, it seems possible that computer-based systems may reduce the potential for bias, not least by collecting the data that allows HR to identify any systematic group differences that emerge – but they cannot eliminate it entirely. If computers are to be brought into the PA process, they should perhaps facilitate rather than replace face-to-face feedback – it seems likely that there will continue to be a need for the latter (and for training in how to handle it) probably in much the same form as appraisal takes now. Quite a lot depends on the broader organisational and work context; computer-based performance feedback systems may be most effective when employees frequently use and have access to computer technology, in which case getting feedback this way will come more naturally. An example of an unusually thorough and carefully constructed online performance management system is given in Box 5.3.

Box 5.3: online performance management at UBS

UBS is a large financial services group employing over 70,000 people globally. It went through ten years of rapid growth, including mergers and acquisitions, and perceived the need to ensure its PM systems were applicable to the new shape of the organisation and that they delivered value. This led to the development of a new PM online system which combined corporate and local ownership. Three core competencies (Client Orientation, Teamwork and Professional Behaviour) were identified, along with a number of supplementary, flexible competencies; all parts of the business included the core competencies in their PM, but they were free to choose amongst the latter those that were most valuable and relevant to them. Each competency is defined in terms of four levels of performance, and each level is described by a set of observable behaviours. Business leaders, HR and Managers can create and define the role profiles they see as critical and determine the competency expectations for each of these – a degree of flexibility and sophistication that would be difficult to achieve in anything but an IT-based system. When it comes to making an assessment of an individual's performance, the system collates multiple raters' assessments and generates a performance 'skyline' to highlight strengths and weaknesses. The line manager assigns his or her own ratings in light of this information and their own view of the person's performance. The system allows the appraiser to see how the level of competence being shown matches the level required by the role. It also generates a recommended overall rating by calibrating managers' ratings against required competency levels.

The UBS PM system allows for continuous access to update and adjust objectives and will soon allow appraisers to enter notes and observations on performance or goal achievement at any point in the year, and for the person appraised to obtain that ongoing feedback. It also facilitates HR giving feedback to line managers about the distribution of their ratings and how these compare to other, more widely-based distributions of ratings. HR are also able to take data off the system to identify 'blind spots', which are skill gaps for teams or departments, and to assist in developing action plans to deal with them.

The flexibility allowed by the UBS system is considerable, and there are many other aspects of it than can be outlined in this brief description. The organisation has already found that the new approach is superior in terms of providing a more accurate picture of employee development needs, and they are rigorously evaluating the system in other ways; so far, results have been reassuring in terms of its acceptability to users.

One more caveat –

With personal (including performance) data stored on a PC, there is a danger to confidentiality, which is of course the reason for the UK legislation enshrined in the Data Protection Act. Those appraised may reasonably seek reassurance as to who will have access to their appraisal data held on an IT system, and what security is in place to protect it. In her study, Hirsh (2006) confirms this concern and found that managers saw a further disadvantage of computerisation in that it simply encouraged HR to ask for yet more information on skill profiles etc.

So, the potential for further applications of IT in the appraisal field is considerable, but as yet the impact of them is unclear; there seem to be potential advantages and also perhaps some disadvantages. Two things we can be sure of – the first, that some people will herald them as the answer to all previous problems; the second, that they are not. We will probably learn about their best use the hard way, as usual. Some companies will rush into applying them, and we can all stand back and watch and learn from the results. It is always tempting to think that a system or a new piece of technology can get us off the hook when it comes to the messy business of handling relationships at work and managing performance, but while it can help, it will never do more than that.

In summary

The changes that organisations have gone through in recent years, and their continuing evolution, make it even more essential that appraisal practices are developed that offer a degree of tailoring to the context and circumstances of the different parts of an organisation. Consultation with the main stakeholders in formulating the appraisal scheme is key to the success of this. The shift in organisational structures – and in particular the move to more 'flat' hierarchies – has implications for who contributes to the appraisal of an individual. The range and level of staff covered by appraisal arrangements has increased, and this also requires a more flexible approach to ensure that the process is relevant to their varying needs. The administration of appraisal schemes is still often too cumbersome with an excessive emphasis on forms. Whilst the growing role of IT in delivering the appraisal process can lead to swifter and more efficient operation of the scheme, the more ambitious use of computers in appraisal – for example in delivering feedback on a more regular basis – raises many issues to which we do not at present have answers.

Discussion points and questions

How do we get 'buy-in' to appraisal during the design stage?

Who should contribute to the appraisal of an individual employee? Is there a role for self-assessment – if so, how much reliance should we place on it?

What can information technology contribute to performance appraisal – will it make the process more objective, will it help in making feedback more acceptable?

Key references

Antonioni, D. and Park, H. (2001) The relationship between rater affect and three sources of 360 degree feedback ratings. *Journal of Management*, 27, pp. 479–495.
Mabe, P. A. and West, S. G. (1982) Validity of self-evaluation of ability: A review and meta-analysis. *Journal of Applied Psychology*, 67, pp. 280–296.
Stanton, J. M. (2000) Reactions to employee performance monitoring: Framework, review and research directions. *Human Performance*, 13, pp. 85–113.

Chapter 6

Multi-level, multi-source feedback systems

The previous chapter looked at the issue of who should appraise, and touched on the issue of multi-level, multi-source appraisal. The latter has undoubtedly taken off in a big way in the last few years, usually under the banner of 360-degree feedback. This generally means an individual being rated by subordinates, peers, superiors and – sometimes – clients or customers, as well as doing a self-assessment. A few British companies began using it, sometimes in a more limited form that was essentially upward feedback from subordinates, in the early 1990s. Mention of these schemes in the press sparked off great interest: one of the organisations involved had more than 500 calls and letters from other companies as a result of a few column inches on their system in a national newspaper. Since then, 360-degree feedback systems have spread with tremendous speed across both public and private sectors.

Strangely enough, the idea of multiple-source assessment is not by any means new. Perhaps the earliest documented example of such an approach in the UK is that adopted on an experimental basis by Gulf Oil some years ago (Stinson and Stokes, 1980). This was designed to be additional to the existing appraisal scheme, and was limited to 30 senior managers in a number of countries. (As noted in the previous chapter, geographical spread makes it hard for any one appraiser to monitor subordinates' performance effectively.) Each member of this group chose between five and eight colleagues at any level who they felt were in a position to make a valid assessment of their performance. The raters so chosen completed the appraisal forms anonymously, and then sent them to the HR department. The latter drew up a summary for the individual concerned, who prepared a self-appraisal in light of it. The appraisee's boss was also given the summary to help in preparing for the appraisal, which then took place. In general, this multi-source appraisal was well received by all concerned. The London Business School and Henley Management College were also early users of such feedback for students attending courses they ran.

In many respects, what has evolved more recently differs relatively little from the Gulf Oil scheme. Why then did it take another 15 years or so to become more widely adopted? A clue to this is the fact that it has a much longer history in the US (Redman and Snape, 1992), where there is traditionally a rather more robust attitude to giving and receiving feedback. This, along with a readiness to accept a process that, to some extent, represents a challenge to normal hierarchical concepts of management, are perhaps preconditions for such a development to become possible. The changes in UK organisations described in Chapter 5 created a new environment and changed ideas about management, with the result that 360-degree feedback was an idea whose time had come. To some extent, the acceptability of multi-source feedback is influenced by wider cultural differences (see Chapter 12). All the indications are that 360-degree assessment in one form or another is likely to be used more widely – it is not some temporary fad. The actual proportion of companies applying it is hard to gauge, but one report (Kandola and Galpin, 2000) indicated that in a survey of 60 HR departments, over 75 per cent were using it, confirming its growing popularity. A later, international, study (Brutus *et al.*, 2006) suggested not only a continuing increase in use but also a more diverse range of applications. Perhaps most interestingly of all, many top level staff in organisations are participating in it; it was a requirement for all members of the UK senior civil service to go through a 360-degree exercise, and it will be a part of the ongoing assessment process for medical consultants in Britain (see Chapter 11).

The typical 360-degree feedback system

Although there are many minor variations, most systems of this kind are rather similar. The main elements, and how they are handled, are as follows.

The questionnaire

This generally presents a series of statements about the 'target' manager's behaviour and effectiveness, and often is linked to the key competencies described in that organisation. Each competency will be described by a set of behavioural indicators of the sort we saw in Chapter 3 (pages 27–30) and each of those will be rated in terms of the effectiveness of the individual in relation to that behaviour or the frequency with which it is displayed (see Box 6.1 for examples of the kind of rating scale typically used).

So, if there are eight competencies thought relevant to that role, there might be something like five to eight questions asked in relation to each of

Box 6.1: typical rating formats used in 360-degree feedback questionnaires

Rating Scale – example 1
The individual is simply rated on their level of effectiveness in terms of each specified behaviour:

  Extremely effective
  Very effective
  Effective
  Mostly effective
  Partially effective
  Not effective

Rating Scale – example 2
This focuses on the frequency with which a behaviour is demonstrated, rather than the level:

  Always displays this behaviour
  Nearly always displays this behaviour
  More often than not displays this behaviour
  Sometimes displays this behaviour
  Seldom displays this behaviour
  Never displays this behaviour

them, giving a rating form of around 40 to 50 questions. Some companies mix all the questions up together; some group them under their relevant competency heading. The better examples of such systems offer the respondents the alternatives of saying, in relation to any particular question, either that they think this is not relevant to the job or that they have not had the opportunity to assess it, so allowing them to skip that rating. Other variations on the rating task include such practices as asking raters to rate the relevant attribute in terms of actual level displayed, and then in terms of desirable level for the job in question. Most forms also provide a free-written section in which other observations may be made. These are sometimes helpfully structured by asking such questions as, 'What should he (or she) do more of?' or 'What should he (or she) do less of?'

The raters

The focal manager (i.e. the individual on whom the feedback is being given) completes a self-rating while being rated by others. Many organisations allow the focal manager to choose who contributes to the rating process, according to who is in the best position to comment on their performance. The number of raters ranges from three to as many as twenty, depending on circumstances. One view frequently taken is that there should be a minimum of five people giving ratings, so that a degree of anonymity can be maintained. Usually, the raters will be peers, subordinates, and the immediate boss; other superiors in a position to comment on performance may also sometimes be included, which is especially helpful when the focal manager has been working in several project teams. Clients or customers, generally but not necessarily external to the organisation, figure in some systems. The focal manager's self-ratings are not entered into the aggregate of the ratings of others but put alongside them to point up any differences.

The feedback process

There are three main elements to this. The first is the person who collects the feedback; the second is the feedback report and how the data is represented within it; and the third is the manner in which this information is conveyed to the focal manager. The completed rating forms normally go either to a designated source in HR or to an external consultant; less often, they go to a senior manager. Whoever collects them has the task of collating the ratings in a form that will be helpful to the recipient. Most often, this simply means aggregating the ratings and presenting an average 'score' on each competency, broken down by rating group (peers, etc.) perhaps putting the self-rating alongside it. Providing the numbers in each group are sufficient, this preserves anonymity for the respondents. In some cases, where the number of colleagues contributing feedback is few and breaking them down into groups would make them individually identifiable, their ratings are simply put together and presented as overall figures. This is understandable, but has the cost of failing to identify any differences in perspective between subordinates, peers and others involved, which may have considerable significance in terms of development implications. The other problem with averaging ratings either within or across rater groups, is that information about the range of assessment is lost. It is quite possible for someone to come out as rather middling on an attribute because one group of, say, subordinates assessed him or her as high and another group as low on that behaviour; such a difference can stem from favouritism or from different role relationships, for example. It thus seems desirable to represent the ratings of different groups separately. This should not compromise anonymity, providing there are enough raters in each category. Quite reasonably, there is usually less concern over the immediate boss's ratings being identifiable.

Free-written comments can be listed verbatim, though it is more useful for a summary of the themes emerging to be included in the report. This can help illuminate the ratings, and give some leads in terms of development needs. It is not uncommon for 360-degree feedback systems to specify a criterion level of performance, defined by ratings above a certain value, and to highlight ratings that fall short of this or that significantly exceed it. Various profile charts, graphs etc. are frequently used to present the information in a more striking manner, especially when the system is delivered through computer input.

Just how the assessment is communicated to the manager does to some extent reflect the background and purpose of the feedback process. In organisations in which there is still considerable sensitivity about this kind of feedback, the report may simply be sent to the target managers and the initiative left with them as to whether they show it to, or discuss it with, anyone else, and whether they choose to take any action on it. More often, though, the report is given to the individual by whoever has been charged with collecting the information in the first place (e.g. a consultant), and then discussed with that person with a view to producing a development plan based on the feedback. A few organisations – BP Oil and the former Child Support Agency, for example – have in the past operated a process whereby the contents of the feedback are actually discussed with some or all of the raters present, the event being facilitated by an HR manager. Another example of this kind of approach is reported by Storr (2000) in Humberside TEC. In these cases, the concern over preserving anonymity is obviously rather less! However, open discussion of the content of the feedback does have the major advantage of allowing clarification. Ratings alone can often be a little ambiguous. One manager said to me, 'I was accused of not giving enough credit to my subordinates, but I still don't know whether this was because I did not thank them enough for work done well or if it really was down to the fact that I did not recommend two of them for promotion last year.' Note his use of the word 'accused'.

An interesting and well-presented case study of the introduction of a multi-source feedback system is provided by Clifford and Bennet (1997). They describe how initial work on management standards in the Automobile Association was used as a basis for implementing a 360-degree system to bring about a culture change. A 50-item management standards questionnaire, with the response to each question given on a clearly described six-point effectiveness scale, was used to gather feedback. Each participant sent the questionnaire to their boss and to their first-and second-level reports; respondents were encouraged to explore what they valued most, or least, about the participant. Feedback was handled by internal HR staff and line managers specially trained for the purpose. The aim was for each participant to emerge with a prioritised development plan. Clifford and Bennet's account gives a picture of a carefully handled process systematically monitored in terms of its operation and impact. Box 6.2 below presents a further illustration of such a scheme, this time operated within the context of a specific management development programme.

Box 6.2: an example of 360-degree feedback used in the context of management development

This was an application of 360 as part of a career review workshop run for middle managers in a public sector organisation that deals with financial strategy and regulation. A key element of the workshop was the input to participants provided by psychometric test data and colleague feedback, and how this could help inform their thinking about future career development. The 360 questionnaire covered seven competencies and consisted of 41 items rated from (6) extremely effective to (1) very ineffective. The participants were given the questionnaires to distribute 3–4 weeks before the event, and when completed they were returned directly to external consultants who compiled a report for each manager. On the afternoon of the first day of the workshop, a consultant led the group through a session on psychometric tests (their pros and cons, and how they should be interpreted), before distributing confidential details of their scores on the personality and cognitive tests taken pre-workshop to each participant. After they had looked at these and had a chance to raise general questions, the session moved on to look at 360-degree feedback, and how it should be interpreted. The participants were then given their feedback reports and dispersed to read through them individually. The final session of the day was given to talking through general issues and questions arising from the feedback, and how it might relate to the psychometric data.

Prior to the second stage of the workshop process, which was a week later, each participant – having had some time to consider the test data and the feedback – had an individual session with a consultant to discuss the implications and possible development steps. After this, they attended the final group elements of the workshop.

One feature of this organisation's use of 360 feedback was the care they were willing to go to in checking that the questionnaire used did what it was supposed to; in other words, they carried out an analysis to see:

- whether raters were using the full range of the rating scale
- whether different rater groups showed any specific biases
- whether the items related to each competency were correlated with each other rather than with items relating to other competencies
- whether there were any items respondents found difficulty in replying to

In light of this, they were able to do some fine tuning of the questionnaire. Particular strengths of the approach taken to using 360 here were the way it was integrated with psychometric data to give a broader picture, and the extent to which support and assistance was provided to participants in helping them understand the information and its implications, and in formulating development plans accordingly.

Why has it caught on?

Having briefly described and illustrated the kind of process involved, it is worth asking – why has it become so widely adopted, why have diverse organisations seen it as a worthwhile activity? The reasons they usually offer revolve around:

- *Empowerment*: Feedback gives subordinates a 'Voice' in how they are managed, peers a voice in how this person relates to them as a member of the team, customers a voice in how they are dealt with. As such, 360-degree feedback is an empowering mechanism that gives people an input and a degree of control they might not otherwise have.
- *More Rounded Assessment*: Traditional approaches to appraisal and assessment are top-down and inevitably limited in perspective. The use of multi-source feedback is inherently fairer and gives a more rounded and balanced perspective on the individual. This does NOT necessarily mean a more objective one, though, as we shall see.
- *Enhances Awareness of Competencies*: Many organisations have spent a fortune on developing competency frameworks, but the problem then is getting people to understand what they mean and to use them as the performance language of the company. Basing the 360

questionnaire on the competencies and their descriptors can help raise awareness of them and make staff more familiar with the wording and concepts used.

- *Powerful Learning Potential*: This really is at the heart of most applications of feedback – the impact it can have and the potential for using this to generate behavioural change. Feedback is hard to get on a day-to-day basis, and the higher in an organisation one goes, the more this is true. So 360-degree assessment may represent the first real feedback an individual has received in a long while, and coming from all his or her colleagues, it is hard to ignore.
- *Improved Self-Awareness – and Performance*: One of the explicitly stated aims of 360 is to increase levels of self-awareness, on the grounds that holding a view of oneself that is sharply different from the way other people see you is likely to be detrimental to performance. So, the notion is that 360 provides a chance to compare self-assessment against the perceptions of others, and to gauge the 'gap'. Over successive feedback episodes, the notion is that people become more realistic in their self-perceptions and hence the gap between their assessments and the assessments made of them by others becomes smaller. As will be seen below, the research evidence supports the notion that greater self-awareness *is* associated with better performance.

The burning issue – appraisal or development?

Right from the start, most applications of 360-degree feedback have been set in a developmental context, but more recently there has been a marked shift towards using it as a direct input to appraisal. Appraisal and development are not mutually exclusive of course, but which of these purposes gets the greater emphasis in a multi-source feedback scheme has a bearing on a number of important decisions as to how it is operated:

- *Is it to be mandatory or optional?* If it is an aspect of the appraisal process, it is more likely to be mandatory: you can hardly have a number of people opting out of part of the appraisal. Actually, both practices can be found in the same organisation, e.g. a large company in the telecommunications field has it as mandatory for top management layers and optional for middle management (where they report around 60 per cent take-up).
- *Is it to be done annually?* If it is part of appraisal, then presumably it will be an annual event, with the implications this has for the resources needed to administer it. But as a development event, it could reasonably be done on a more intermittent basis, or even as a one-off.

- *Who decides who is to contribute to the assessment process?* As we have noted, the target manager often chooses his or her own assessors – in developmental schemes. But is this acceptable in an appraisal context? There must be some dangers here. Allowing people to choose who makes an input to their appraisal process can offer an opportunity for the more Machiavellian-inclined to bias the process by arranging a reciprocal process of back-slapping. Whether this actually happens, at least in any significant proportion of cases, is not known.
- *Who is responsible for follow-up action?* In development, the target individual often works with an HR manager or consultant to develop an action plan. But in the context of appraisal, the individual's boss is more likely to be involved.
- *If it is to be part of an appraisal process, is it to be linked to rewards?* In a minority of UK organisations, such as parts of BAe, this link has existed for some while (Handy *et al.*, 1996). It has also been related to pay in some US companies (e.g. Federal Express) and their UK operations for some years.

360-degree feedback and appraisal: the pros and cons

Some HR practitioners and management writers have expressed concern about having 360 feedback as an input to appraisal, with the attendant possibility of a link with pay, so it may be worth running through the arguments for and against. Before doing that, though, it may also be worth reminding ourselves of some of the reasons why top-down appraisal schemes have failed so often in the past:

- They are perceived to be unfair by appraisees, in part because they reflect the limited perspective of one person (the boss).
- They have been found to be poor assessment devices: appraisal ratings predict little and are subject to many distortions.
- Appraisals seem too often to result in demotivation and defensiveness, with the result that they are avoided by both parties.

On the face of it, 360-degree feedback seems to offer a way round some of these problems. So let us look first at the case for making it part of the appraisal process. The arguments go like this:

- Teamwork and managing staff are vital aspects of most managerial and professional jobs. If this is the case, then should they not be assessed by those people who are in the best position to comment – namely, peers and subordinates – and should that assessment not be part of the appraisal of performance?

- Much is said (see above) about 'empowering' employees. By putting subordinates' feedback into the appraisal process, one is indeed empowering them: they are able to exert some influence over how they are managed and treated.
- Making 360-degree feedback part of appraisal overcomes the problem of potential bias in an appraisal that rests on one person's assessment. In theory, multiple levels and sources of appraisal data should lead to a more objective, well-rounded picture of the individual's contribution, strengths, and development needs. It should consequently promote higher levels of trust in the fairness of the process. Thus, assessments from a wide range of colleagues and the decisions made on the basis of them may be legally – and possibly ethically – more defensible.
- Finally, if 360-degree feedback is all it claims to be, why should it not be included in appraisal? Doing so is a useful way of sending a message to people that this process, and what is reflects, is something the organisation takes seriously.

Well, this all sounds quite convincing; but what about the other side of the argument? Here are the reasons offered for keeping 360-degree feedback as purely a development tool:

- Once you put it into the appraisal system, it will undermine the trust of those giving the ratings, which is necessary for the whole thing to work. The result will be poorer-quality information from subordinates in particular, and probably peers too. There is some research evidence to back this up; peer ratings given as an input to appraisal tend to be less reliable, less valid and more lenient than when they are given for developmental purposes (Pollack and Pollack, 1996), and subordinate ratings have been found to be of lower quality when used for appraisal purposes (Greguras *et al.*, 2003).
- Associated with this, target managers will become more defensive and less ready to accept the feedback because of the potentially damaging consequences for them; its potential to generate constructive development activity will be reduced. Again, there is evidence to support this (see Fletcher, 2001).
- It could lead to political game-playing. You might get subordinates asking for rises, changes in duties, etc. just prior to the time they and their manager know that they are going to be asked to contribute their assessments. Managers might be tempted to court popularity.
- To run the system on an annual basis is time-consuming and costly. Even those giving the assessments may suffer rating-fatigue.
- Is the accuracy and quality of the assessment ratings provided in 360-degree feedback *really* better than what tends to come out of a

traditional appraisal system? Or are we just swapping one set of biased perceptions for a whole raft of them, which, far from arriving at some objective truth, simply obscure the picture? For example, we know that the extent to which appraisers like appraisees influences on their assessment of them (Lefkowitz, 2000) – is the same true for peers and subordinates giving ratings in a 360 exercise? Unfortunately, the answer seems to be 'yes' (Antonioni and Park, 2001; van Hooft *et al.*, 2006). Indeed, Bailey and Fletcher (2002a) found that there was even an effect in the opposite direction – the quality of focal managers relationships with feedback givers influences the former's perceptions of the credibility of the feedback being offered. There is also evidence that 360 assessments are no more immune to ethnic bias than other forms of appraisal (Alimo-Metcalfe and Alban-Metcalfe, 2003).

Now the whole question looks a bit less straightforward, doesn't it?

In a way, the arguments matter little, because the fact is that some organisations do incorporate 360-degree feedback in appraisal, and more are intending to. Perhaps the most important thing is at least to consider the issues flagged above and to monitor how the system operates in the appraisal context. As will be seen below, there is certainly great cause for concern about the accuracy and quality of the ratings provided, although fortunately this does seem to be open to remedial action. It is the link with rewards, though, that should give rise to the greatest hesitation.

The debate here is really no different to that in relation to appraisal in general. For 50 years or more, the research literature has been pretty consistent in suggesting that direct pay links do little for the quality and effectiveness of appraisal; reward issues get in the way of constructive discussion of development needs. There is no reason to believe that this will not happen to some extent if there is a pay link to 360-degree feedback. Some organisations say that this does not happen in their experience – but you need to look rather carefully at how thorough the 360-degree systems they operate actually are, and precisely what the pay link is. Obviously, if the relationship with pay is very indirect, it may exert little influence. Quite apart from the reactions of staff to links with pay, though, is the justification for linking with pay. This rests on the assumption that 360-degree ratings are accurate and psychometrically sound, which, as we shall now see, may not be sustainable.

The quality of 360-degree feedback

Concerns about the quality of conventional appraisal ratings can be found at various points in this book and in the research literature (e.g. DeNisi,

1996). Unfortunately, many of the same problems seem to arise with 360-degree feedback, as is exemplified by a study in a multinational oil company carried out by myself and some colleagues (Fletcher *et al.*, 1997). In this case, the company had wisely introduced its scheme (which was designed for them by an external consultant) on a pilot basis in just one division, and then asked us to evaluate it. The scheme looked like a lot of others, with 80 performance descriptors rated by peers, subordinates, and clients nominated by the target manager, as well as by the immediate boss and the individual concerned. The performance descriptors were meant to relate to three broad competencies that the company used. When we analysed the ratings from this system, along with other data, we found:

- the behavioural descriptors did not correspond to the competencies they were meant to
- they were so intercorrelated that, in effect, most of them were redundant and all that was being measured was an overall dimension of 'good–bad'
- the ratings did not show a relationship with any other criterion measure of performance used in the company
- there seemed to be systematic biases that affected specific groups of raters.

The inescapable conclusion from this analysis of the pilot scheme was that any development plan arising out of the feedback process could be seriously misguided. If such ratings had been fed into an appraisal process, and possibly been linked to reward decisions, the basis for the assessment and the equity of those reward decisions would have been called into question. All is not doom and gloom, however. On the basis of the analysis, we were able to redesign the scheme which, among other things, involved cutting the rating form to half its original length and rewording a number of items. When the revised scheme was piloted and evaluated, it showed vastly superior psychometric qualities compared with the original; the behavioural descriptors lined up with the competencies and the ratings correlated with the external criterion measure of performance. The company's careful approach to 360-degree feedback was thus justified. Instead of launching a system across the organisation on the basis of blind faith and a superficial appearance of relevance, they had taken it one stage at a time and looked critically at what they were doing. They ended up with something that was less time-consuming and much more effective than what they started out with; indeed, what they started out with was not effective at all.

What this example suggests is that 360-degree feedback systems are rather like psychometric tests. Their value is difficult to assess on the basis of appearance alone; 'face validity' is not a guarantee that they are actually doing what they claim to be doing. Also, like tests, they may have a powerful impact on the recipient of the feedback, and could lead to important job and career consequences for those assessed. If we take this analogy further, then it seems reasonable to advocate that 360-degree feedback systems should be subject to the same kind of design process and monitoring that one would associate with properly developed psychometric instruments. They should be able to demonstrate that the assessments they offer are acceptable in terms of their psychometric properties; that they do reflect the dimensions or competencies they claim to, that they can show some relationship with other measures of performance, and so on. At present, my suspicion is that very few UK 360-degree feedback systems meet such a specification, or at least they are unable to produce any evidence to that effect. In the longer term, if they become part of the appraisal process without following this path, it seems quite possible that they will face the same kinds of legal challenges that have been encountered by tests – and deservedly so.

Effectiveness: What the research says

If we want to evaluate this kind of feedback process, what criteria might we use? The first issue is one we have already touched on above – does the questionnaire measure what it claims to, or to put it another way, is it valid? The way to check this is to see how ratings given as part of 360 correlate with other, independent, measures of performance. There is certainly some supporting evidence here. Conway *et al.*, (2001) report a meta analysis showing that peer and subordinate ratings account for significant and unique variance in objective performance measures (profit, productivity, etc.). Erickson and Allen (2003) found that store managers' MSMR ratings correlated with store revenues, sales and profit margins. There are some less positive findings in terms of correlating with simulation exercises or tests (van Hooft *et al.*, 2006), but these are in a sense less relevant criteria. In addition, various studies (Beehr *et al.*, 2001; Ostroff *et al.*, 2004; Smither and Walker 2004) have found positive relationships between feedback ratings and performance appraisal ratings. There have been studies that did not find correlations with appraisal ratings (e.g. Brett and Atwater, 2001), though they are in a clear minority. But appraisal ratings are perhaps less convincing as 'proof' of the validity of 360 feedback as there is always the possibility of some contamination (that is, the feedback may have influenced the appraisal assessment). Also, there would seem to be little point in having 360-degree feedback if what came out of it correlated highly with appraisal ratings – the whole point is to capture the viewpoints of different groups on the expectation that they *will* differ in some respects.

So, there is plenty of support for the potential validity of 360-degree feedback ratings if the questionnaire is constructed properly in the first place. But quite apart from whether these systems are accurate, in the sense of measuring what they say they do, what do they actually *achieve*? Certainly, many managers receiving this kind of feedback feel it is potent, and they seem to have a broadly positive attitude to it (Fletcher and Baldry, 1999), but does that mean they respond constructively and modify their behaviour and style? In the UK, Tyson and Ward (2004) found that senior managers significantly improved on competency ratings after such feedback. Smither *et al.*, (2005) did a meta analysis of 24 studies that had examined changes in 360-degree feedback episodes over successive applications. This was a large sample, consisting of up to 7,000 managers, and some of the studies covered incorporated control groups in their design. Overall, they found that focal managers' ratings from all feedback giver groups tend to improve over successive feedback episodes, though not by a huge amount and there is also quite a lot of variability in how much change is observed. Interestingly, they also found that where feedback was used for development it resulted in greater behavioural change than when it was used as an input to appraisal. Whilst this may support those who feel 360 should not be part of the appraisal process, it could also be interpreted in quite another way – perhaps those giving feedback for appraisal were more conservative and realistic in assessing the extent to which the focal managers' performance had improved.

One other, more indirect, point should be made on the research. It was noted earlier that an aim of feedback is to make the recipient more self-aware, with the underlying assumption that having a wide disparity between one's self perceptions and how others see you is probably unhelpful in performance terms. The research supports this; there are a number of studies showing that people who are self-aware (i.e. their self-assessment is broadly in line with how others see them) are also assessed more highly on independent measures of performance (Fletcher, 1997; Atwater *et al.*, 2005).

Asking a more complicated question

In terms of evidence, it looks promising. But the extent to which people change their behaviour following feedback is, as noted above, neither great nor completely consistent. Instead of asking the very broad question as to whether 360-degree feedback is effective, we should probably be asking a rather more complex and refined question – more like, what kind of feedback, delivered in what manner, from what source, given to which managers will bring about which specified improvements? There seem to be a number of factors that impact on the effectiveness of the process; here are just some of them –

1   What people do with the feedback

London and Smither (1995) followed up 252 managers over a five-year period and found that those who discussed the feedback with those who had provided it showed significantly more improvement in ratings than those who did not. Somewhat similarly, managers who work with a coach to review feedback and set development goals show more improvement than those who do not (Smither *et al.*, 2003). Tyson and Ward (2004) confirm the importance of building-in coaching follow-up to feedback.

2   Initial level of performance of the focal manager

Some studies (e.g. Walker and Smither, 1999) have found that managers who initially received less favourable ratings put more effort into sub-sequent development activity than those whose ratings were higher – presumably because there was more need for them to do so. Bailey and Fletcher (2002b) found that, over time, feedback led to a perception of increased competence and lowered development needs. Of course, much depends on the nature of the organisation and the resources available for following up the development implications of the feedback.

3   The credibility of the feedback source

If we look at the feedback literature in general (Kluger and DeNisi, 1996) we find that over and over again the credibility of the source – the degree to which those receiving the feedback have trust in that source – comes through as being a very important factor in acceptance of the feedback. Is that true for 360 systems too? In which case, do some sources of feedback have more impact than others? Bailey and Fletcher (2002a) conducted a study in public and private sector organisations, and found that the most accurate feedback was perceived as coming from direct reports, and that the extent to which it was seen as accurate (or credible) was influenced by the amount of contact the reports had with the focal manager and the quality of relationship between the two of them. However feedback from the boss was seen as the most important, even if it was not accurate! Perhaps there is good reason for this – if, in your eyes, your boss has the wrong idea about your performance (and this is not likely to be a case of you worrying that he thinks you are too good), then all the more important to know so that you can do something about it. Rather ironically, then, despite 360 being used to give a more rounded and fairer assessment than the boss alone can provide, the boss still remains the most important input to it – power counts for more than accuracy or credibility!

4   The gender of the focal manager

There is some reason to believe that gender differences will be found in the operation of multi-source, multi-level feedback systems. Typically, the self-ratings of female managers are found to be closer to the ratings made of them by their colleagues than is the case for male managers; the latter tend consistently to overrate themselves compared with how they are seen by others (Fletcher, 1999). This needs to be taken account of in the interpretation of the feedback ratings; it should not be assumed that this lower level of agreement in the case of male managers implies less accuracy or validity of the ratings made of them. The more realistic interpretation is that quite a few male managers are not quite as self-critical as they should be!

The cultural background of those giving and receiving feedback is likely to be significant. There are well-recognised differences between cultures in attitudes to communication; some cultural groups may be much more reticent about giving frank feedback, especially to superiors; and the attitude to receiving it is also likely to reflect this (see Chapter 12, pages 176–177). As noted at the beginning of this chapter, differences within Western culture and even in organisational culture may be part of the explanation of the variations in why and where the idea of 360-degree feedback has been taken up. But these broader and deeper cultural differences are likely to be represented within organisations, especially multinational companies, and so the response to 360-degree feedback may be far from consistent even within one organisation or one division. This needs to be recognised in any preparation and training given by way of introducing the scheme.

There are many other factors that could be listed here – including the quality of the 360 questionnaire measure itself (already dealt with earlier), and a whole host of individual differences – such as self-efficacy (Bailey and Austin, 2006) or other aspects of self-evaluation (Bono and Colbert, 2005) – and contextual variables.

In summary

The next few years will probably see the shift in emphasis from 360-degree feedback as a development device to its use in appraisal. The arguments for and against this have been rehearsed earlier, and so will not be repeated here. It can be used for both purposes, though if it is to be part of appraisal, one would hope that it would be treated as just one input to the process, rather than taking centre-stage. It would perhaps be unfortunate if its use in this context encouraged a swing back to a predominantly assessment-oriented approach to appraisal.

The enthusiasm and the speed with which 360-degree feedback has been embraced is remarkable. Fortunately, there is a growing body of evidence suggesting that, if it is well designed and implemented, this kind of process can lead to changes in behaviour, increased competency levels and other desirable performance outcomes. However, the level of success achieved will depend on a wide range of variables that need to be taken account of in design and application of multi-source feedback.

The concept of multi-source, multi-level feedback seems to suit the move towards the less hierarchical, more flexibly structured, and knowledge-based organisations of the future. But the parallels with psychometric testing are striking. Tests are often presented as easy to use, but actually they are only easy to use badly. And the merits of any one test are difficult to judge on superficial characteristics alone. The rush to use tests in the 1980s is similar to the wholesale adoption of 360-degree systems. In the case of tests, it led all too often to poor practice, the presentation of deficient instruments to the market, and – ultimately – to increasing legal challenges. There is every chance that 360-degree feedback systems will follow the same route if they are not introduced more carefully and examined more critically than is usually the case at present. In view of this, the next chapter is devoted to outlining what we can now recognise as 'best practice' in the field.

Discussion points and questions

Should we use 360-degree feedback as an input to appraisal, or just employ it as a development tool? What are the arguments and evidence you would use to argue either way?

How would you evaluate 360-degree feedback – what do you feel are the most important things to look for, and how would you go about it?

What factors are likely to determine whether 360-degree feedback will have a positive effect with any particular individual focal manager?

Key references

Fletcher, C. (1997) Self-awareness – a neglected attribute in selection and assessment. *International Journal of Selection and Assessment*, 5, pp. 183–187.

Ostroff, C., Atwater, L. E. and Feinberg, B. J. (2004) Understanding self–other agreement: A look at rater and ratee characteristics, context and outcomes. *Personnel Psychology*, 57, pp. 333–376.

Smither, J. W., London, M. and Reilly, R. R. (2005) Does performance improve following multi-source feedback? A theoretical model, meta-analysis, and review of empirical findings. *Personnel Psychology*, 58, pp. 33–66.

Tyson, S. and Ward, P. (2004) The use of 360 degree feedback technique in the evaluation of management learning. *Management Learning*, 35 (2), pp. 205–223.

Chapter 7

Best practice and current trends in multi-source feedback

Some years ago, the author wrote an article on 360-degree feedback in an HR magazine, only for a consultant to write in to the letters page a couple of weeks later saying it was 'not rocket science' and line managers could be trusted to be given the tool and allowed to run with it themselves. He was of course, quite right – it is not rocket science. However, as we saw in the previous chapter, it is all too easy to design a 360 questionnaire that does not measure what it claims to. And it is also quite possible to do a degree of damage to individuals by not handling feedback carefully. Indeed, some people working in this field use the acronym SARAH to describe the pattern of reaction some focal managers go through on receiving their feedback –

Shock
Anger
Rejection
Acceptance
Help!

The trick is to get the feedback recipient to the point of Acceptance, because some never get passed the first two or three stages, and can suffer accordingly. Those who get angry and reject the feedback are storing up trouble for themselves and others, and need some help to move on. And the research (e.g. Brett and Atwater, 2001) is clear in telling us that less positive feedback does not magically become more acceptable when it comes from sources other than the boss. So managing the feedback at the individual level is not so straightforward either. In light of this, the Department of Trade and Industry in the UK was sufficiently concerned to set up a working party to draft Best Practice Guidelines on multi-source feedback so that they could be widely disseminated. Both the British Psychological Society (represented by the author amongst others) and the Chartered

Institute for Personnel and Development (CIPD) contributed members to that working party. What follows in this chapter echoes the guidelines produced.

Planning to introduce a 360-degree programme

The timing and culture of an organisation have to be right for the introduction of these feedback processes. The adoption of a full 360-degree approach needs to stem from a steady evolution in appraisal and development practices. Many organisations have for some years included a few very mild gestures in this direction, e.g. headings on the appraisees' preparation form inviting them to identify things that 'management' could do to help them improve performance. It is very unlikely that a 360-degree scheme would be accepted where there has been little or no history of appraisal of any kind: it would represent too radical a step.

Even where there is an ample history of appraisal, one of the main problems is how apprehensive many potential 360 participants feel about it in advance. Frequently voiced concerns by the managers being assessed are that they feel their position may be undermined and that subordinates and even peers can use the opportunity to exercise any grudges they hold. Subordinates, on the other hand, may fear some retaliatory punitive action by the managers. If high levels of mutual trust exist, such problems may not arise, but it seems that mutual trust is more the exception than the rule. Thus, as we have seen, most feedback schemes promise anonymity for the raters. But at least as important as this is the need to consult participants in the scheme, feedback contributors as well as focal managers, about it in advance – about how the scheme should be structured and operated, aspects of its content, who will have access to the feedback reports and so on. Only by following that kind of approach are fears likely to be allayed and enough trust built up to let the scheme flourish.

Developing the questionnaire

The main points to follow here are:

- Focus as far as possible on rating observable behaviours. It is no use asking (most) subordinates to comment on their boss' strategic thinking capacity – first, much of it may not be visible, second, it may not manifest itself to more junior staff anyway. Make sure that respondent groups are asked to comment on what they are likely to be able to offer a judgment on, namely behaviour that they are in a position to observe and capable of making an assessment of.

- Do not ask those giving feedback to rate too many competencies – concentrate on the key competencies for the feedback purpose. Some feedback questionnaires are insufferably long. It might be OK to ask a 100+ questions on a one-off basis, but if you are going to ask people to complete such questionnaires for a number of colleagues, and maybe more than once for each of them, then 'ratings fatigue' will set in fast! It is usually best to focus on just a few key competencies, and these are probably mostly going to be in the interpersonal domain, because that is what 360 feedback is especially good at accessing. It is probably best to aim for a maximum of around 40 questions – so, at 5–8 per competency, that means no more than 6–7 competencies.
- Check that the questions do indeed relate to the competencies. This goes back to the issues highlighted in relation to the oil company example mentioned in the previous chapter (page 79). At its most basic, it means checking to see if there is more correlation between the answers to the questions within a single competency than there is between them and questions relating to other competencies. For further details, see Fletcher *et al.* (1997). If this kind of analysis is beyond the expertise of anyone in your organisation, an external consultant should be able to carry it out, or (more cheaply) a student on an MSc course in Occupational Psychology might do it for their MSc dissertation research.
- Ensure the rating scale allows for sufficient range of response. The author recalls seeing a financial services company 360 system that was great in most respects, except that its output failed to identify anyone as having any development needs! The reason for this was the wording of the rating scale for each item – it basically left the feedback-giver the choice of saying that this person was either really good in terms of the specific behaviour, or poor! Most people when responding to these questionnaires do not want to sound too critical or undermining in their comments, and for the focal managers, it is easier to take feedback that says they are doing generally OK but there are some things to work on. The rating scale, then, has to be worded to make it possible for some weaknesses to be conveyed in such a way that it is acceptable to both parties. As indicated in the previous chapter (page 70), one form of wording frequently adopted presents the questions in terms of how often the focal manager has demonstrated the behaviour or how typical it is of them (Not at all/To a small extent/To some extent/To an adequate extent/To a large extent/To a very large extent). An alternative is to frame the rating in terms of levels of effectiveness, and to add the development implications (e.g. Reasonably effective: Some development need indicated). Apart from the wording of the rating scale, it is also important to allow respondents the opportunity to say either that

they have not had the chance to observe the behaviour or that they feel it is not relevant to the role.

• Include scope for qualitative comments as well as ratings. There are some feedback systems that consist *only* of free-written comments, and some (more) that have only quantitative ratings. Most, however, are based on ratings with some provision for additional written comments at the end, perhaps in relation to each competency covered by the questionnaire. As noted in the previous chapter, the inclusion of this qualitative feedback can flesh out the ratings and help explain some of them more fully. There is a risk, though – allowing written comments is opening Pandora's box – you do not know what you will get. The danger is that people can use the opportunity to say things that are irrelevant, tactless or hurtful, or just not constructive. Whilst this seldom happens, it is a possibility. Research (Atwater and Brett, 2006) suggests that combining normative (i.e. rating-based) and textual feedback is most effective.

Implementation

The first thing to say is – do not try to roll it out across the organisation in one go. 'Right First Time' is not something that works terribly well with 360. If at all possible, like the oil company case described on page 79, do a pilot run in one division first, and monitor that carefully. If all goes well, much of what needs to be done is reasonably straightforward. Those giving feedback need to be told what the timescales are; just sending out questionnaires and asking for them to be returned soon is a recipe for non-completion. Usually, respondents should be asked to return them within a week. Who these people are, how many of them, and how they are to be approached are things to be decided. Sample size (the number of raters) is an issue on two counts. First, the assessment has to be based on a big enough sample to ensure that it is valid; if it is small, there is a danger that one individual rater's bias or prejudice will have a major impact on the average rating. Second, the sample of raters has to be big enough that individual sources cannot be identified; a minimum of four or five subordinates is usually suggested from this point of view. The implications for the time and administrative effort involved are clear.

The number and identity of the raters may have been agreed at the consultation stage. Often, the focal manager decides who to ask and gives out the questionnaires, but where the exercise is linked to appraisal the choice of respondents is generally determined by the focal manager and their boss together. Whoever is responsible, it is likely that they will appreciate or need guidance from HR on how many to give out and to which categories (i.e. how many to peers, subordinates etc.). All those completing questionnaires have to be told who or where to return them to, and be given a means to do so. Although on the face of it, all this is simple enough, there will inevitably be queries and problems that arise, including those that stem from actually trying to complete the questionnaire, and in some organisations it has been found helpful to establish a help line when the exercise is started.

Report and follow up action

Some 360-degree feedback reports, especially those generated by software packages, produce reams of paper – endless charts, tables and text, to the extent that the recipient may feel rather overwhelmed by the sheer volume. It is important for the report of the feedback received to be sufficient to give a clear picture, but not in such detail as the focal manager will have difficulty seeing the wood for the trees. Most such reports include the following information:

- Bar charts showing the average rating given on each competency by each group of raters (peers, boss etc) as well as the self-rating
- Where the questionnaire is reasonably short, a similar analysis to that above, but this time in relation to the individual behavioural items which make up each competency
- A highlighting of the highest rated competencies, and the lowest-rated
- If this is not the first feedback episode, a comparison of ratings this time with the previous occasion
- Identification of specific behaviours that have been rated as less effective and/or requiring development action
- A listing of free-written comments relating to each competency (should the system have allowed for these)
- Analysis of behaviours that feedback givers have felt they could not make a rating of for one reason or another.

The extent to which the second of these is important varies – if it is a long questionnaire, it can lead to a lot of graphs. But the individual items that attract low ratings do need to be flagged up. The use of average ratings is understandable and useful, but it is unfortunately not enough on its own. This is because one can have an average subordinate rating of 5 on a scale that goes from 1 (low) to 7 (high) – which sounds fine in itself – but it can be arrived at by having three subordinates rating you as 3 and another three rating you as 7, which is rather less fine. This is not uncommon – it may arise from bias, with a manager treating subordinates differently, having an 'out' group and an 'in' group, or it can arise from different subordinates seeing different aspects and samples of their boss' behaviour. Whatever the reason, it is important to know the range and spread of the ratings given, not just the averages.

Feedback reports vary also in the extent to which they provide any interpretation or commentary on the ratings. Some will provide a 'gap' analysis, focusing on the degree of match, or mismatch, between self-ratings and ratings from others. This is a crude but useful measure of self-awareness. Where a report is being sent directly to the focal manager, especially if it is to be left to the individual to decide whether to share the content with anyone else, it is essential that some help is given in understanding the feedback and in putting it in a context. Without this, the focal manager might have some difficulty in assessing the meaning of what is being conveyed – is it the results of an opinion survey, is it like a psychological test, is it common for subordinates to see you differently from your peers, and if they do what does that mean? These and many other questions can come to mind when reading the output from 360, and focal managers need guidance to use it.

The most important advice, though, is to encourage the recipients of the feedback to share it with someone else, and if at all possible build this into the system from the outset. The discussion might be with a consultant, someone from HR or even with a peer. Better still, however, is if the focal manager has the confidence to go back to the sources of the feedback; as we saw in the previous chapter (page 82) there is evidence that this produces better long term outcomes (Walker and Smither, 1999). However, neither the individual nor the culture might be ready for such direct discussions. The purpose of discussion is not just to clarify and understand what has been said, but also to decide what action is appropriate. Again, most focal managers (and their bosses, come to that) need some help in thinking through the kinds of development activities that might be appropriate and available, and then in putting them together in the form of a development plan. Some software based systems automatically raise a list of potential development steps in relation to each competency the 360 questionnaire has covered. It follows on from this that for any 360 system to be useful, the resources have to be in place to facilitate the development action that arises out of it. Tyson and Ward (2004) confirm the value of coaching being integrated into the feedback process.

One issue that is seldom if ever addressed is the extent to which the feedback given is positive or negative in overall tone, and the extent to which it deviates from the individual's own self-view i.e. the extent of the 'gap' in the gap analysis mentioned above. It has long been known that most people have a limited tolerance for criticism in a conventional top-down appraisal, and as was pointed out at the beginning of this chapter, the same is probably true in relation to 360 feedback. If a feedback report shows that an individual's self-view is substantially more positive than the feedback given, then it would be wise to have some mechanism for identifying this at an early stage – preferably before the individual has been given the feedback – so that some kind of support strategy can be put in place. This might either be in the form of arranging for a facilitator to be present when the report is given or in terms of the text provided around the feedback.

Using norms

Where the sample of managers and feedback givers is large enough, it is possible to develop norms – in other words, to show the average rating achieved on any competency (broken down by feedback group if desired) and, in some cases, some measure of the distribution of ratings e.g. standard deviation. This kind of normative data can be useful to the individual, to see how their ratings compared with colleagues or with equivalent groups within the organisation. It can also be valuable for an organisation if a consultancy company providing the 360 system can show the distribution of ratings on some or all of the questionnaire items that has been accumulated from applications in other, similar organisations – this can afford a degree of benchmarking, so that a company can see how their focal managers as a group fare against similar groups elsewhere. Here the dividing line between psychometrics and 360-degree feedback can become a little blurred.

As indicated, normative data can be very informative. But to obtain it, the organisation may have to trade off the desirability of having a set of questionnaire items that are tailored to its culture and needs against the need to have some fairly generic set of items that have been used across a range of different companies. The other caveat is that many aspects of organisational context – including the background reasons for deploying 360 and the way it was introduced – may vary from one company to another, and these could well impact on the pattern of feedback ratings that emerge in any one place. In which case the whole point of using normative data to make comparisons is undermined.

Evaluation

A lot of time and effort can go into setting up and running a multi-source feedback system, and given the strong feelings and reactions it can generate amongst participants, it is wise to make evaluation a rather more urgent priority than it might be with some other HR processes. Some of the research evidence on the validity and effectiveness of 360 feedback was presented in the previous chapter (pages 80–83) – here the focus is more on the *practical* guidance on what to look for and how to go about it. The criteria against which to evaluate 360 break down into short, medium and long term outcomes.

Short term evaluation

Perhaps the most pressing thing is to get some quick feedback on the feedback, so to speak. It is vital to identify anything going wrong as early as possible. The kind of information that needs to be sought in the short term is:

- Is the system acceptable to the users? In other words, how did those giving the feedback and those receiving it feel about the process, how it worked, what came out of it, and so on? Getting initial reactions to these basic questions is worthwhile, because it may allow remedial action to be taken early before the system has rolled out to other groups.
- Does the system identify development needs? The main purpose is to get feedback to encourage improvement where it is necessary, so are any potential areas for improvement identified for most people? There will obviously be some for whom little improvement is possible or necessary, but these should be very few. Do the majority of focal managers report that they got useful development directions from the exercise?
- Has the feedback questionnaire functioned effectively and measured what it set out to measure? This is a bit trickier, because it involves the kind of statistical analysis that was mentioned in the previous chapter in relation to the oil company example. See page 88 for suggestions on this.

Medium term evaluation

This level of evaluation is unlikely to take place if 360 is used as a one-off development exercise, but if it is applied more than once, it becomes very relevant. There are two aspects to it:

- Do focal managers show an increase in self-awareness? Given that increasing self-awareness is an oft-declared purpose of 360, this is something we might be very interested in. If the data from each application of 360 is kept, it is possible to see if the level of agreement between focal managers' self-ratings and the ratings of others has increased, i.e. if they have become more 'realistic' in their perceptions of their competencies. Whilst there are several quite sophisticated ways of computing this self–other rating gap measure (see Fletcher and Bailey, 2003), the simple subtraction of the self-rating from the ratings of each other group on each competency should be enough to show if there has been a shift. It will obviously also be of interest to see if the ratings of the focal manager have increased in favourability over time, as this might indicate perceived improvement.

- Has there been development activity recorded as a result of the feedback? It is one thing to check, in short-term evaluation, if development needs have been identified, but quite another to see if they have been acted upon. After a reasonable amount of time has elapsed following the feedback, it should be possible to either ask the focal managers (or their bosses) what action was taken and/or to see what record of development activity relating to the feedback exists in the HR department.

Long term evaluation

Few if any organisations do long term evaluation, though fortunately there is some research into this as we saw in the previous chapter. The kind of outcomes that are longer term in nature are:

- Do ratings of managers by others show a pattern of improvement over time, with successive feedback episodes, in relation to the areas that needed such improvement? Are there any hard measures of performance that show improvement? The latter are notoriously difficult to come by, and even when they are available, so many other factors impact on performance that it may not be realistic to expect 360 to show a direct effect on it.
- Are there any signs of a culture change? This is even more difficult, but since 360 is a culture change instrument, it is reasonable to ask whether after some applications of it there are signs of people becoming more comfortable with seeking, giving and accepting feedback. For example, do the focal managers show a greater likelihood of talking to the feedback givers directly about their views?

Some current trends and issues in multi-source feedback use in the UK

The trends and issues described here mostly arise from data the author collected as part of a wider study (Brutus *et al.*, 2006) – though not reported in that paper – and are based on the views and experiences given him by the HR managers and consultants he interviewed on this topic. First, some trends:

- There is less of a 'sheep-dip' approach to using 360-degree feedback. Initially, organisations tended to invite everyone at a certain management level or in a specific part of the organisation to take part. Now, application tends to be more focused on particular groups or for more specific and less 'catch-all' purposes.
- An example of the above is the use of feedback as a diagnostic tool in team development, or as a team-building aid in itself. Also, it may be called for in relation to the coaching and development of an individual senior manager, whose coach may personally approach and interview a whole range of people who work with this manager. This usually provides very 'rich' information, though of course it usually does not present anything in normative form. The coach typically analyses the themes emerging and records verbatim (but usually anonymously) the comments made under each one.
- A number of organisations have chosen to depart from constructing their own feedback questionnaires – perhaps because of the doubts about their effectiveness – and instead use 360-degree format versions of existing psychometric measures, such as the Emotional Intelligence Questionnaire (Higgs and Dulewicz, 1999).

Another fairly new application of the process is in relation to the validation of medical practitioners, but that is dealt with in Chapter 11. Moving to some of the current issues highlighted by people working in this field:

- There was almost too much demand for 360 feedback interventions in some organisations – HR was being bombarded with requests for bespoke questionnaires for specific teams, individuals, bits of the company and so on! Apart from the danger of multi-source feedback being seen as a panacea and applied rather blindly, this can place quite a strain on resources.
- Improper use of the process was noted occasionally. For example, a Health Authority accessing feedback information which had been collected under a 'development only' guise, and then using it in a disciplinary process against the individual concerned. Clearly, this is unethical.
- Some consultants complained about being asked by their clients to help implement a 360-degree feedback system built around the

client organisation's existing competency framework, which in the eyes of the consultants was unsatisfactory or inappropriate in some way.

- Should the boss always be included as one of the feedback givers? As was noted on page 82 when the study by Bailey and Fletcher (2002a) was described, the feedback from the individual's line manager seems still to be given the greatest importance, even if it is viewed as inaccurate. Some organisations have noticed this and deliberately removed the line manager's input, as they fear it tends to 'swamp' the feedback messages from peers and direct reports and hence to detract from the attention paid to them.

In addition to these three issues, there is also of course the ongoing debate – described in some length in the previous chapter – about the desirability or otherwise of using 360 feedback as an input to appraisal.

In summary

Best practice in multi-source feedback demands attention be given to careful preparation of the ground for all parties before it is introduced, expertise in designing the questionnaire, staged implementation, and the provision of an appropriate report and follow-up support mechanisms for those receiving the feedback. There are other aspects of good practice that are not dealt with here – for example, in relation to using software in this field (Atchley *et al.*, 2001). However, the above will be enough to demonstrate that such feedback processes are certainly not straightforward, and although there are potential benefits from applying multi-source assessment and feedback, failure to think it through carefully at the outset can lead to no positive outcomes being achieved, or worse still some actual damage being done. In view of this, putting evaluation strategies in place is essential, and these may focus on the short-, medium- and long-term impact of feedback.

Discussion points and questions

How does the use of 360-degree feedback in your organisation match up to the best practice guidelines – what are the strengths and weaknesses?

If someone was devising a feedback questionnaire for you in your role, what questions do you think it would be relevant to ask, and how would you word the rating scale?

How would you prepare the ground for the introduction of a 360-degree feedback process? What sort of consultation would you do, and with whom? What kind of briefing and support would you want to put in place?

Key references

Bracken, D. W., Timmreck, C. W. and Church, A. H. (2001) The Handbook of Multisource Feedback. Jossey-Bass: San Francisco, CA.

Fletcher, C., Baldry, C. and Cunningham-Snell, N. (1998) The psychometric properties of 360 degree feedback: An empirical study and a cautionary tale. *International Journal of Selection and Assessment*, 6, pp. 19–34.

Fletcher, C. and Bailey, C. (2003) Assessing self awareness: Some issues and methods. *Journal of Managerial Psychology*, 18, pp. 395–404.

Chapter 8

Training, and the implementation of appraisal

The role of training in determining the success of an appraisal scheme cannot be overestimated. Fletcher and Williams (1992b) have shown how the effectiveness of performance appraisal is related to the training effort put into it by the organisations concerned. Surveys show that training is offered to appraisers by nearly 80 per cent of UK organisations (Industrial Society, 2001). Unfortunately, this does not mean that the training was taken up by all appraisers; another survey of managers themselves indicated that 30 per cent of them had not been trained (Strebler *et al.*, 2001). Nor does it say anything about the quality of the training. On both these criteria, there is great room for improvement. One of the main failings of appraisal training in the past has been the emphasis on the procedure and paperwork rather than on the process and the skills needed to carry out appraisal in a sensitive and constructive manner. It is, of course, important that everyone knows what the scheme consists of and how it is to be operated, but this is really the easy part. Because it has a high 'comfort factor', there is a tendency to focus on the report forms etc. as if they were the main purpose of the exercise, which they are not – in fact, they often just get in the way (Hirsh, 2006).

Most of this chapter is rather atheoretical and will concentrate on the practical issue of how the behavioural skills needed in appraisal can be imparted; some further guidance on training, specifically in the context of professional groups, is given in Chapter 11. We will also consider the training needs of the appraisees – usually significantly neglected. Before that, however, it is worth addressing the issue of where to start the ball rolling. The conventional wisdom seems to be right – to introduce appraisal at the top and to work down, on the basis that (a) top management have to be seen to be taking it seriously, and (b) it is a salutary experience for someone to have been appraised before they themselves appraise anyone else. There is some evidence to support the first contention. A review study by Rodgers and Hunter (1991) has demonstrated the importance of senior management involvement, though in the context of MBO schemes rather than appraisal as such. It found that organisations introducing MBO with a high level of senior management commitment achieved average productivity gains of over 56 per cent, compared to average gains of just over 6 per cent in the case of organisations where such commitment was lacking. By analogy, since more appraisal schemes now take in director-level staff, there is reason to hope that the commitment will be present.

Background briefing and documentation

This element of appraisal training can be run as part of the appraisers' skills course or as a separate, preliminary session (the advantage of the latter is that it allows for larger groups to be dealt with at any one session than would be possible on a skills course). Its purpose is to tell all the appraisers what the thinking behind the appraisal scheme is, what it is trying to achieve, how it is structured and implemented, and to introduce and explain the forms and paperwork. If there has been a good consultation process in developing the scheme, then all this will be that much easier to put across. Without it, the sessions will probably take longer to run as there will need to be more time allowed to raise questions, allay anxieties and debate issues. In these cases, the briefing session is actually doubling as a commitment-gaining exercise. The aim is not just to inform but to sell the scheme to the appraisers.

The briefing sessions should normally be held fairly shortly before the appraisal training courses (if these are separate) and the first round of appraisals. It is often helpful to start by giving a short description of the recent history of appraisal in the organisation, and why there has been a need to change and/or to develop the new scheme. The aims of the new scheme and how it is to be operated can then be outlined. Either at the start of the session, or at this point, many organisations ask a member of top management to speak briefly in support of the appraisal scheme, to indicate high-level commitment to it and to emphasise that it is a worthwhile activity. It is not uncommon to find organisations inviting some external speaker – often a consultant or a prominent academic in the field – to make an input here as well. Their role is again to reassure the participants that the scheme is a good one and to draw some lessons from elsewhere (such as prestige, high-performing organisations) as to the value of effective performance appraisal. It is worth reiterating that if a genuine consultation process has allowed appraisers and appraisees to have a say in the design of the appraisal system, much of this selling effort will be unnecessary.

Something that can make life more or less difficult here is the way the briefing groups are made up. If any control can be exercised over this, it is

probably best if any appraisers who are known to have particularly negative attitudes to appraisal and who can be very defensive about it – sometimes dubbed the 'awkward squad' – are spread round the groups. This
way, their influence can be diluted and they may even be swayed to a more
positive approach by their peers. If they are allowed to collect in one group,
however, they usually just reinforce each other's prejudices and fears. The
other question about group composition is whether it is better to make it
representative of the organisation as a whole, by getting a cross-section of
appraisers from different departments to each session, or to run separate
sessions for each department or division. Each has its pros and cons, but
if there is to be any kind of flexibility in the way the scheme operates to meet
local needs, then the latter approach is clearly better.

The content of the briefing sessions varies according to how far they are
intended to serve as part of the training proper. If they do have a function
beyond informing and gaining commitment, then it usually involves
taking the participants through any guidance notes that are issued and
maybe giving some instruction on rating and report form completion.
These topics will be dealt with below when the training itself is considered.
Also, the question of briefing appraisees will be covered later in the broader
context of what training might be given to them.

Training the appraisers

It is not just the 'awkward squad' who are apprehensive about appraisal.
Many managers do not have a great deal of confidence in their ability to
handle appraisal interviews effectively, and so tend to cling to the paperwork. Some have an exaggerated idea of what appraisal involves and what
it demands of them (this is especially true if they have little or no experience of it). They see the appraisal as being akin to professional counselling,
and feel ill-equipped to take it on. Others try to reduce their anxieties by
minimising the importance of appraisal, seeking to make it sound trivial
or unnecessary. This usually gives rise to the kinds of comment every trainer
who has run an appraisal course has heard umpteen times – 'This is
only what I do on a day-to-day basis anyway', 'Good managers (i.e. those
like me) don't need appraisal', etc. The implication is that appraisal is a
superfluous and redundant addition to the dialogue that is already taking
place. However, both research (Fletcher, 1978; Nathan *et al.*, 1991) and
experience suggest very strongly that this is not true. It is precisely those
managers who have frequent communications with their staff who have the
most productive appraisals.

The extent of the appraisers' concerns about their ability to conduct the
appraisal will depend on its content and aims, and how much say they have

had in them. But even where they have participated fully in the design stage, there will still be a fair number who need to have their confidence built up through the training process. Training here is as much about giving that confidence as it is about teaching specific skills. For this reason, it is vital that

- the training is organised so as to ensure that there is enough time for participants to see they they are capable of doing a good job. If there is time for just one practice session, the appraiser often does not handle it well and then has no opportunity to learn from the feedback and improve both performance and confidence.
- the training is delivered as close as possible to the time of the first appraisals.

Neither of these is very easy to arrange. The ratio of participants to trainers on any one course should not really rise above 4:1 if there is to be a supervised practical element and effective feedback. Unless the organisation has a lot of trainers, this means that it will take some while to train everyone. So those going through on the first courses might have some time to wait before conducting their appraisals, if the organisation is working on a common starting date and the principle that no one will appraise unless trained to do so. In addition, the time commitment needed for good skills training makes it rather costly.

The time problem is particularly acute for senior managers, as it is difficult, if not impossible, to get them away from their desks for two days. There are three main options open to cope with this. First, run shorter courses for more senior and (in theory) more experienced people. The problem here is that they give the lead, and if they do not demonstrate their belief in the importance of the scheme, the message will get through to those below them. Also, being more senior and more experienced does not mean being more competent in handling appraisal. As has been observed on many occasions, 20 years' experience can often be one year's experience repeated 20 times. A better, second option, if at all possible, is to try to break up the training for senior managers so that they can attend on a couple of separate sessions. There is another difficulty in delivering training to the most senior levels, though. Top managers are not noted for their willingness to expose any of their real or imagined failings in front of peers. As a result, skills training conducted by in-house trainers is often politically unacceptable at these higher levels. One way round this is to find suitable externally run, open courses pitched at senior management level. Increasingly, though, there is another option available, thanks to developments in IT (see Chapter 5). This is to make available to appraisers a training package which is delivered through their PC and which they can work through in their own time. E-learning of this kind allows self-pacing and gets round the problem of senior managers feeling exposed in a training situation. Moreover, it allows the user to not only revisit aspects of appraisal they feel they need to reinforce their learning on but also to ensure that the learning is fresh in their minds by doing so immediately prior to actually holding the appraisal sessions. There are a number of such software programs available; an example of one multi-media package is described in Box 8.1. Ideally, of course, this kind of approach would supplement conventional skills training.

Box 8.1: performance appraisal – getting it right: an E-learning approach to training

This is a CD-based learning package (also deliverable through the internet or intranet) that is marketed by Robertson Cooper Ltd (RCL), and for which the author provided the technical content. The Appraiser programme first takes the individual through such subjects as assessing competencies, setting and review- ing objectives, avoiding bias, and using 360-degree feedback. It then moves on to preparing and planning the appraisal interview, and then (the greater part) handling the interview itself. This last element focuses strongly on feedback skills. There is also a special section on dealing with difficult situations e.g. an appraisee losing their temper, or complaining about lack of promotion. Indeed, one of the aims of the video sequences throughout was to portray 'real' reactions of participants, rather than bland scenarios that make appraisal look very easy to do. This learning resource uses graphics, video sequences and voice-overs to present the material, and is highly interactive; it requires the manager to respond to ques- tions as to how to handle a situation, and shows the consequences of different approaches that might be taken. At the end of each module is an assessment quizz for the individual to gauge how effective their learning has been. To work through the whole of the appraiser programme takes an individual around three hours, but because it is modular, a manager can decide whether to cover all the modules or just choose the ones that seem more important for their needs. There is a video/DVD Trainer's pack to complement the package.

A special feature of this package is that it also includes a separate CD for Appraisees. In the space of 30–40 minutes this takes them through the purpose of appraisal, raises their awareness of their own attitudes to the process, and helps them prepare for it, inluding doing a self-assessment and setting objectives. It goes on to guide them through the interview itself, helping them understand the importance of non-verbal behaviour, the need to participate and take ownership, and how to react to less positive performance feedback.

The main aim behind this learning resource is to help in making the face-to-face aspects of the appraisal situation as effective and positive as possible. The problems that arise in this context tend to be common across appraisal schemes, no matter what their format.

Assessment skills

Where the orientation of the appraisal scheme has a strong assessment component, this will need to be reflected in the training by:

- describing the dimensions on which the appraisees are to be assessed
- providing some exercises to help course participants to correctly identify the behaviours relevant to each dimension, and to assess them appropriately
- outlining some of the main rating/assessment errors.

The first of these seems straightforward enough, but is worth spending time on. How the dimensions were arrived at, and precisely what they mean, needs to be gone into fairly thoroughly. The less the detail given on the appraisal form, the greater the time needed to discuss the behaviours the dimensions are dealing with. Without this, the appraisers will work to different interpretations of the dimensions and the scale points on them. With BARS or similarly based assessment devices, there is much less danger of this.

Course participants usually find exercises in using the assessment dimensions extremely helpful. One type of exercise is to give them a pen picture of an individual and to ask them to complete the assessment ratings on the basis of this. The ratings are subsequently discussed with the trainers and other course members. Alternatively, they can be given a written list of behavioural observations and asked to decide which assessment dimension each one relates to. If the observations are quite detailed, they can be allocated a rating on the dimension as well. A step up from this is to present the course members with videos showing work episodes that illustrate the behaviours underlying the appraisal dimensions, then have them do the assessments on what they have seen. One advantage of this approach is that it can also be done on a distance learning basis; appraisers do not have to attend the course (or that element of it) at all.

The purpose of exercises of this kind is not only to ensure that appraisers gain a common understanding of what is being assessed and the standards involved, but that they also learn about some of the problems and pitfalls of assessment. At some point in the training process, they need to be made aware of the biases and distortions that can creep in. This can be put over in written form, and reinforced through the examples that arise – fortuitously or by design – in the course of doing the practical exercises. Some of the most frequent assessment errors and their sources are described in Box 8.2 (another, prejudice and discrimination, will be discussed later). One final point about providing this kind of assessment training: experience suggests that it pays dividends even outside the immediate context of the appraisal, helping managers develop assessment skills they can use in a range of situations.

Box 8.2: sources of bias and error in assessment

Halo effect. This is the tendency to allow one or two favourable attributes of an individual to colour one's judgment of all their other attributes. The result is to produce an overall, rather un-discriminating positive assessment – a 'halo'. The opposite phenomenon is sometimes called the 'horns effect'; this is where some unfavourable attribute of the person appraised leads to a generally negative impression being formed. This kind of error is one of the most commonly encountered, in selection interviews as well as in appraisal.

Attributional error. Before this is described, try a little exercise for yourself. Think of an incident recently where you did not perform as well as you would have hoped; why did this happen, how would you explain it? When you have mulled that over, move on to another incident, this time one where one of your subordinates (or, if you do not have any, a peer) did not perform as well as you hoped – again, why did this happen, how would you explain it? No cheating now; do not read on until you have analysed the two incidents!

Have you displayed 'fundamental attributional error' (to give it its full name)? This refers to a pervasive tendency we all have to take much more account of the situational circumstances in explaining our own behaviour – especially when we have been less than successful – than we do in explaining other people's behaviour. When it comes to understanding why others have acted the way they did, we are much more likely to make dispositional attributions. In other words, we see other people's actions as being caused by their personality and abilities and we play down the importance of the situation, the context of the behaviour. The implications of this for appraisal are clear: the danger is that the appraiser will be too ready to see a lack of goal achievement as being due to the appraisee's deficiencies and will not make enough allowances for other factors (of which the appraiser may well be one).

Biased sampling. There are two main forms of this. First, the tendency to base the appraisal on the last month or two of the period under review, because that is what dominates in the memory. Things that happened earlier, in what is the greater part of the appraisal period, are forgotten. The second form, which sometimes occurs in combination with the first, is to recall only the times when things have gone wrong, when the appraisee has not performed well. The extent to which this happens is demonstrated by the large number of people in organisations who work on the philosophy of 'no news is good news'.

Faulty implicit personality theory. Most people, without being conscious of it, have some ideas about personality and how it is structured; they have an implicit personality theory that guides them, and which may not always be built on sound foundations. You can see this in how untrained assessors rate candidates in group exercises: the candidates who talk most easily are often judged as being the highest on emotional stability. Actually, there is no good reason for assuming that an articulate person is also a stable one, but although faulty, it is a common inference about personality. Another frequent error is to assume that an assertive individual is also more organised and more intellectually able than someone who is not. These kinds of ideas about personality traits and the relationship between them can be a source of distortion in the way appraisers assess their staff.

'Similar to me' effect. This is very common in interviews and can affect appraisals, too. It is where a similarity in attitudes, preferences or background between the appraiser and appraisee influences the former to be positive in response to the latter, even to the extent of being unduly favourable in assessing performance. It is a kind of 'halo' effect, and one based on a very human tendency; similarity attracts – we are inclined to like people we see as being similar to ourselves.

Appraisal interview training

The training given to cover the conduct of the interview itself needs to deal with a variety of skills required in:

obtaining information
giving feedback
problem-solving
motivating
counselling.

A full discussion of these skills is beyond the cope of the present chapter; the reader who wishes to go into this subject in depth is referred to books such as that by Gillen (1998). We shall focus here chiefly on the kind of training necessary to impart process skills relevant to appraisal.

Many courses include a video or training film, either produced in-house or obtained from external sources (e.g. as mentioned in Box 8.1), to illustrate teaching points. Some of these are very useful, not least in promoting discussion amongst the course members. However, they do need to be professionally made and presented to be really effective – amateurish efforts simply give the more sceptical amongst the audience further ammunition to ridicule the appraisal scheme. There is little doubt, though, that appraisal interview training can best be tackled through practical exercises where the participants get feedback on their performance from trainers and fellow course members. One of the most commonly used techniques is the role play interview. Typically, this involves one course member appraising another on the basis of a written brief that describes the situation and their different perspectives. An alternative is to ask the individual playing the role of the appraisee to base it on a real problem case known to them. However, this kind of exercise exacerbates the inevitable artificiality of the training situation, and allows the favourite escape clause of 'Well, of course, I would not have handled it that way in real life.'

A much better approach, and one that generates a higher level of realism and course member involvement, is to get the participants to perform a task that they are then appraised on by their fellow course members. There are a number of ways of doing this. They may work on a group project – often akin to an assessment centre group decision-making task – then appraise one another on their individual contribution and performance. Depending on the numbers involved and the time available, they may all be given a turn at leading the rest of their syndicate in a task (building structures from Lego bricks, etc.) and then be appraised on that. A third variation is to get one course member to give a short presentation on a topic, have a second one appraise them on that, the third participant appraises the second on the handling of the appraisal, and so on. There are as many permutations on the exercise theme as the trainers' imagination permits.

The point about exercises of this kind is that, whilst they only allow the appraisal of performance in one isolated event, they do offer an opportunity to practise appraisal skills on genuine behavioural examples. The course members are ego-involved to the extent that they find it a demanding task, with the minimum of artificiality. True, the nature of the task that they are appraised on is not specifically and directly job-relevant, but this is not a disadvantage – a task that is very complex or involved in the work of the organisation runs the risk of focusing too much attention on content and detracting from the real point of the exercise, which is about process.

The usual format in running such exercises is for the syndicate tutor to ask the appraiser and then the appraisee for their feelings and observations on how the practice interview was conducted, followed by feedback from the tutor and the other syndicate members. The latter may have been given a behavioural checklist to guide their observations and the tutor may divide the monitoring and feedback between them so that they individually concentrate on different aspects of the way the appraiser handled the session. Whichever way this is done, however, it provides another valuable opportunity to practise much the same feedback skills as are needed in an appraisal situation. This needs to be pointed out before the practice interviews commence, and some guidance given to course members on how to go about giving feedback to one another. Box 8.3 presents some general guidance on giving feedback in this context (and, indeed, on conducting an appraisal interview itself). More detailed guidance on feedback skills can be found in Egan (2001). The value of having a course which permits each participant the chance of doing at least two practice interviews is that they have a chance to learn from the first and to improve their skill and confidence in the second.

Exercises of the kind described give the opportunity for practising skills in collecting information. The appraiser should be asking the right kind of questions to find out why the appraisee approached the task in the way they did, and so on. Skills can also be practised in giving feedback and, to an extent, in counselling on how to improve. The exercises may be a vehicle for demonstrating skill in problem-solving, though this will not necessarily be the case unless some deliberate effort has been made to build this in from the inception. Perhaps the one area in which they do not give adequate opportunity to develop skills is that of motivation. This is such a neglected topic in appraisal training that a separate section is devoted to it later in this chapter.

The practical component of an appraisal course needs to be supported with some written notes for guidance to reinforce the message conveyed in the training. These can be taken away and referred to by the appraisers to refresh their memories before they do their appraisals. An example of the kind of thing that might be given is presented in Appendix A. Apart from going over the basic points again, guidance notes can deal with issues that there may not be time for on the training course; for example, how to deal with special problem cases. There is an understandable desire amongst some attending appraisal courses to be told how to deal with every conceivable reaction and problem. Clearly, it is not possible to provide answers to this; the aim of the training is usually to impart generic skills and techniques that can be adapted and applied to a range of situations and needs. Course exercises normally focus on examples of typical appraisal content and interaction, since this is what most appraisers have to deal with most of the time. But there are extreme cases that occasionally arise – appraisees becoming overly emotional, or aggressive, or seeking to be manipulative, for example. The appraisers' concerns about these make them loom larger in their minds than the probability or frequency of them happening actually warrants. But they cannot be ignored. Even if they are the exception rather than the rule, when they *do* occur, they can cause the appraiser a disproportionate amount of trouble. If the time available for practical exercises is too limited to deal with them, then the alternatives are (a) to include some advice on the handling of problem cases that the individual appraiser can keep – as for example, in the CD learning resource described in Box 8.1(b) to provide advice through a video presentation on the course (c) provide a 'helpline' that appraisers can ring to seek advice, usually from the HR department.

One last point on the training of appraisers: it is valuable if they can be offered the opportunity to attend some kind of follow-up session run by training and/or personnel department staff. This might be in the nature of an 'appraisal clinic', where they bring back for discussion specific problems or issues that they have encountered in carrying out their interviews. It could also take the form of a review group made up of the original course membership convened at the end of the appraisal cycle where (for an hour or so) they can raise any particular difficulties and seek advice. Both of these serve a further purpose in acting as monitoring devices for the appraisal scheme as a whole.

Box 8.3: some general points on giving feedback

The purpose of feedback is to help the person to whom it is directed. To this end, it should be given in such a way that the person (a) understands it, (b) accepts it, and (c) can do something about it. How can this be achieved? There are some general rules to follow that can help here:

- *Be tentative* – seldom are things so clear-cut that observations take on the mantle of indisputable fact, to be conveyed as such.
- *Be willing to listen* – individuals may well have observations to make that throw new light on the problems under discussion. They should be encouraged to put their views. Even where their reaction is more emotional than 'reasoned',

it is probably better to let people get if off their chests rather than try to cut them short.

- *Be concrete* – discuss specific behaviours and examples to illustrate and support the points being made.
- *Be respectful* – try to communicate acceptance and understanding of the individual; you are talking about their performance of a task, not discussing their personality and values.
- *Identify both the positive and the negative aspects of performance* – resist the temptation to harp on about the deficiencies alone.
- *Be constructive* – offer suggestions as to how the situation might have been tackled differently and how problems might be tackled in the future.
- *Do not try to make too many critical points* – apart from the danger of generating defensive reactions, people can only take in and deal with just so much at one time.
- *Concentrate your observations on the aspects of performance that the individual can do something about* – there is little sense in focusing on deficiencies that will be impossible for the person to remedy.
- *Make sure your value judgments are identified as such* – and not presented as facts.

Training appraisees

Training appraisees is still far from commonplace; a survey (Industrial Society, 2001) showed that 62 per cent of UK organisations gave appraisees details of the mechanics of the appraisal scheme, 40 per cent offered formal training (how much or how positively the offer was made we know not), and 25 per cent did nothing for them at all. This is probably a major flaw in appraisal provision. If appraisal sysems ask appraisees to make a self-assessment prior to the appraisal, and to think about their objectives (as most of them do), why should the appraisees not be given training to help them in this? Arguably, they should need it more than their more senior appraisers. If the appraisees are to have a significant input into the appraisal process, then they should be given some help in making it effective. Of course, many appraisers are, in their turn, appraised by their own bosses. For them, the appraiser training will probably fulfil most of the needs from the appraisee perspective, though a short session specifically focusing on this could be included in the appraisal interview course. It is no bad thing to give appraisers an opportunity to put themselves on the other side of the desk and see how things look from there.

Frequently, appraisee courses are simply briefing sessions, with no real practical component. They sometimes take place within the broader context of induction courses, and in contrast with appraiser courses, there is seldom any pressure to attend. One county council I spoke to had found that the take-up rate of places on appraisee courses was so low that they eventually withdrew them. This is rather disappointing and fairly unusual, perhaps caused by a lack of understanding of what was on offer. The content of appraisee training to some extent mirrors that of the appraisers. It can include the following:

- *Backgrounding briefing.* At very least, they need to know what the aims of the scheme are and how it is to run.
- *How to prepare.* This may be simply providing an agenda, or giving a preparation form, or it may include how to complete a self-appraisal form that is an integral part of the process.
- *Guidance on objectives.* This should encourage the appraisee to think in advance about what these might be for the year ahead, and give some training on how objectives should be framed.
- *Discussion of self-assessment.* This should look at the strengths and weaknesses of self-assessment, and review its place in appraisal.
- *Combating anxiety.* Interviews of all sorts create a degree of apprehension, and some cognitive-behavioural techniques (imaging, relaxation, etc.) for reducing anxiety can be taught where needed.
- *Assertiveness training.* Some basic guidance can be given to help appraisees put their own point of view across to a superior without being unduly emotional or defensive.
- *How to respond to criticism.* One of the concerns uppermost in appraisees' minds is the prospect of criticism and how they will react – talking through the issues here can help them respond more constructively and confidently if and when it happens.
- *How to get action.* The appraisees can be encouraged to take the initiative in following up action recommendations to ensure that they are implemented.

Many of these can be presented in the form of discussion topics, though there is plenty of scope for practical exercises if desired. Training appraisees is something that can add a significant impetus to the effective running of an appraisal scheme, in that if they are empowered to drive it from their side, the appraisers will find it hard to do anything but respond with their best efforts. Again, if running (or indeed, attending) appraisee courses presents difficulties, an alternative is an e-learning solution of the kind outlined in Box 8.1.

Other issues in appraisal training

Appraising diversity

Where appraisees and appraisers are from different cultural or ethnic groups, there can be the potential for misunderstanding and poor communication. A business services organisation found evidence of this and did all they could to make sure that their new appraisal documentation was framed in language that was understandable to all. Piloting it with representatives of all the groups involved helps here. This is an issue that is worth sensitising appraisers to in training if they are likely to appraise staff of very diverse cultural backgrounds (or, indeed, educational levels). There are different styles of interpersonal communication and self-presentation that have been found to characterise different cultures (see Chapter 12 for a fuller discussion of this topic). Hofstede (1980), for example, studied differences within IBM across over 40 countries and identified many variations, centring around such things as:

- the extent to which power was centralised or dispersed, with its implications for how authority is perceived and accepted
- the degree to which deviance from norms and values would be tolerated (e.g. less in Greece than in Sweden)
- the balance between individualism and collectivist, more group-centred attitudes (e.g. Australia being high on the former and Pakistan high on the latter).

These and other factors have an impact on individual behaviour. Individuals from, say, a Chinese background may not feel it appropriate to assert their views with superiors, as this is regarded as impolite within their culture (see Chapter 12). Appraisers dealing with culturally diverse groups – which now applies to many managers, not just those in international businesses – should have some part of their training focused on likely culturally based differences and the need to adapt appraisal style accordingly. For instance, it is possible that it will take considerably more effort to encourage self-appraisal and two-way communication with some groups, and the appraiser should be prepared for this. The training of appraisees is also important here. Many of the elements of appraisee courses listed earlier can be given special emphasis where the cultural mix indicates that it is likely to be needed.

Another aspect of having a diverse workforce is that it can produce the bias and prejudice that gives rise to unfair discrimination, on the grounds of race or sex. While there is a need to monitor the output of appraisal schemes for this, there is also a need to tackle it from the other end, the input. Bias does not always show itself in the form of ratings or of the assessment of target achievement (if the latter is as objective as it is supposed to be, then there is hopefully less opportunity for this to happen). It can be more subtle than that, but just as damaging. Going back to the concept of attributional error, Garland and Price (1977) found that successful performance in female managers was attributed by prejudiced male managers to either luck or to the task being an easy one, whereas unprejudiced managers put it down to high ability and hard work. Similar distortions in the explanation of good or poor performance can arise where the appraisees are members of ethnic minorities and the appraisers are racially prejudiced.

This kind of bias can be illustrated in various ways. One approach is through assessment exercises – for example, appraisers can be given written descriptions of individuals and their performance and asked to react to them in some way (e.g. by rating the people described or explaining their likely motives for behaving the way they did). Half the appraisers can be given the description containing a female principal character and the other half given the same one but with a male character. Comparing the ratings and accounts of the two groups – without identifying individuals – often brings out into the open the kinds of stereotypes and assumptions that are part and parcel of bias. Needless to say, though, this requires especially sensitive handling on the part of the trainers.

Finally, one other mistake that male appraisers in particular need to be alerted to was identified by HR staff in a large local authority. This was a tendency to equate working late in the office with quality of work and commitment, which was then reflected in PRP recommendations. The most frequent losers from this were women who, having worked the full day, then went home to their families.

Diversity is a broad issue, and the reader who wishes to go into it further is referred to the book by Fullerton and Kandola (1998).

Training to motivate

Many, perhaps most, appraisal schemes pay at least lip service to the aim of motivating those appraised. For some of them, it is one of their main purposes. Yet if you look at the content of appraisal training courses, you seldom find any mention of the word motivation. There seems to be an assumption that simply doing the appraisal is enough to motivate the appraisee, and if that is not the case, then it is down to the performance-related pay to do the job. What does motivate people at work, and how can this knowledge be built into appraisal courses?

There is no single, universally accepted theory of motivation that explains the differences between people in the effort and commitment they put into their work (for a good general introduction to this field, the reader is referred to Hollyforde and Whiddett, 2002). The two main theories that have found favour and a fair amount of empirical support are Goal-Setting Theory and Expectancy Theory. The former deals mainly, as the name implies, with the motivating qualities of goal-setting and how to maximise them. The evidence – reviewed by Locke and Latham (1990) – shows over and over again how goal-setting is effective in raising performance levels. Few findings in occupational psychology are more reliable than this one – more than 90 per cent of all studies on goal-setting show positive effects. To elaborate a little further, this research shows that:

- More difficult and more clearly quantifiable goals encourage achievement to a greater extent than do easier and vaguer goals. Exhortations of the 'do your best' variety are of no value.
- For performance improvement to take place, there has to be adequate feedback on goal achievement – but feedback alone, without there being goals set (as one finds in many appraisal systems) does not lead to improvement.
- Commitment to the goals is necessary for the goals to affect performance, and that commitment is affected both by the expectations of success in achieving the goals, and by the value placed on that success.

The last of these points brings forward the other best-supported theory of work motivation, namely Expectancy Theory (see Donovan, 2001; Arnold and Schoonman, 2002, for description and evaluation). This stresses the need for individuals to be able to see a clear and positive relationship between the amount of effort they put in, the performance improvement it brings about, and the way that improvement leads to valued outcomes. Only if all these conditions are met is the individual likely to be fully motivated. Whilst appraisers cannot bring about all of these conditions, they can play an important role in influencing them.

These two theories do not explain all work motivation, but together they offer a sound basis for moving forward. Any appraisal system that is intended to motivate would benefit from exposing appraisers to these concepts as part of the training, and inviting them to explore the implications for the appraisal scheme and what they as appraisers can do at the practical level to make the appraisal a motivating experience. This is where another ingredient needs to be added – consideration of individual differences. Following the broad principles of goal-setting and expectancy theories will be a good guide, but there is still the need to understand the make-up of the individual appraisee. When discussing the place of appraisal within a performance management framework (pages 43–44), it was noted that people vary greatly in what motivates them, and that different things were important to the same person at differing career stages. The appraiser needs to be aware of this, and to know what, in expectancy theory terms, are the outcomes the individual values. If the organisation runs an appraisal scheme that allows managers some latitude in dispensing rewards – and the emphasis here is at least as much on the non-financial variety as the financial – and the manager knows the appraisees well enough, then the appraisal process can be successful in motivating performance improvement. Appraisal training, then, can facilitate this by directing course members' attention to the nature of individual differences in this respect. Brain-storming some ideas about what rewards appraisees *and* the appraisers themselves value can be a useful course exercise that provides a basis for more creative thinking about appraisal as a motivational tool.

One last point here: most of what has been said about motivation in this section hinges on providing the impetus for improved performance through appraisal. Whilst it is important to include this as part of appraisal training, it also has to be emphasised in training that this alone is not enough. Motivating subordinates to improve is one thing, but without the empowerment and development to allow them to, not a lot will be achieved.

Who does the training?

This used to be a fairly straightforward matter, and probably remains so for many organisations where appraisal falls directly into the lap of the HR and training departments. There is also increased reliance on self-development, with the provision of resource centres for managers to use as and when they need. Things are less simple, though, where appraisal is part of a performance management system and is owned by line management. If the latter have had some part – possibly a major one – in designing it, then they may also have some role in the training. The problem is that they may not be very good at training! Rather than abdicate this role to the line, the best solution may be for the HR department to work in collaboration with line representatives to tailor and deliver the training required by local circumstances. This can be through jointly designed and presented courses, or through a system of cascaded training, where HR staff train a cadre of line managers (self-nominated and/or nominated by local management) to go out and train their colleagues, providing them with the necessary back-up materials (OHP transparencies, handouts, and so forth). This group of managers can then adapt the basic package to the way appraisal operates in their own divisions. One of the advantages of this approach, reported by organisations that use it, is that these line managers – if they are well-chosen – have a high level of credibility with their colleagues, and are the most effective representatives for the appraisal scheme. The initial training provided for them by HR has to be of the highest standard, though; they have to go away convinced of the value of what they are doing if they are to gain the commitment of their colleagues.

On a rather different theme is the relative virtue of in-house versus bought-in training. At very senior levels, for reasons given earlier, it is often necessary to go outside the organisation to arrange suitable courses. For the rest, much depends on the training resources available. If there is no expertise in-house, then getting external help is the only option. This does not necessarily mean buying places on courses; it can be much better to hire a consultant to work with the organisation and run courses specifically for it. In fact, buying places on externally run public courses is probably the least attractive and least effective form of training. Such courses can be of a high professional standard and put over generic appraisal skills in a competent way, but what they cannot do is to cater for the unique characteristics of the organisation and the way appraisal operates there. They therefore tend to be seen as rather remote and lacking in relevance to the appraisers' context.

In summary

Training makes a substantial impact on the quality of appraisal. It should start with running briefing sessions to help those involved understand the appraisal scheme and its aims, before moving on to actual skills training. The latter will include both making an accurate assessment and holding an appraisal interview. It is also desirable to help line managers who are going to appraise their staff to understand their motivations and to be sensitive to differences between one person and another in what they are likely to respond to. There are many elements and different approaches in training that may be relevant, including the use of e-learning solutions, and these have to be chosen and adapted to meet the level and needs of the appraisers. Whilst training efforts have traditionally been centred on the appraisers, there is good reason (and evidence) for thinking that much more should be done to help appraisees prepare for the session and to get the most out of it. One of the most important considerations in delivering training is to ensure that it addresses the issue of diversity, raising awareness of the kinds of biases and misunderstandings that can arise in the appraisal context.

Discussion points and questions

How would you adapt appraisal training to the needs and context of different level management groups in an organisation?

What steps can we take to identify and then to reduce or eliminate bias and unfair discrimination in performance appraisal?

If you were devising a training programme to help staff who were going to be appraised to get the most out of the experience, what elements would you include and why?

Key references

Egan, G. (2001) *The Skilled Helper: A Systematic Approach to Effective Helping.* 7th edn. Counselling series. Brooks/Cole: Pacific Grove, CA.

Gillen, T. (1998) *Handling the Appraisal Discussion* (Management Shapers). Institute of Personnel and Development: London (now CIPD, London).

Industrial Society (2001) *No 86 Managing Performance.* Managing Best Practice series. The Industrial Society: London.

Chapter 9

Monitoring and maintenance

The chief personnel executive of an organisation employing more than 50,000 people and which had introduced comprehensive performance management and appraisal policies, when asked what he would do differently if he were to start again, replied that he would lay more emphasis on the importance of maintaining them. He was putting his finger on one of the eternal problems of appraisal – how to keep it alive and well. Great effort is often expended on setting it up in the first place, with very little thought given to the follow-through action needed once it is up and running. Yet the frequency with which organisations encounter difficulties with their appraisal schemes should give ample warning of how essential it is to monitor them from the outset, and to modify and correct any deficiencies at the earliest possible stage. If problems do arise, they have to be caught quickly, or the whole appraisal scheme rapidly generates scepticism and disillusionment that is hard to dispel – and which can make any effort to modify the scheme an uphill struggle.

Most of what is dealt with in this chapter, like the previous one, is centred very much on practical rather than theoretical aspects of appraisal. Moreover, what is said here implies a central role for the personnel or HR department, despite the emphasis elsewhere in the book on moving away from monolithic, centrally driven appraisal schemes. It is certainly desirable, as ever, to evaluate appraisal in a manner that involves line management and others. But the complexities of the exercise and the need, in many respects, for a broader perspective indicates that this is an area where personnel have to act as the driving force and prime facilitators.

Performance indicators for performance appraisal

How do we recognise excellence in an appraisal scheme? What are the criteria by which an appraisal scheme might be judged successful or unsuccessful? These can be broken down into short-term and long-term criteria, with the former being much easier to define than the latter.

Short/Medium-term criteria

As far as monitoring the effectiveness of the appraisal scheme in its first year or so of operation is concerned, it is obviously the short/medium-term criteria that are relevant. These include:

- *Completion rate.* The most basic measure of all is whether the appraisals are actually carried out. Research over the years has shown just how often appraisals are not done, and how far managers will go to avoid them; an Industrial Society survey in 1997 showed that less than one-third of UK organisations achieved a two-thirds completion rate. If the appraisal scheme has been well-designed, with a good level of consultation, this should not happen. Where all appraisal forms go to central personnel, it is relatively easy to check on completion. Contemporary trends in appraisal, however, mean that it is less often the case that personnel are automatically sent copies of appraisal documents. They tend to reside with the appraisee and appraiser as working documents to be referred to when, say, objectives are subject to interim review or development needs are discussed. There is a lot to be said for this practice, as it makes appraisal reports live documents rather than just file fodder. But it need not preclude the emailing of a simple action sheet to the personnel division indicating what action recommendations, if any, have been agreed. This can serve the triple function of notifying personnel that the appraisal has been done, informing them if there are some action recommendations that fall within their sphere of responsibility, and providing them with a means of checking on the subsequent implementation of action recommendations.

  There will always be a few appraisals that are not done for one good reason or another, but any sizeable shortfall should set alarm bells ringing. The MD of one business services organisation decided to give a further encouragement to the prompt and full completion of appraisals; he made it a pre-condition for considering promotion applications from the appraisers.

- *Action generated.* Another useful indicator of how things are going is the extent and type of action recommendations generated by the appraisal. If appraisal documents produce few agreed action points, then something is not quite right, the more so if there is any indication of development needs – how are they going to be dealt with? The nature of the action recommended is as important as the quantity. If the bulk of the action is to be taken outside the immediate job context – such as external training courses – then it may be an indication that the appraiser and appraisee are not looking hard enough at what they can do together to improve performance. Indeed, if most of the recommendations coming forward relate just to appraisers or to appraisees, the question needs to be asked as to whether the system is working as intended. It is reasonable for the majority of action following appraisals to be for implementation by the appraisees (overall, that is – clearly there will be individual cases where this is not so), but not all of it. If appraisers are taking responsibility for nearly all the post-appraisal action, then the suspicion arises that they are not getting their appraisees sufficiently involved in the process.

- *Quality of written reports.* Where the appraisal scheme entails the completion of a formal written report, the content of this can give some indication of how the process is operating. At its simplest, the issue is whether the report is being completed in the manner required. More searchingly, the written content can be evaluated in terms of how much is recorded, whether there are any inconsistencies or deficiencies (e.g. weaknesses being identified but no remedial action mentioned), and the frequency and nature of the dissenting comments recorded by appraisees. The general tone of the comments can reveal a great deal. For example, I can recall an appraisal report written after the appraisal interview by a senior civil servant which said: 'I would not like to see Jones at a promotion interview on this showing.' It was not hard to imagine that the appraisal session had been conducted in a rather gruelling fashion, more akin to a promotion interview than an appraisal interview. Analysing all written reports, especially in a systematic way, is usually far too time-consuming to be worthwhile. It is more realistic to do it on a sampling basis, or to rely on the corrective input from other appraisers where more than one manager is involved (e.g. where the appraisal is done by the appraisee's immediate boss but also seen by the boss two levels up) – though in the latter case, this function needs to be emphasised in training as part of the second appraiser's role.

- *Attitudes and the perceived value of appraisal.* From action to reaction – how appraisers and appraisees feel about the scheme once they have been through a round of appraisals, what they see as the benefits and outcomes, what they see as the problems, are all important indicators of how the scheme is working. Depending on when they are collected, these reactions can be short- or long-term criteria. If the participants feel positive about the scheme and see it as leading to useful developments (e.g. performance improvement, knowing where they stand, greater role clarity), then there is some cause for optimism. Although these might be subjective responses, they are as important as any hard data; the commitment of the participants rests on them. Any reported difficulties in the way the appraisals were conducted (too much emphasis on objectives, insufficient recognition of work done well, avoidance of giving feedback on the part of appraisers, and so on) from the perspective of either appraisers or appraisees, can be investigated and remedial action taken.

- *Equity.* The concept of equity in relation to monitoring performance appraisal has two main aspects. One is the way reward decisions are made and the spread of assessments that give rise to them. Do certain sections of the organisation fare significantly better than others in terms of assessments and rewards, and if so is it justifiable – are they really better? The other aspect concerns equal opportunities and unfair discrimination. Are the distributions of assessments, and the content of appraisals generally, similar for both sexes and across ethnic groups? Inequity in either of these domains is likely to pose severe problems, not least in the area of law, for the organisation and its appraisal scheme. Appraisals have not only to be fair, they have to be seen to be fair. For a more academic perspective, the attention given by management writers to organisational justice theory bears directly on the question of equity in appraisal (e.g. Erdogan *et al.*, 2001; McDowell and Fletcher, 2004).

Long-term criteria

It could be argued that there should not be any long-term criteria for the effectiveness of an appraisal scheme, because no scheme should continue in the same form for a long period if it is to remain relevant to the changing circumstances of the organisation. But given that there is likely to be some continuity in the appraisal arrangements – most changes in appraisal schemes are more in the nature of evolution than revolution – it does seem reasonable to look at the longer-term benefits the appraisal and related processes have produced. In fact, it is probably worth considering what the long-term criteria might be even if there is no intention to actually try to measure them. The rationale for this is simply that it often clarifies the organisation's thinking about appraisal to formally identify what the long-term success of an appraisal scheme might look like. It is, of course, possible that such a process will bring to light the fact that the organisation sees appraisal as an activity that has only short-term pay-offs. For those – hopefully the majority – who do see appraisal as having a strategic contribution to make, four broad criteria that might guide their evaluation are outlined below. None of them are determined solely by the effectiveness of appraisal, but in each case the appraisal scheme has a role to play and can reasonably be assessed in that context.

- *Organisational performance.* There are obviously many factors that influence the basic indices of organisational performance, and some of them (such as government policy or the state of the economy in general) are more potent in their effect than appraisal can ever be. None the less, appraisal policies – particularly within a performance management framework – should have some effect. Perhaps the clearest indicator of their impact on organisational performance in the broadest sense is the extent to which the targets set for individuals are seen as being achieved. If they are, and if those targets relate in a systematic way to the business plan, then the appraisal process might fairly be judged to be making an effective contribution.
- *Quality of staff.* One of the main functions of appraisal is, or should be, the development of staff. If it is successful in that, then the organisation will find either that it has enough trained employees to meet its normal requirements at any given time, or that it can readily identify where gaps are likely to occur (which might arise through problems in recruitment) and take remedial action. In other words, one of the criteria that can be used is whether the promotion vacancies or new posts can be filled from within the organisation by staff of acceptable quality.
- *Retention of staff.* Appraisal is a communication device, and in the process of discussing performance and meeting development needs, problems that might cause individuals to leave the organisation can be detected and (sometimes) dealt with. If the appraisal scheme is an effective vehicle for motivating people and raising job involvement and job satisfaction, it can help to minimise the wastage rate and boost staff retention, so saving the money that might otherwise be used in recruiting and training new staff.
- *Levels of commitment.* As implied by the last point, an effective appraisal system should eventually – not overnight – lead to more positive attitudes to the job and to the organisation. Thus, levels of job involvement, job satisfaction and organisational commitment are all indicators that are relevant to judging how well an appraisal system is operating and the kind of impact it is making in the long term (measurement of commitment will be discussed shortly).

Methods and sources of evaluation

To say what the evaluation criteria might be is one thing, but how to actually collect the data is quite another. The methods of evaluation are implicit in most of the criteria outlined above, however, more needs to be said about evaluating three of them: attitudes and perceived value, equity, and levels of commitment.

Measuring attitudes to appraisal and its perceived value

There are two main methods available here, the interview and the question-naire, and both can be targeted on appraisers and appraisees alike. Inter-views produce richer data – the interviewers can ask probing questions and follow up on interesting observations, and will be able to grasp the nuances of the appraisal process and its context for the people they are interview-ing. The three drawbacks of this approach are: (a) it is time-consuming, and this inevitably limits the sample size; (b) it is sometimes difficult to analyse and summarise this kind of qualitative data; and (c) it does not give the respondents anonymity, which may inhibit their frankness. The pros and cons of the questionnaire method are just the opposite. On the positive side, it allows for larger samples, quantitative analysis, and can afford anonymity to the respondents. The cost of this is that it does not yield the richness and detail of observations that come from interviews. Also, not all organisations have the resources or expertise to run questionnaire surveys, or can afford to commission them from outside consultants (a cheaper alternative to the latter is to approach an occupational psychology depart-ment or a business school in a university and ask if any students would care to run an evaluation study as a project – the disadvantage here being that the company loses some control over the evaluation process).

The core content of the evaluation is much the same whichever method is used. The areas to be covered are likely to be:

- background details of the respondent (age, sex, job)
- what was discussed in the appraisal
- perceptions of the effectiveness, fairness and outcomes
- overall attitudes to the appraisal scheme.

The exact content and framing of questions will depend on the nature of the appraisal system and the level of the respondents. As most organisations have a lot more experience of interviewing than of mounting questionnaire surveys, the basic steps involved in the latter are described in Box 9.1. IT makes it much easier to mount web based surveys, and indeed where elements of the appraisal process itself are delivered this way it becomes possible to capture much more data on the distribution of ratings etc. and to check for biases (see the section on Equity above).

In any evaluation study aimed at investigating attitudes and perceptions, whether by interview or questionnaire, the quality of the information obtained will, in part, depend on the degree to which the respondents cooperate. If members of trade unions or staff associations are involved, then these bodies should be consulted on the evaluation exercise and asked

Box 9.1: running a questionnaire-based evaluation study

It is not as difficult to run questionnaire surveys as might be imagined; most medium or large organisations should be able to cope with them. The sequence to follow is this:

1 The aim of the survey and when it is to be carried out are the first things to consider, as the two questions are linked. If the chief objective is to find out what went on in the interview and whether the appraisers followed the training guidelines they had been given, then the survey has to be done as soon as possible after the interviews have taken place (otherwise, people simply forget and do not report accurately). If, on the other hand, the main concern is the effects and outcomes of the appraisal process, then the questionnaires have to go out long enough after the appraisal for some effects to have been observed – perhaps three to six months at least. Ideally, both types of information are sought. This means either having two separate surveys or staggering the distribution of the questionnaires, some going out immediately after the appraisals and some rather later. The latter is probably the more economical approach, but care has to be taken that the time elapsed since the appraisal is taken account of in analysing the data and interpreting the findings.

2 Decide on the sample. To a large extent this depends on the size of the organisation and the resources available. In small companies, it should be possible to cover all appraisees and appraisers (though a decision has to be taken about whether staff who find themselves in both roles are to be burdened with completing two questionnaires, one as appraisee and one as appraiser). In larger organisations, some kind of sampling will probably be necessary. The sampling can be done on a random basis from personnel records, or various divisions can be chosen and all staff in them covered. The main thing is to ensure that the sample is (a) as representative as possible in terms of age, sex, level, function and geographical area, and (b) large enough to give worthwhile information – it is important to remember that the response rate may be as low as 50 per cent, though hopefully it will be more like 75 per cent.

3 Develop a pool of questions on the basis of what you want to ask about the appraisals and what effects they have had. One set of items will be for appraisers, and the other set – on a separate questionnaire – will be for appraisees. Keep in mind the length of the questionnaire and the time it takes to complete; most people will not spend more than around 20 minutes on it at most.

4   Put the items together in questionnaire format, paying particular attention to the instructions (on how to complete the questionnaire) and the wording of the items. In the case of the instructions, are they clear and appropriate to the kind of response format (e.g. ticking one of a series of response alternatives)? And in relation to the item wording, avoid asking two questions in one, e.g. 'Did the appraisal lead to an increase in your job satisfaction and performance?' (Whatever the answer, you will not know if the respondent was referring to satisfaction, performance, or both.)

5   Pilot the draft questionnaires by giving them to a small group of staff at the target levels. When they have completed them, discuss the content and format of the questionnaire with the pilot sample. Were the instructions and the questions clear? Was any item especially difficult to answer or posed problems in some way? Was anything omitted that they felt was important? Did they have a common understanding of what the items meant? How long did it take to complete?

6   Redraft the questionnaire in the light of this feedback, and send it out (either electronically or on paper) to the sample with a suitable covering letter. The latter should:

- make clear the purpose of the exercise
- say who will receive the output from it and how it will be used
- if possible, guarantee anonymity for the respondent
- state who has authorised the evaluation study
- explain how the sample has been chosen
- ask for the cooperation of the person receiving the questionnaire and give an indication of the (short) time it takes to answer it
- indicate where to send it on completion.

7   In the case of large samples, the data can be analysed using any one of a variety of statistical packages available. For smaller sample sizes, it is possible to do the analysis manually. Often, simple percentage response breakdowns on each question will provide the information necessary, though further analysis using simple statistics like chi-squared will help bring out any significant differences between the various staff groups (i.e. analysing the data by sex, age, function and so on).

for their suggestions on its content. This will not only help to gain their support for the study, and so encourage their members to participate, but will also increase their interest in the findings and in implementing changes as a result of them. Senior management involvement and backing should be sought for the same reasons. After gaining all this support, employees can be informed of the impending study, told that it has been sanctioned by the various interested parties, and asked for their cooperation through the medium of in-house publications (newsletters etc) or departmental meetings.

When it comes to interpreting evaluation data of this kind, a number of issues arise. It has to be recognised that the observations collected are subjective, although they represent the reality for the people concerned and will determine their reactions to the appraisal process. But there will be some inconsistencies, not least between appraisers and appraisees. The objective truth, such as it is, usually lies somewhere between the two. More difficult is to ascertain what constitutes a satisfactory set of results. For example, is it good to have 30 per cent of appraisees feeling that the appraisal helped improve their performance, or is that rather low? Can we realistically expect a 100 per cent positive response? The best way to answer questions of this kind is to have some 'norms' – a picture of what average results look like – so that the organisation can compare their results against them and see if they were higher, lower or the same. Data collected by the author and his colleagues in evaluation studies across seven organisations of varying size in public and private sectors go some way towards providing this basis for comparison. The figures given in Box 9.2 below are based on responses from 5,940 appraisees and 1,332 appraisers (the response rates in the studies was generally high, 75–95 per cent). The quality of the appraisal systems and the adequacy of the training offered varied a good deal from one organisation to another, and it can be seen that even with the better ones there was still room for improvement in several respects.

Once the evaluation results are in and have been analysed, their implications for the way the appraisal scheme is operating and how it might be modified have to be considered. The general principle of encouraging ownership and participation in appraisal can be followed through here by arranging group feedback sessions in which small groups of appraisers (and possibly, in separate sessions, appraisees) are presented with the main findings of the evaluation and invited to discuss them and their implications. This both provides feedback and acts as a vehicle for generating improvement. If problems in the way the appraisal scheme is running have been identified, some action has to be taken – there is not much point doing the evaluation if the will to act on the findings is lacking. This may entail additional training (possibly targeted at certain groups or particular skills), clarification of the written guidance, or changes to the nature of the scheme itself. Most important is that something should be seen to be done, and done quickly.

Box 9.2: comparison of evaluation data from studies in various organisations

% of cases in which –	Best result achieved	Average result achieved	Worst result achieved
The appraisee was given some notice beforehand	99	91	67
The appraisee did some preparation beforehand	83	62	16
The appraiser spent an average of not less than half an hour preparing for the interview	95	69	34
Weaker aspects of performance were discussed in the appraisal	81	54	40
Training needs were discussed in the appraisal	70	47	21
The appraisee reported their job satisfaction as being higher after the interview	40	30	15
The appraisee felt their performance had improved (or was likely to) as a result of the appraisal	54	40	20

Measuring levels of commitment

If introducing or revising performance appraisal is a significant organisational development intervention, then it should have broader and longer term effects on communication, staff attitudes to the organisation and their levels of involvement in their work. All these and more can be tapped by a questionnaire survey, but there is a basic problem. To be meaningful as an evaluation of the changes brought about by appraisal, or any other intervention, there has to be a base-line measure against which to project those changes. In other words, you need a before-and-after measurement strategy.

Rather than constructing questionnaires from scratch, an alternative is to use one or more of the standard measures of job satisfaction, organisational commitment and similar variables. This saves time and effort and, more importantly, has the advantage of offering the opportunity to compare the organisation's scores on these measures with those published from other organisations. This makes it possible to look at the changes that have taken place within the organisation *and* at whether the levels of job satisfaction etc. are higher or lower than elsewhere. Research (Fletcher and Williams, 1992b, 1996) on performance management using this approach demonstrated how the differing quality of performance management schemes was reflected in the scores on such variables. This has been extended and replicated by the Audit Commission in their research on performance management in local government (Audit Commission, 1995a,b). Acquiring these kinds of measures is not very difficult. They are readily available in the occupational psychology literature and can, in most cases, be used without having to purchase them. Some specific measures that are relevant and the references for them are listed in Appendix B. Also, the Audit Commission Management Handbook (Audit Commission, 1995c) presents in full the questionnaire constructed by the author and used in their study. However, it may be wise to get some guidance from a chartered occupational psychologist if the organisation is contemplating incorporating measures of this type in its long-term evaluation of appraisal.

Assessing equity: the fairness of the distribution

The basic task here is to collect all the relevant data from the appraisal documentation and recommendations. This is usually done by the central personnel department, monitoring the distributions of ratings and pay recommendations and checking to see that there are no unjustifiable variations between staff groups.

It may be that the differences in the distribution of assessments are entirely justifiable. However, if a group of workers from a particular ethnic background do less well on performance ratings than do the majority of appraisees, the question is whether this genuinely reflects attributes of the appraisees or whether it is due to biased perceptions on the part of the appraisers. If there is evidence that this group of appraisees have less experience or lower educational levels, this could be the reason for the lower performance levels. On the other hand, if no such differences between them and the rest are observable, and no development action for them (or less than for the majority) was recommended by the appraisers, there would be cause for suspicion and concern.

A frequently encountered instance of where justifiable inequities can arise is in reward decisions. It is probably unrealistic to assume that all parts of the organisation are performing effectively, and this will be represented in the PRP recommendations. The problem is one of determining whether the higher levels of PRP awards being put forward by managers do reflect superior performance or just excessive leniency in assessment. As suggested in Chapter 3, the best way of sorting this out is to leave it to the line managers themselves to justify their pay recommendations to their peers, with personnel providing any statistical information that is relevant (e.g. changes in divisional output, expenditure, and so on over the year).

While variations in appraisal data may be a function of sex, race, division etc. and have to be investigated, there is a broader level of evaluation and monitoring that needs to be done. This is checking to see if the *overall* distributions of ratings and merit pay increases look right, which implies that there is some idea at the outset of what they should be. This is clearly essential if pay costs – and employee career expectations – are to be kept under control. The case of a major UK bank illustrates this. It started out with the expectation that 10–15 per cent of staff would be assessed as having exceeded their targets, 60–70 per cent as having met their targets, and 10–20 per cent as having fallen short of target. They did not get quite this kind of distribution, as the actual proportion of staff in each category was 22 per cent, 69 per cent and 9 per cent. This is not far off what they wanted, but the impact on the pay bill is worth pointing up. The top group, which contained 7–12 per cent more staff than anticipated, got a 10 per cent bonus, while the bottom group, which had 1–10 per cent fewer staff in it than anticipated got a 2.5 per cent bonus. If the distribution had departed much further from what was expected and desired, the consequences could have been fairly serious.

Sometimes the overall distribution produces quite a different problem. The overall performance rating for 6,000 middle range administrative staff in a large county council after one year of a new appraisal and PRP scheme looked like this (Fletcher and Williams in CIPD, 1992):

Highest Rating	1	2	3	4	5	Lowest Rating
% Staff	0.01	5.2	93.1	1.0	0.01	

The problem here is one of almost everyone being rated in the middle. Given that the rating is a basis for PRP decisions, this is very unhelpful as it fails to discriminate effectively between differing performance levels (unless one makes the unlikely assumption that there were virtually no differences amongst 6,000 staff). The fact that PRP was new in this organisation may have contributed to the excessive caution of the appraisers. In cases of this kind, those who have responsibility for appraisal within the organisation have to take some corrective action. Again, the best way to do this is by group feedback sessions backed up by written guidance.

The general point then, is that it is helpful (essential in the case of PRP systems) to have some idea of what the rating distributions should be overall, and to communicate this to the appraisers – and probably to the appraisees (as a restraint on expectations). Monitoring appraisal assessments, and checking to see if there are unexplained variations in them, is a key part of the evaluation process. Neglecting to do so can cost the organisation dear in more ways than one.

Why is there so often a lack of evaluation?

It is not easy to carry out evaluation exercises, and one is often struck by the contrast between organisations' willingness to commit considerable human and financial resources to setting up personnel systems – be they psychometric tests in selection, assessment centres, appraisal schemes or whatever – and their extreme reluctance to commit a fraction of those resources to seeing if they were getting their money's worth. It may be the difficulty of doing evaluation work, it may be that the organisation does not think it has the expertise, but I have a terrible feeling that, in quite a few cases, it comes down to not wanting to know. Some managers responsible for designing systems have an understandable resistance to finding that what they have done is not actually working very well, with all the implications that has for their self-esteem, their standing with the organisation and the subsequent effort they have to put in to get things right. Small wonder that they show little enthusiasm for evaluation, with the risks that it may carry for them personally. To overcome this, it needs to be publicly recognised from the outset (the design stage) – by everyone involved – that it is the exception rather than the rule for appraisal schemes to run perfectly from day one, and that evaluation and further improvement is a normal expectation.

In summary

If an appraisal system goes wrong in some way, it usually happens quite early in its life, and a sound monitoring and evaluation system will pick it up before too much harm is done and the system becomes discredited. The more immediate criteria on which to assess the appraisals revolve around completion rates, development action generated, participants' attitudes to the system and perceived fairness. Longer term one might look for achievement against targets, staff retention and organisational commitment. Much can be learned by questionnaire surveys, and there are various standard attitude measures that are available which may afford an opportunity for benchmarking results against those obtained elsewhere. The other vital aspect of evaluation is its role in monitoring the equity of the assessments made, and assuring that there is no evidence of systematic bias against any particular group.

Discussion points and questions

Why is it important to evaluate appraisal systems – and when should you do it?

What do you feel are the most important aspects of an appraisal system to evaluate, and why?

How can we assess whether an appraisal system supports diversity – what sort of data do we need to collect?

Key references

Edwards, J. E., Scott, J. C. and Raju, N. S. (2003) *The Human Resources Program-Evaluation Handbook*. Sage: Thousand Ocks, CA.

Erdogan, B., Kraimer, M. L. and Liden, R. C. (2001) Procedural justice as a two-dimensional construct: An examination in the performance appraisal context, *Journal of Applied Behavioural Science*, 37, pp. 205–222.

Fletcher, C. and Williams, R. (1996) Performance management, job satisfaction and organisational commitment. *British Journal of Management*, 7, pp. 169–179.

Appraising, identifying and developing potential

Most of the content of the previous chapters has focused on the appraisal of performance, albeit with an eye to motivating and developing individuals over the review period. Traditionally, however, appraisal has a longer-term perspective in contributing to the assessment and development of potential. In recent years, with the 'war for talent' (Michaels *et al.*, 2001), this has been given greater attention and prominence, and that is reflected in the more lengthy treatment of the subject here than might traditionally be associated with a book on appraisal.

In times of economic uncertainty – which is just about all times now – development and career planning are often seen as less important aspects of appraisal. This is perhaps not surprising as it is harder to project ahead and to envisage growth with confidence; many organisations have delayered and downsized and consequently have fewer promotion opportunities on offer. The pattern of career progression is thus less stable for many people, and less likely to be continued within the same organisation. However, these circumstances – far from suggesting that promotability and potential should be taken off the appraisal agenda – indicate that the career progression of the individual needs to be addressed with much greater care. If there are fewer promotions to be had, then it is even more essential that the process of deciding who will get them is seen to be fair and effective. If career development opportunities increasingly lie outside the organisation, then the latter cannot rely quite so much on the loyalty and company commitment of individual employees as a motivating force. The 'old deal' whereby organisations offered cradle to the grave employment in return for loyalty and motivation is no longer sustainable in many companies (Sparrow and Cooper, 2003). Moreover, the nature of career development, either inside or outside the organisation, is changing. With flatter organisations and fewer senior positions, for many people development is going to involve sideways moves or job enlargement rather than a straight promotion. In effect, a new contract has to be instituted, whereby the organisation undertakes to assess individuals' potential and to help them develop – ultimately, if necessary, outside the organisation. As part of this, self-development needs to be encouraged; if organisations are less able to guarantee future opportunities, then individuals can be provided with the experiences and skills to become more autonomous in facilitating their own career progression (for a wider discussion of this, see for example Conway and Briner, 2005, or Sturges et al., 2005). This is the so-called 'new deal' – development in return for commitment while employed. There has to be some balance between organisational and individual needs in appraisal, and only by retaining the assessment and development of potential as part of the appraisal process (in the widest sense) can this be achieved.

Deciding the best methods for assessing and developing potential is not at all straightforward, however. One obvious basis to work from is present performance, as reflected in appraisal and other data. But the reason for having an assessment of potential is precisely because present performance is by no means a completely reliable indicator of future performance. It is certainly true in nearly all cases that if an individual is not performing well at the existing level, they are very unlikely to do better at more senior levels, and will probably be even worse. The question is, which of the majority of staff who are performing satisfactorily in their current jobs have the latent ability and aptitude to progress further and to be successful one or more levels higher in the organisation? How are those latent abilities and aptitudes to be assessed? The main methods for doing this are described and evaluated below. Before looking at them, though, there is another broad issue to consider: What is it, from the organisation's viewpoint, that people are being assessed and developed *for*?

One way of explaining this is to give an example from my own experience. I was approached by the newly appointed personnel director of a large company, who was seeking assistance in implementing a psychometrically based assessment and development programme for all middle and senior managers in the company – a big project given the numbers involved. The aim was to assess the managers' potential and to find some way of developing them. All very worthy, but developing them for what, I asked? Potential for what? Essentially, the answer took the form: 'Because it's a good thing, isn't it?' It rapidly became evident that (a) there was no idea of what abilities or competencies were needed to be effective at senior levels within the organisation, (b) there was no willingness to try to find out what these might be, (c) there was no idea about where the company was going in the next few years, the implications for the kinds of skills and attributes they would then need in their managers, and how this would inform development efforts now, and (d) there were insufficient resources to handle the development activity that would follow from such a large-scale assessment process.

Although more career development than before will lead to movement between organisations rather than simply within them, it remains important for organisations to try to identify what their needs are likely to be. If they do not, then there is a good chance that they will end up with the wrong mix of abilities and competencies for the situation they find themselves in a few years down the line. Techniques for analysing their requirements are largely those discussed in relation to competency-based appraisal in Chapter 3. However, they will also be mentioned again below in relation to some of the methods of appraising potential, specifically those that are focused on longer-term potential rather than short-term promotability.

The conventional appraisal process as a means of assessing potential

For a long time, the appraisal of performance and promotability and/or long-term potential were both parts of the same exercise and recorded on the same form – and indeed still are in a good number of organisations. The problems of linking the discussion of current performance with rewards, which include promotion, led to many appraisal schemes separating the two functions out. As a result, it has become common for the appraisal of potential to be carried out at a different time of the year and to be written on different report forms from the appraisal of on-going performance.

The main role for appraisal in the context of career development is as an opportunity to discuss short-term training and development needs and for the appraisee to talk over career aspirations with the appraiser. But the conventional appraisal process has been found severely wanting as a means of assessing long-term potential, though it does have a more worthwhile contribution to make to immediate promotion decisions. The problems of using performance appraisal in this context are numerous:

- As a means of assessing current performance – which is the basis of the promotion/potential judgment – its accuracy leaves a lot to be desired.
- The direct linking of promotion or other rewards to the performance discussion has detrimental effects on the latter.
- Managers are sometimes reluctant to lose their best people, and it is not unknown for this to affect their written assessments of potential.
- The manager's own style may inhibit the opportunity for a subordinate to demonstrate potential.
- Where judgments about long-term potential for senior management levels are needed, line managers are not necessarily the best people to

comment, as they may not have reached that level themselves and therefore not possess first-hand experience of what is required.

- The limited breadth of perspective of individual managers can mean that they are unaware of the performance standards required for promotion and of the range of opportunities available – which may give rise to the creation of false (unduly high or low) expectations in the appraisee.

Several of these problems (and particularly the last one) are accentuated in appraisal schemes that are highly devolved and line-owned, which suggests that in such circumstances it is especially unwise to let the assessment of potential rest solely on the appraisal process. However, even in centrally driven appraisal schemes, given all the other demands and burdens placed on the annual appraisal, it does not seem very sensible to add this one. Perhaps the best contribution the annual appraisal can make is as a short-listing mechanism: if appraisees are consistently performing at a high level (and perhaps have demonstrated this with more than one boss), then they are worth considering for promotion by whatever other review or assessment method is used. This way, the line manager still has a direct influence on promotion decisions, but not the deciding one. An example of how appraisal can be used in combination with other inputs and methods is reported by Catano *et al.* (2007) and is summarised in Box 10.1.

Box 10.1: an example of an appraisal-based promotion system

The Royal Canadian Mounted Police carefully developed a new appraisal system with a view to using it in making promotion decisions. Officers were appraised on a set of eight core competencies, which themselves had been arrived out through an extensive and systematic process of development. Each competency was described in different behavioural terms according to differing rank/responsibility levels. Candidates completed a Performance Report for Promotion (PRP), giving two examples that illustrated their performance level on each competency (i.e. 16 in all). An independent referee was approached to verify the examples given by the officer. The PRP also contained a set of BARS (see Chapter 4, pages 00) for each competency. Again, these had been developed through a careful and systematic process. The officer's immediate boss completed these ratings, and could add further comments if he/she wished to. The officer had the opportunity to see the ratings and to record agreement or disagreement on the form; if there was a disagreement that could not be reconciled, the officer could record what he or she thought the rating(s) should be.

The next step is for the PRP to be viewed by a Promotion Review Board consisting of three senior officers. Their purpose was to resolve any disgreements over ratings and also to act as a check on over- or under- rating by individual line managers; they thus exercised a moderating function and could enhance consistency of standards. The Board's final set of ratings were summed and fed directly into the promotion decision, which rested on a combination of the rating score, the score from a job simulation exercise (JSE) – the latter presented the candidate with a set of 48 scenarios that might be encountered at the next level up (the level being promoted to) and asks which of a set of alternative responses would be the most effective and appropriate in dealing with them – see the section on Behaviourally Based Interviewing later in this chapter. Again, this JSE was the result of careful, empirical development and offered objective scoring. So, in effect the promotion process offered an assessment of past performance and competence (the ratings), including a self-assessment, and a future-oriented measure of how an individual might perform at a higher rank (the JSE), with each of the two components being given equal weight in the final decision.

Considerable emphasis was given to providing training to all participants in the promotion process, and the promotion process was subject to thorough evaluation. For an full and excellent account of this work, see Catano et al. (2007).

Career review panels

One of the most common methods of making assessments about potential and feeding them into career planning is through the use of career review panels (CRPs) (also known by a variety of other, similar names). CRPs usually consist of a panel of senior managers, convened by the personnel department, who periodically review either all managers at a specific level, or on a selective basis. Their task is to make some assessment of the promotability of individuals and to draw up a career plan for them. In doing this, they will have access to appraisal forms and possibly to additional reports made by appraisers specifically for this purpose. They may also interview staff if they feel this would be helpful. Throughout their deliberations, they have input from HR, which should help inform them of the range of opportunities available, the people who might fill them, and the manpower planning situation in the short and medium term.

The advantages of this approach are that it is flexible, it provides a wider perspective than can be achieved by any one appraiser, it still involves line management, it has credibility because of the senior level of the people on the panel and it does not interfere with the normal appraisal process. The limitation of CRPs is that they remain largely dependent of the input from the performance appraisal to assess potential (though that input might relate to a broader time span and the appraisee's performance under more than one appraiser). They are still in the position of trying to judge potential on the basis of present performance. Also, some or all members of the panel may have little or no direct contact with the people whose potential they are trying to assess. Looking at the pros and cons of CRPs overall, whilst they are helpful in making decisions on short-term promotions, the method seems to have most to offer where it is used as a career planning mechanism based on assessments of potential done by other means.

The interview in assessing potential

The interview still seems to be the most popular way of deciding suitability for promotion to a specific post. The form of the interview may vary, from a one-to-one interview with the manager who has a vacancy to fill, to a panel interview where HR and other departments are represented. How candidates are chosen to attend for the interview can be based on personal applications to the manager concerned, on appraisal data, and on psychometric test results. Leaving the last-mentioned of these aside for the moment (it will be dealt with in depth below), the use of the interview usually takes a fairly conventional form. Typically, questions centre on:

- the individual's career so far, and the reasons for the decisions they have taken
- the attraction of the position they are applying for and how they would tackle it
- the way they perceive the fit between their experience and abilities and the position they are applying for
- future career aspirations and direction
- various hypothetical questions of the 'what would you do if' and 'how would you do such-and-such' variety.

The advantages of interviews are that they are fairly easy to arrange, and that they are usually considered to be an essential part of the promotion process, if only so that the manager with the vacancy to fill can have a say in who is appointed, and the candidates can meet the person they would be working with. Alas, all that might be said of interviews in general applies to them in this context too. The typical, unstructured interview by the untrained interviewer remains an abysmal selection tool, for the many reasons that the research spanning three-quarters of a century has demonstrated. The outcome is as likely to be determined by the biases of the interviewers and what they have failed to find out as by anything more positive. Happily, this does not mean that the interview is devoid of value in contributing to the assessment of potential, as more recent developments in interview techniques show.

Behaviourally based interview methods

It has long been known that more structured approaches to interviewing increase its effectiveness. There are now a number of behaviourally based interviewing techniques that are applicable in assessing promotability and potential and have been shown to be valid – in other words, they predict performance with some success (Eder and Harris, 1999). There are two basic types, one which focuses on past performance, which is sometimes called the past-behaviour interview (PBI) though probably more often simply referred to as a competency-based interview, and one which focuses on future behaviour, which is called the situational interview.

Competency-based interviews

If the competencies or dimensions relevant to effective performance in the post are known, then it is possible to develop a structured interview around them. Thus, if it is known that organisation and planning are key elements in the job, then a series of questions on this theme can be drawn up to assess the extent to which the candidate has demonstrated a capacity for planning and organisation.

Examples might be:

> 'Tell us about how you establish the priorities in your present job.'
> 'Can you outline an example of how you have achieved a difficult goal through careful planning?'
> 'Describe how you go about planning and organising your own work and time.'
> 'What was the most difficult planning task you have had? Tell us about it.'

Questions of this kind yield useful information and are targeted on the important aspects of the job, and they do deal with actual rather than anticipated behaviour. But they all relate to what the individual has done in the past, at a lower level, with the limitations that implies. Nonetheless, there is considerable evidence in support of their validity (Taylor and Small, 2002).

Normally, a 45-minute interview of this kind will cover three to five competencies; trying to deal with more leads either to very superficial coverage or very long interviews. As has been implied above, you are dealing with a kind of 'scripted' interview here, drawing on a pool of maybe six or seven questions per competence. It would not be the intention to ask all the questions under each heading, but simply to ask enough to get a measure of the individual's capability. Although the initial question list is set, the interviewers do of course ask probing follow-up questions for clarification. The reasons for having a pool of questions are (a) that some questions are not relevant to the experience of some candidates, or that the latter have little to offer in answer to them, and (b) that the questions may otherwise become too predictable and well known within the organisation. At the end of the interview, the assessors make ratings of the individual on each competence, based on the evidence of the behaviour the person has described (and *not* on his or her behaviour in the interview). It is best to have two interviewers if possible, so that one can be concentrating on making notes on the answers while the other asks the questions; they can swop round on this responsibility from competence to competence or from interview to interview.

Competency-based interviews yield useful information and do deal with actual rather than anticipated behaviour. A potential criticism of the method is however that it reflects individuals' work approach at present or in the past – and possibly when they were operating at a lower organisational level – rather than what might be demanded of them in the future. Several other concerns have been raised, too. First, there is sometimes a degree of initial resistance from those doing the assessment to the idea of having their freedom limited by the straitjacket of pre-set questions. This does not seem to last long, though; they quickly become quite comfortable with it and like not having to think up questions for themselves. They also appreciate the thoroughness and fairness of the method. But there is another perspective here: the candidates. What do they think? Research suggests a mixed reaction; many of those assessed this way feel that competency-based interviews are fairer. They also see them as more obviously job-related than alternative approaches – which they are.

On the downside, though, candidates who have encountered competency-based interviews on more than one occasion complain that the interviews were 'boring' and easily fakable. If the style and content of interviews become too predictable, it does not take very much intelligence to 'manufacture' convincing episodes showing how one demonstrated achievement orientation, interpersonal sensitivity, etc; the danger of synthetic behavioural evidence seems very real. The only way round this is to spend more time on each question, probing the answers in such detail as to make faking very difficult to sustain.

Situational interviews

The situational interview is quite a sophisticated technique and one that takes some time to develop – it is described in Box 10.2. One of the strengths of the situational interview is that it seeks to project candidates forward into their anticipated behaviour in the role they are being assessed for. It is true that because people say they will act in a particular way when faced with a situation it is not necessarily the case that they do so in reality. However, the evidence of the validity for the situational interview is some reassurance here (Day and Carroll, 2003). Apart from anything

---

Box 10.2: the situational interview

This novel approach to interviewing requires the organisation first to carry out, or have access to, a critical incidents job analysis of the position to be filled (see page 15). The incidents identified will describe various situations and problems that typically arise in the job. The steps in constructing the situational interview are then as follows:

A group of managers familiar with the job and level at which the vacancy or vacancies exist select a number of incidents that they agree on as being characteristic of the job and as sampling the main attributes necessary to perform effectively in it. So, for example, they may choose a reported incident where a manager had a problem with a subordinate because of a complaint about sexual harassment from another member of staff. The manager concerned passed it on to personnel to handle rather than deal with it personally.

These incidents are turned into questions. In the case of the example given, it might be: 'One of your subordinates comes to you with a complaint about sexual harassment from another of your subordinates. You suspect it is true, though you have no other evidence to go on. What would you do in this situation?'

The group of managers would then be asked to say, independently and on the basis of their knowledge of staff of varying standards at this level, how good, mediocre and poor performers would deal with the situation outlined. When they have done this, they discuss their answers to check that there is a good level of agreement in each case. In the example used here, they might come up with a set of benchmark answers like this:

• *Good performer:* try to deal with the situation themselves, but gather further information from the parties involved before coming to a judgment about what action is appropriate.

- *Mediocre performer:* passes the matter on immediately to personnel without any attempt to gain further information or taking any responsibility for it.
- *Poor performer:* calls in the party alleged to be doing the harassing and issues a stern warning without seeking further information and without giving them an opportunity to answer the allegation.

Answers reflecting these three strategies might be scored 1, 3, and 5 respectively. A complete set of questions and graded answers is arrived at through the same process, in such a way that all the key dimensions of the job are covered. The example used here might reflect both judgment and supervisory ability.

The interview takes place and candidates are posed the questions. Their answers are taken down by one of the interviewers (the method requires a panel of at least two).

Candidates' answers are scored, preferably independently by two or more raters, in terms of how they relate to the benchmark answers. The raters then discuss their marks and come to an agreed assessment.

This approach to interviewing sounds just like presenting a set of hypothetical questions, and it is – but with some crucial differences. It is based on job analysis, the questions are chosen to cover the important performance dimensions, and the answers are quantitatively rated on how they compare with good and poor performers in the job. It is certainly a more demanding form of interview in terms of time and managers' involvement, but it has been shown to have good validity if used appropriately (Latham and Sue-Chan, 1999) – so at least it is time well spent. Also, it probably sounds more daunting to construct than it actually is.

It may strike the reader that this sounds rather like an orally-administered questionnaire, and so it will be no surprise to learn that it can indeed be delivered and scored in pencil and paper (or computer administered) format – sometimes called a Job Simulation Exercise – see Box 10.1 above.

Latham *et al.* (1980); Latham (1989).

else, at least the situational interview tells you whether the candidates *know* what the right answer is, irrespective of whether they will really act that way.

There is some evidence that different types of behaviourally based interview may predict different outcomes in a selection situation. Specifically, competency based interviews give better indicators of an individual's cognitive ability, task performance and managerially relevant personality attributes, while situational interviews are better at predicting the fit between the individual and the organisation in terms of work styles and values (Krajewski *et al.*, 2006). Perhaps the best advice is to use a combination of both. Whatever the relative merits of the various approaches to behaviourally based interviewing, all such structured interviews are likely to be better at yielding accurate assessments than unstructured interviews (Wright *et al.*, 1989). Panel interviews also seem to be superior to one-to-one interviews in this respect (Weisner and Cronshaw, 1988). Without the use of behaviourally based methods, the interview as a means of assessing potential is likely to be little more than an exercise in impression management.

Using psychometric tests in assessing potential

Psychometric testing is a complex topic, the full scope of which is beyond this book – readers are referred to Toplis *et al.* (2004) for a fuller treatment of the subject. Any organisation willing to invest the money in either buying in external consultants or in getting their own staff trained in testing can make use of the methods described below. Companies producing tests offer good (but fairly costly) training, and it inevitably tends to focus on their own particular products. It is therefore advisable first to get some independent advice as to what, *if any*, are the most appropriate kinds of tests for the situation and whether it is going to be more cost-effective to get company staff trained or to have it done by an external agency. The British Psychological Society publishes a directory of chartered psychologists, which is available online, and by identifying within this those that are qualified as Chartered *Occupational* Psychologists, you will find the most appropriate guidance.

How can tests assess potential?

The huge growth in the use of psychometric tests over the last ten years or so (Wolf and Jenkins, 2006), both here and elsewhere in Europe, has included an increase in their use to assess promotability and potential. What is the basis for thinking that psychometric tests can contribute to the assessment of potential? There are two broad categories of tests that need to be looked at here: one covers cognitive (intellectual) abilities and the other deals with personality attributes – though, strictly speaking, the latter are not 'tests' as they do not involve right or wrong answers. The argument that cognitive tests have something to say about potential is the strongest, or at least the most straightforward. It goes something like this:

- In many administrative, managerial and professional roles, a good level of intellectual ability is needed to perform effectively.
- The higher individuals go within these roles (up to a point), the greater the demands made on them, and the greater their ability needs to be to cope.
- We therefore need to know that any candidates for higher responsibility levels have the intellectual potential to perform effectively, which can be assessed by comparing their cognitive abilities against those of people already successfully performing at such levels.
- Because they can show whether an individual matches up to the intellectual level associated with people already at higher levels, tests can also give some indication as to whether individuals who are performing well in their present job are actually at their ceiling or whether they have the intellectual resources to progress further.

The question might be asked as to whether educational qualifications might not serve the same purpose. They can, but not nearly so well. The advantage of tests is that they often show up intellectual potential that is not evident in academic achievements. There are all sorts of reasons for this, but essentially it comes down to the fact that educational qualifications reflect a great deal else besides intellectual ability – home background and opportunity, parental attitudes, motivation, adolescent problems and rate of maturity, quality of teaching, and so on. Not surprisingly, then, psychometric tests given to adults are very often found to be more predictive of job success than are educational qualifications. Moreover, with grade drift and a tendency for more people to get high exam grades at all levels, academic results become less useful as a means of discriminating between differing levels of ability. The evidence, both in the UK and the US, shows a strong relationship between cognitive test scores and measures of both training and job performance, especially in more complex jobs (Bertua *et al.*, 2005).

It is a little more difficult to specify the role of personality measures in assessing potential. In terms of promotability to a particular job, the case is fairly straightforward. Here, the demands of the job and the person specification for it will suggest some personality attributes that are likely to be essential for effective performance and some that are likely to be counterproductive. A personality questionnaire may thus be useful in providing some data on these qualities. However, when the issue is one of longer term potential to perform effectively some years in the future at a higher level and across a range of jobs, the requirement is much less clear-cut. It is less certain what personality attributes will be needed. There are two main alternatives to follow. One is to give personality measures to existing high performers at this level and see if any particular pattern emerges. The problem here is that any profile that emerges tells you about how things are now, not necessarily about how things should be or will be in the future. This can be illustrated by an example from my own experience.

I was asked to carry out individual, psychometrically based assessments on the board of directors of a medium-sized company that had just been acquired by a large engineering and electronics firm. The tests showed a remarkably consistent pattern: most of the directors were intellectually highly able, but operated in a style that seldom exploited their potential in this direction. They were all strongly task-oriented, extremely high in drive and energy, quick to react, disinclined to think strategically, individualistic and uncooperative. The one exception to this was the MD, who was intellectually less capable than his colleagues but was the only one of them who had some capacity for teamwork and was probably the only one who could get them to move in the same direction. It was not difficult to see how the nature of the work in that company and the tendency for people to be attracted to (and promote) individuals like themselves had brought about this group of directorial clones. The recipe had worked for some time, and the company had grown rapidly to become very successful. Unfortunately, when the market changed and competition increased, they did not seem to have had the resources within the board to respond to it; they all continued to charge ahead in the same way, without thinking through a new strategy. The point of this example is that if one took the personality pattern of the high performers in this organisation as the model for assessing the potential of more junior managers, the result would be pretty disastrous in a few years' time. It does not mean that there is no value in taking account of the personality pattern of senior managers (quite apart from anything else, it may say a lot about the organisation and how it is likely to function), but to be guided entirely by that would be a mistake. An analysis of future directions and needs has to be built in to the picture.

The other alternative for guiding the use of personality measures in assessing long-term potential is reasonable deduction (or informed guesswork). It is probably going to be the case that some characteristics are *not* going to be helpful. People who are emotionally unstable, extremely low in drive, excessively aggressive, and so on are much less likely to make progress to the top. People who are flexible, dynamic, outgoing, emotionally stable, etc. are more likely to be effective and to perform at higher levels. However, there are obvious limitations to this kind of approach, and it will only be helpful with some of the more extreme cases.

A competency analysis of the work conducted at this level will help, and also give some pointers as to what will or will not facilitate performance. But trying to relate personality questionnaire data – and, indeed, other psychological test scores – directly to competency descriptions raises some problems. The root cause of the difficulty is that competency frameworks and psychological test dimensions usually describe behaviour at different levels. An individual competency description typically focuses on a broad pattern of surface behaviour relating to some aspect of work performance. To take the example used earlier, a competency labelled 'organisation and planning' will be described in terms of such positive and negative behaviours as 'can link own plans with wider strategic objectives', 'prioritises demands made on his/her time', 'carefully monitors progress', 'initiates action without thinking it through' (all these are taken from actual examples of descriptors for such a competency). When the psychologist looks at this range of behaviour, several different psychological constructs are likely to seem relevant: thoughtfulness, analytical thinking, caution, impulsiveness, and so on. In other words, the psychological dimensions are often much narrower in nature, and several different ones may be relevant to any one competency. Even with very work-focused personality measures this remains true.

So it becomes quite complicated to line up the psychological test dimensions with the competencies. In a few cases, there are actually no very clear or close relationships between the two; competencies that revolve around the notion of business sense or business awareness often come into this category. More usually, though, a number of psychological constructs seem to be relevant to each competency. A common problem that then arises is that no single psychometric test can be found to fit the bill: no one of them will offer measures of all the psychological dimensions that the analysis of the competency framework throws up. This being the case, the choice is either to use a lot of different tests – not attractive in terms of time or cost – or to decide to prioritise and perhaps use just one or two that cover as many of the key competencies as possible; the latter is normally the course adopted.

Another, perhaps more fundamental and difficult, issue that arises is when the psychological analysis of what is involved in the competencies suggests that the competencies do not make psychological sense. Either the psychological qualities required for different behaviours described under a single competency conflict with each other, or the same thing is true across two (or more) different competencies – implying that it is unlikely that an individual could be high on both. By way of illustration, take a competency called *achievement orientation*: the behavioural descriptions frequently include such things as 'sets targets beyond those required', and 'wants to be the best'. The psychological profile for individuals with very strong achievement motivation is not always one that fits very comfortably with the teamwork and interpersonal competencies, which often emphasise the capacity to put personal credit to one side in favour of the team, or imply giving higher priority to team cohesion and individual well-being than to personal goals.

Yet another issue that can arise stems from almost the opposite phenomenon, namely the same psychological factors contributing to different competencies. A common example would be a trait like Emotional Control contributing to the assessment of such competencies as customer relations, resilience, interpersonal sensitivity, and so on. Having the same psychological factors relating to different competencies can cause problems in being able to discriminate between the latter and assess them independently. Sometimes the problem lies in the quality of the original work done in identifying the competencies. But in other cases it goes deeper, and reflects an unrealistic expectation of what people can achieve. The underlying assumption of some frameworks is that the competencies are all compatible and that it is possible to be strong in all of them. Psychologically, there are grounds for challenging this assumption. More pragmatically, though, the advice might be to leave plenty of time to think through the use of personality questionnaires and other psychometric tests in this context, and to realise that they seldom map neatly onto competencies. Other assessment methods will be needed. If they are used sensibly, though, personality questionnaires can contribute to the prediction of competency (Dulewicz and Herbert, 1996; Salgado *et al.*, 2001).

One final, general point about personality questionnaires: in the past, there have been some isolated but well-publicised attacks on the value of such measures. It has now been convincingly shown that these attacks are spurious and can be dismissed (Jackson and Rothstein, 1993). Personality questionnaires can be very useful, though they are certainly neither straightforward nor always effective to apply.

The ways in which tests are used

There is a variety of ways in which tests are applied in assessing potential and promotability:

- They may be given to external candidates as part of a selection procedure, not only to assess suitability for the job vacancy but also to get some idea of the individual's potential beyond that.
- Internal candidates for a promotion vacancy may be given a battery of tests to assess their suitability for the promotion in question.
- Individuals may go through a testing session as part of a career assessment process that is not related to a specific promotion or job vacancy, but which has the assessment of potential as one of its aims (see Table 10.3).

- Tests are often included as an element of the assessment centre process, which will be described shortly.

Quite often the testing of candidates is done within the organisation by those appropriately trained. But at middle and senior levels, it is common practice to send the individuals to an outside consultant – usually a chartered occupational psychologist – to conduct the assessment. Apart from the higher level of expertise offered by taking this (possibly expensive) route, the main reason for it is political. Middle and senior management candidates are less happy to be put through such a searching assessment process by someone who may be junior to them in the organisation. The form of these assessments typically includes a battery of cognitive ability tests – numerical, verbal, logical reasoning and (perhaps) creative thinking – and one or two personality measures, as well as an in-depth interview with the consultant. The result is a report to the company which covers various aspects of work performance, and (where appropriate) an assessment of their suitability for a particular promotion vacancy, based on a job description and person specification. If the aim of the assessment has been more general, the report will include an assessment of overall career potential and will review career alternatives against the background of the individual's strengths and weaknesses. There is almost invariably some kind of feedback session with the candidate, where the assessor goes over the findings and discusses them with the individual, who may also receive a copy of the report.

It is never suggested that tests are sufficient by themselves to assess potential. They should always be employed as an additional input to other sources of information, such as existing performance, career progress to date, and possibly an interview. Their results and implications have to be interpreted in the light of all this information. An example of combining them with assessment centres is given in Box 10.3.

Box 10.3: using personality questionnaire input at an assessment centre for promotion

A large international accountancy and consulting firm used the process outlined here for assessing Director-level staff for making the next step up to Partnership. The individuals had to be 'sponsored' by the Partner they worked to in order to go through the assessment process. The first stage was to complete a well known general personality questionnaire (the NEO), which was then followed up with a profiling interview conducted by an occupational psychologist. This would cover the candidate's background and work history, and elicit behavioural examples of situations and challenges they had dealt with. The psychologist would probe any particular areas of concern that had been flagged up by the individual's personality profile.

Within the next week or two, the candidate would attend a demanding two-day assessment centre (AC) where they would be assessed on six competencies. On the third day, the assessors reviewed the evidence under each competency for each candidate, coming to an agreed rating in each case, indicating whether the candidate had performed at Partnership level or still needed development. The psychologist attended this assessment session, his or her function being to outline the strengths and weaknesses observed from the profiling interview on each competence. However, the aim of this was in part to present the candidate in a wider perspective than just their performance in the AC – to reflect a more enduring picture of how the individual had performed in their career so far, and to put their performance in the previous two days into a broader context. As part of this, the psychologist used the personality and interview data to help explain, if explanation was necessary, how and why the candidate may have behaved as they did – for example, showing inconsistency across different types of exercise or between their normal in-the-job performance and how they fared in the AC. This would inform the assessors' discussions and in some cases shade their final competency assessment in one direction or another – especially where there were implications for whether shortfalls in observed AC performance were likely to be easily remediable or not. Thus, although there was not a direct feed-in of personality 'scores' to the assessments made, they nonetheless had an indirect influence in many instances.

Assessment centres

The term 'assessment centre' (AC) is used to describe the process whereby a team of assessors uses an integrated series of assessment techniques to assess a group of candidates. Those techniques typically include psychometric tests, interviews, peer ratings and simulation exercises. It is the last mentioned of these that constitute the core of the AC. They are meant to simulate or sample the kinds of work that an individual has to do at the level being selected for. These can include group problem-solving tasks, individual decision-making exercises (e.g. in-tray exercises), business games, and interview role plays. Again, as with psychometric testing, this is a topic worthy of a book in itself, and the reader can be directed to an excellent one by Woodruffe (2007). The discussion of ACs offered here will be limited to a general outline of their use in assessing and developing potential, examination of some of the main issues associated with this method, and an evaluation of its worth.

Setting up and running ACs

As with so many aspects of appraisal, the first stage is to identify the key attributes for effective performance at the target level – the level in the organisation at which you are trying to assess the potential to perform successfully. This usually involves some kind of competency analysis of the kind discussed several times in this book. Once the necessary competencies or behavioural dimensions have been decided, it becomes possible to judge what kinds of exercises might be used to assess them. The usual practice is to aim to have at least two, and preferably more, AC assessment techniques contributing to the assessment of each dimension. This ensures that the behaviour in question is sampled on separate occasions on different kinds of task, and possibly by different assessors – so providing a basis for making reliable judgments. A matrix is usually drawn up, with assessment exercises across the top and the competencies assessed down the side.

The simulation exercises should represent the work at the target level as accurately as possible, and to this end managers already at that level should be involved in providing material for the exercises. It is possible to buy AC exercises off-the-shelf from various consultancies and test producers, but most organisations rightly want the content and nature of the exercises to reflect their own work and culture as closely as possible – which means constructing them from scratch, probably with some help from a consultant experienced in this field. Once the dimensions, exercises and other assessment methods are devised and decided on, a timetable for the AC event and administrative matters, such as where it is to be run, can be settled. Two other vital issues have to be confronted while all this is going on: who are to be the assessors and how are they to be trained; and how are the candidates to be nominated for the AC?

The assessors should largely be managers in the organisation who are working at the target level, so at least they know the work and demands associated with it at the present time. Their involvement has two other benefits: it ensures input and part-ownership of the AC process by the line, and it gives the AC a degree of credibility with senior line management as a result. Getting this line input is far from easy, as it requires a considerable time commitment from the managers concerned. They need to be trained, and then to be able to act as assessors on enough AC events (assuming that there are a series of them) to maintain a consistent standard. The importance of the training cannot be overstated; the value of the whole AC rests on it. The assessors should have the background and rationale of the method explained, gain some experience of doing some or all of the exercises themselves, and be given instruction in behavioural assessment. In particular, they need to become thoroughly familiar with the competencies or dimensions they are assessing, and what kind of behaviour is covered by each of them, so that they can correctly classify the candidates' behaviour when they see it. Ideally, the performance of the assessors themselves should be monitored, as they certainly differ in effectiveness (Stillman and Jackson, 2005).

Apart from the line manager assessors, there will usually be some HR representatives and possibly also one or more outside consultants. Including the latter is very desirable, for two reasons. First, where occupational psychologists are concerned (and they often feature in this role because of their expertise in devising ACs), reviews of the research evidence suggest that their success in predicting performance from ACs is greater than that achieved by line managers (Arthur *et al.*, 2003). Secondly, even with all the sophistication of the AC method, there is still a danger of the assessors selecting people they see as being similar to themselves. In other words, the AC becomes a glorified cloning process. The presence of external assessors reduces the chance of that happening.

How the candidates for the AC are to be identified is never altogether straightforward. The basic options are:

- self-nomination
- nomination by the boss
- qualification through passing exams etc.

Nomination by the boss has the advantage of being based on current performance, but given the inadequacies of appraisal as an assessment mechanism, relying solely on this source may mean that some good candidates are missed. Self-nomination is the best in terms of scanning all possible candidates who might have potential and who could have been overlooked. However, this can also lead to some very unsuitable candidates putting themselves forward, with two unfortunate consequences: they waste the organisation's resources by taking places on ACs which are costly to run, and they may set themselves up for experiences of failure that could be very discouraging or even damaging to them. There is some virtue in the argument that says that where self-nomination is allowed, there should be a first-stage screening process involving psychometric tests. There are a few organisations where certain objective criteria, typically passing professional exams to some level, are used to determine who should attend ACs. Where there are such criteria and they are relevant to the assessment of potential, then nomination is much more clear-cut.

The typical ratio of candidates to assessors is 2:1 or 3:1, and the number of candidates attending any one AC is normally within the range of five to fifteen. The duration of the AC depends on the number of assessment techniques it contains, but is usually one to three days. The last day or part of it is devoted to the assessors' conference, where each candidate's performance is reviewed in turn; all the information is scrutinised, candidate by candidate; and final ratings on each dimension agreed. The candidate will be given an Overall Assessment Rating (OAR) which generally boils down to a judgment that the individual (a) has high potential, (b) possibly has high potential, or (c) does not appear to have high potential at the moment. The first two of these lead to fast-track development status.

In due course, the outcome of the AC and observations on the candidates' performance in it will be conveyed to them in an individual feedback session. This is usually given by one of the assessors and/or a personnel representative, and the candidate's line manager may also be present – which is important if the latter is to assist the candidate in implementing any development plans. The implications of the AC for career progression will be thoroughly discussed and whatever action is needed put in hand.

Issues in the use of ACs

Some of the practical problems in using ACs have already been mentioned. There are, however, a number of other issues that HR practitioners need to be aware of:

- *Self-fulfilling prophecies.* There is some danger of letting ACs create crown princes and princesses. Once individuals have been identified as having potential, special attention and resources are lavished on them, so it may not be surprising if they do well. The expectation that they will be high performers can also influence perceptions of their actual performance. It is important, then, that such individuals are subject to particularly careful assessment to see that they are living up to their promise. Equally, the judgment in an AC that an individual does not have high potential must not be allowed to become the kiss of death, with no further interest or resources being directed to their career progression. This leads on to the next issue.
- *The feedback process.* The feedback given after ACs leaves a lot to be desired and tends to be one of the weakest features of how they are operated. The primary problem is that it comes too long after the event to capitalise on it. If the feedback is to be meaningful, it has to be given while the experience is still fresh in the participants' minds; a week or more after the event is far too long. Also, it has to be especially

sensitively handled with individuals who have not done well in the AC. It has been found that failure in an AC (one aimed at identifying managerial potential) reduced psychological well-being and some aspects of motivation at least six months after the event (Fletcher, 1991). There is sometimes a need for counselling on a longer-term basis, so that individuals do not feel that their career is somehow over and that they are no longer valued; not everyone can be a high-flyer.

- *Cost-effectiveness.* There is no doubt that ACs are the most expensive assessment process to run. It is impossible to give a precise cost per candidate, since the content and duration of ACs varies so much, as does the number of candidates put through them (obviously, the set-up costs as a proportion of total costs diminish with increasing numbers put through the AC). Utility analysis shows that the financial benefits of better selection using ACs far outweigh the expense of the method; see Woodruffe (2007). This does not mean, though, that it is impossible to achieve nearly as good results through using cheaper methods. The main alternative to ACs is using psychometric tests, which are certainly cheaper and almost as predictive of future performance as are ACs, though perhaps not quite (Krause *et al.*, 2006). The debate about the relative cost-effectiveness of the two methods will go on and on, but in a sense there can never be an answer. The reason is that there is no way of financially evaluating either the superiority of the AC as a development tool or its face validity (the extent to which it *looks* as though it is measuring what it claims to) for both candidates and assessors. However, the experience of being trained as an assessor on an AC seems to improve a manager's assessment skills in other situations, such as performance appraisal – another valuable consequence of the method.
- *Preparing the candidates.* Because of its unique and demanding nature, the AC has the potential to throw some people a little off-balance. It is important to give candidates an idea of what to expect (the Civil Service Selection Board, for example, sends out a booklet describing in some detail what the candidates will be doing over the two days). It is also desirable to break them in gently, by having less demanding exercises, or 'unfreezing' exercises, first. Anxiety generated by the AC itself, which is not generally characteristic of the candidate, can adversely affect and distort performance at ACs (Fletcher *et al.*, 1997), and assessors need to be aware of this. Having said that, even ACs are not immune from candidate impression management tactics (McFarland *et al.*, 2005).
- *The use of competencies/dimensions.* There is much academic debate about these, and whether ACs really measure them in the way they

claim to – the emerging evidence is generally positive (Kudisch *et al.*, 1997; Lievens, 2001). One thing is clear, however, and that is that the assessment dimensions used in ACs should not be too numerous. It has been shown that more dimensions do not mean more refined judgment – quite the opposite. It is probably better to focus on a smaller number of essential competencies and to train assessors to rate them effectively than to go for long lists of 15 or more dimensions (Arthur *et al.*, 2003).

An evaluation of ACs

A lot of the faith in ACs is due to their high face validity – and also because of the scientific evidence in their favour, which is overwhelmingly positive in terms of their ability to predict career potential and success (Gaugler *et al.*, 1987). However, neither of these means that an AC is actually doing a good job. It is just as easy to set up and run a bad AC as it is to carry out a poor interview. There are some appalling ACs being operated in the UK at the present time (Fletcher and Anderson, 1998). So, one cannot generalise with ACs – because some are good, it does not mean they all are. If, however, they are set up and run in a careful and professional manner, and if they are subject to evaluation and monitoring, they are the best and most thorough method available.

The use of the ACs is quite flexible; they can be employed for assessing the potential of:

*   junior and middle managers for more senior levels
*   first line supervisors for junior/middle management
*   scientific, professional and technical staff for general management or for management within their own specialism.

What they are not usually acceptable for is the more senior levels. Whilst there are exceptions, many senior managers are reluctant to engage in AC-type assessment procedures. The politics and status of operating at this level does create difficulties in running and assessing such things as group exercises. Senior managers are therefore more likely to be put through an external, psychometrically based, individual assessment procedure when being considered for promotion.

Development Centres and other approaches to assessing promotability and potential

Some of the issues associated with ACs that were outlined above have led to an increasing use of a rather different version of the method, known as the Development Centre (DC). Essentially, this is similar in format to the AC, but the focus is much more on the training and development needs of the individual than on coming out with an overall rating of potential – indeed, no OAR is provided at all. The idea is to capitalise on the learning potential of the AC exercises and to use the information they generate to build a development plan for each participant (see Woodruffe, 2007, for a full account of DCs). This largely removes the problem of some people being branded as failures or, come to that, as crown princes. The assessors may include more HR, management development and training staff, though senior line managers will often still be involved. A further variation on this theme was developed some years ago in ICL, where they put together Self-Insight Assessment Centres (SIACs). The approach taken here was that the participants themselves helped in assessing one another, with the aim of increasing self-awareness and enhancing personal effectiveness. Other DCs have adopted this principle and include some elements of self-assessment. It is difficult to formally evaluate DCs in the way one can ACs, because their output is individually tailored and there is no clear-cut criterion against which to measure their success. However, such evidence as there is suggests that results are variable and not quite as good as they perhaps should be given the cost of setting up and running DCs (Carrick and Williams, 1999; Halman and Fletcher, 2000).

There are many hybrid approaches to assessing potential, especially where the aim is to identify high-flyers from an already senior and highly-selected group. An example is given in Box 10.4.

Box 10.4: an example of assessing for high potential

Individuals who reach Senior Civil Service status within the UK Civil Service have already progressed a long way and in most cases will have been through several demanding assessment stages. However, it was decided to seek to identify within this cadre a group of individuals who had the potential for accelerated development that would equip them for top management in a relatively short space of time. The appraisal of their capacity to deliver dynamic leadership went through several stages:

I   Individuals could put themselves forward or be nominated within their own department, which would assess them in ways that varied somewhat from department to department, but which resulted in a very limited number of candidates being put forward for the central assessment process run by the Cabinet Office.

2   Each candidate who went forward presented a portfolio of evidence. This included:

   • a quantitative (ratings based) and a qualititive (free written) self-assessment against the competencies being assessed
   • copies of the last three performance appraisal reports
   • an assessment and ranking from their own department
   • a brief CV

3   The candidates completed, online, two psychometric measures, both focused on Leadership.

4   All this evidence was placed before a panel of three interviewers, consisting of a Permanent Secretary (in effect, the Chief Executive of a Government department), a Non-Executive Director of a Government department (who came from a background career outside the Civil Service) and a Consultant Occupational Psychologist – again, none of the latter were civil servants.

5   After reviewing the evidence, the panel conducted a competency-based interview of each candidate lasting 45–60 minutes, made an assessment against the competencies and a recommendation as to whether the individual should be placed on the new High Potential scheme.

Just over a hundred candidates attended the central assessment process in the first year the scheme operated, and around 50 per cent were selected for accelerated development. Those who were chosen subsequently attended a development centre to help tailor a development plan specifically for them, which was followed by a comprehensive series of activities and strong central support to widen and enhance their leadership capacities.

This scheme is an example of using multiple assessment methods and stages in appraising potential, and is notable for the mix of high-level internal and external assessors used (Fletcher, 2006).

In summary

There is still a place for the annual appraisal in assessing promotability, but where the appraisal is of the traditional kind its role is a limited one. The way so many organisations have taken to using psychometric tests and assessment centres in recent years suggests that this point has been widely recognised. As a trend, it looks set to continue and strengthen for some time yet. One of the advantages of this kind of strategy is that it allows appraisal of performance to be very much line-led, but puts the assessment of potential into a wider perspective that cannot usually be provided by line management alone. It also offers a superior level of objectivity and predictive power in assessment. If handled sensibly, tests and ACs can still leave line managers with a substantial role in implementing career development plans and decisions for their staff. Where it is felt that tests and ACs are not the most appropriate techniques, the development of behavioural interviewing has a lot to offer.

Whichever approach to assessing potential is used, it remains essential that there is an attempt to identify the needs of the organisation in the years ahead (see Chapter 3, pages 30–31, for an outline of metacompetencies in this context). The competencies or skill dimensions arrived at through such a process can be built into the appraisal of performance *and* potential, and a clearer picture will emerge of the likely career opportunities and pathways. With this information, both the organisation and its employees can take decisions and make plans. If the latter know what the options are, and have also been put through assessment methods that give them feedback about their skills and strengths, they are in a much stronger position to direct their own careers. Various techniques such as career planning workshops and workbooks and development centres can further help them in this respect.

Discussion points and questions

What useful contribution can performance appraisal make to promotion decisions – and what are its limitations in this respect? How can we use other methods to compensate for those limitations?

How would you differentiate a Development Centre from an Assessment Centre? Why do you think such methods have become widely used – and should they be?

Crticially evaluate the systems for making promotion decisions and for identifying high potential amongst existing staff in either your own organisation or one you are familiar with. What changes would you make to improve them?

Key references

Catano, V. M., Darr, W. and Campbell, C. A. (2007) Performance appraisal of behavior-based competencies: A reliable and valid procedure. *Personnel Psychology*, 60, pp. 201–230.

Sparrow, P. and Cooper, C. L. (2003) *The Employment Relationship: Key Challenges for HR*. Elsevier: London.

Woodruffe, C. (2007) *Development and Assessment Centres: Identifying and Developing Competence*. Human Assets Ltd: London.

Chapter 11

Appraisal with professionals, and in the public sector

The attitudes and characteristics of professional and scientific staff are often so different from those of administrative and managerial staff that they represent a special case in appraisal – to the extent that they warrant a separate chapter. Much of what will be said here will be in the context of the public sector. This is because there is a far higher proportion of professional staff in the NHS, the teaching profession, higher education and (to a lesser extent) local government than in the majority of commercial organisations. None the less, a fair amount of what is said about the appraisal of professional groups is applicable to their employment in the private sector also. Before addressing the general and specific issues associated with the appraisal of such staff, it is relevant to make some points about public-sector appraisal and where recent developments have led.

Appraisal in the public sector

Accepting for the moment that talking in terms of the whole public sector is lumping together a wide range of fairly disparate organisations, is there any real reason for expecting appraisal to be different here than in the private sector? It could be argued that the vagaries of government policy and the way it affects the public sector are probably no greater than those of the market place and the City and their effects on the private sector. Large parts of the private sector are providing services, just as the public sector is. The types of organisational structures found in the two sectors have become more similar, too.

But there are some important distinctions to be drawn. To list just some of the main ones:

- Assessing the output and effectiveness of public-sector organisations is much more complex than with the private-sector. How society should judge the effectiveness of an individual police officer and of his police service as a whole is generally seen as a more contentious issue than how the effectiveness of managers and commercial companies are assessed.

- Much of the public sector has had to run appraisal on very limited resource budgets.
- More significantly, in many instances – teaching and higher education are notable examples – appraisal has been imposed directly as a result of government policy. This is certainly not a promising backdrop for setting up an appraisal scheme.
- In the health and educational fields (as we have already noted) there are large concentrations of professional staff organised in structures that have few hierarchical levels and where the concept of 'management' is somewhat alien.
- The values of those working in these organisations are sometimes different, and in some cases very strongly influential in why and how they are working there.

The thrust of these differences is that it is often more challenging to make appraisal work well in the public sector; much of what is said here also applies to the voluntary or not-for-profit sector. Despite these problems, as far as performance management schemes are concerned, there is some reason for believing that many public-sector organisations – and particularly those in local government – are at least as advanced as those in the private sector (Audit Commission, 1995a, b, c). Perhaps one of the most interesting and potentially difficult areas for appraisal is its application to the medical profession; as Box 11.1 shows, however, this is an area of great

---

Box 11.1: developments in the appraisal of UK medical practitioners

The old joke about doctors burying their mistakes has presumably worn thin, as it would be difficult to find a greater transition in application of appraisal practices than that currently occuring in the medical profession. From a situation where there was little or no formal appraisal, the performance of doctors is now coming under scrutiny from several different angles:

- Performance appraisal has been mandatory for hospital consultants from April 2003.
- Government White Paper and Reports (Department of Health, 2006, 2007) make it clear that revalidation, based on a portfolio of evidence collected over a five-year period, will be necessary for doctors to maintain their registration with the General Medical Council (GMC). Both appraisal records and multi-source feedback will be inputs to the revalidation process.

- The National Clinical Assessment Service, an arm of the National Patient Safety Agency, has been set up to deal with cases where a doctor is seen to present a performance problem but where there is no immediate question of risk to patients or of cancellation of registration. Their assessment process includes psychometric testing, interviewing and multi-source feedback.

Clearly, the appraisal of doctors in both hospitals and in primary care settings is being taken very seriously. Nor is this a phenomenon limited to the UK, as similar developments can be found in the US, Australia and New Zealand.

The GMC framework for good medical practice covers seven main areas:

1 Good clinical care
2 Maintaining good medical practice
3 Teaching and training
4 Relationships with patients
5 Working with colleagues
6 Probity
7 Health – the doctor's own, that is!

In addition, where relevant two other areas may be included – management activity and research. These elements are used in both appraisal and in the revalidation process. Clearly, (4) and (5) above especially lend themselves to some form of 360 feedback.

That perhaps points up one of the features of developing appraisal in the medical profession – it has spawned its own literature on competencies (e.g. Patterson *et al.*, 2001), appraisal (e.g. Peyton, 2000; Wilkinson *et al.*, 2002; Lyons *et al.*, 2006), multi-source feedback (e.g. Wensing and Elwyn, 2003; Archer *et al.*, 2005) and assessment centres (e.g. Randall *et al.*, 2006). Good as all this is, one sometimes gets the impression that in the process the medical world is taking little notice of the accumulated research and experience in non-medical settings. To be sure there are some important differences between doctors and, say, middle managers, which have to be recognised and addressed. However, a reading of the medical appraisal literature quickly brings to light the similarity in the problems faced, such as reconciling the individual-level need for a developmentally oriented process and the organisational need for a more assessment focused one.

This is an area that is developing quickly and with some thoroughness, for which the medical profession are to be congratulated and for which most patients will breathe a sigh of relief! Moreover, as we will see in Chapter 12, there is a tangible benefit of good appraisal practices in the most fundamental performance measure of all – mortality rates.

progress on a number of fronts. Doctors are a prime example of the issues in appraising professionals, and it is to that topic that we now turn.

Appraisal issues with professional and scientific staff

The key to understanding some of the potential difficulties in making appraisal work with professional groups is to contrast the ethos of the professional with the ethos of organisations. The former is typified by:

- high levels of autonomy and independence of judgment
- self-discipline and adherence to professional standards
- the possession of specialised knowledge and skills
- power and status based on expertise
- operating, and being guided by, a code of ethics
- being answerable to the governing professional body.

There are other attributes, but these are the main ones. Where professionals operate within the context of a private practice or some other small professional grouping, there is no serious problem as all are working to the same model. Not so, however, where they work as part of a much larger and more general organisation. Listing the characteristics of the conventional organisational ethos immediately shows the conflict of value systems:

- hierarchical authority and direction from superiors
- administrative rules and procedures to be followed
- standards and goals defined by the organisation
- primary loyalty demanded by the organisation
- power based on legitimate organisational position.

Small wonder professionals experience role conflict at times, with different expectations and demands from their profession and from their organisational employers. For example, doctors and university lecturers are apt to see their work as being determined by the needs of their patients or students respectively, and by their professional training, rather than by the pragmatic considerations that drive so many organisational decisions on how resources are allocated. One university vice-chancellor summed up the problem very graphically and succinctly: he said that managing academics was like trying to shepherd a flock of cats! Much the same could be said of many professional groups; they do not take easily to the idea of being managed. There are of course variations in the extent to which this is true – for example, engineers are perhaps more used to working within commercial organisational management structures than are some other professions.

Appraisal is likely to fall right into the centre of this 'ethos gap'. It represents an organisational procedure that is embedded within a hierarchical authority structure; it frequently implies that some external agent or process is necessary to motivate and guide the individual's work; and it is the mechanism whereby the organisation's goals are imposed at lower levels. The kinds of performance measures that enter into appraisal discussions may well reflect outcomes that are of primary importance at organisational level but which seem misleading, crude or irrelevant to the professional. Thus, measures like the number of students enrolled, the number of patients seen or the number of social work cases covered are of limited importance to the professionals concerned without some meaningful check on how well quality has been maintained. The professional's aspiration is, more often than not, to achieve the highest standard possible and to extend professional skills and expertise in doing so. The organisation's goals, on the other hand, tend to be more about cost-effectiveness and delivering a reasonable product or service rather than the best possible, even in these quality-conscious days.

On top of all this, the appraisers may or may not be fellow professionals. Where they are not, there is a serious danger of a communication gap between the two parties; they start from different positions and speak different languages. Where professionals appraise one another, this problem does not usually exist, but instead, the organisational agenda for appraisal may well be ignored. Also, it is often the case that the whole process is perceived as embarrassing, as being inappropriate or even distasteful by both parties – with the consequence that it is not treated seriously and is carried out in a superficial manner.

The result of the differences between professional ethos and organisational ethos is to make appraisal far more difficult to introduce and run successfully. It is simply no use to try to operate the appraisal of professional and scientific staff as if they were no different from any others. Quite apart from the points already made, it has to be remembered that this is a group who have usually been through an extended qualification process, and they have a far higher level of educational achievement than most. This alone might serve to make them a more challenging prospect as far as appraisal is concerned. We can look at the detailed implications of all this for how appraisal functions with members of professional and scientific groups later in the chapter. But for the moment, a more general point has to be made. If performance appraisal in one form or another is to be part of the way these staff groups work and are managed, then it would be better to face head-on the issues of the conflicting value systems outlined above before any practical appraisal arrangements are put in place. If both the professionals concerned and the non-professional elements of the organisational management can discuss their expectations and differences at the outset – in seminars, consultative sessions, organisational development workshops or whatever – many of the problems can be addressed and perhaps minimised. They will not be eliminated, but raising awareness of the differing expectations can help in achieving some of the compromises necessary between organisational and individual goals if the appraisal process is to be constructive. The general requirement for performance appraisal to recognise the needs and values of appraisees and appraisers, rather than just the organisation's aims, is even stronger with professional groups.

Designing and implementing appraisal for professional staff

Designing appraisal

As can be gathered from the preceding paragraphs, getting the aims of appraisal right is both more difficult and even more crucial when professional groups are concerned. Potentially, appraisal can serve the same functions for this group as for other employees. However, two points need to be kept in mind:

- Professionals tend to be fairly high on self-motivation, and an overt emphasis on appraisal as a motivating device may cause it to be rejected as unnecessary.
- Assessment against professional and personal standards is acceptable, but is usually perceived as being more relevant to development than to deciding on rewards.

The organisation will generally want appraisal to be a means of directing the efforts of professional staff in such a way that they are in line with the main organisational objectives and priorities. This is far from straightforward: as we have seen, the kinds of performance criteria and outcomes that the organisation values are not always reflected in the views of the individual professional. What all this means is that the *presentation* of the aims of appraisal becomes almost as important as the aims themselves.

Appraisal is more likely to be acceptable if it is seen as a means of facilitating effective cooperation in achieving common goals and as a mechanism for improving professional development than if it is perceived as a way of assessing and motivating professionals to drive organisational performance. In the final analysis, there may not be much difference between these two perspectives in what they actually entail, but there may be a world of difference in how they are thought of. The language and terminology is thus of some significance here. The word 'appraisal' seems to have more negative connotations with professionals than it has for most people, probably because it is seen as something to do with industry and not relevant to their approach to work. Consequently, it may be wise to look for alternative terms. The most popular tend to be variations on a few themes:

- individual development interviews
- work planning and review sessions
- professional development interviews
- performance development sessions
- job progress reviews.

Any title that diminishes the implication that the session is about assessment is an improvement (of course, staff may still call it the appraisal anyway!).

So far, this discussion has treated all professional groups as being much the same. Whilst their similarities might outweigh their differences, the latter do exist. It cannot be assumed that where there is more than one professional group, they will all react in the same way. This was illustrated in Chapter 5 when it was recounted how local government engineers and social workers had been found to have rather different styles and preferences in relation to appraisal. These differences, too, have to be addressed in the design process, by ensuring that all the professional groups concerned are represented in the consultation exercise, and that they are made aware of the differing views of their colleagues in other professions. This is particularly beneficial, as professionals do sometimes need reminding that their own particular profession does not have a monopoly on wisdom. The main point here, though, is that it may make the consultation and design stage of appraisal slower where professional groups are involved than would normally be the case. That slower progress should be built in to the planned timetable for introducing appraisal. Trying to rush into implementation by short-cutting the discussion process is liable to leave a residue of problems. See Box 11.2 for a case study of a professional group who have, rather like doctors, been amongst the last to embrace the concept of appraisal – lawyers.

It was noted earlier that the hierarchical authority structures of organisations do not always fit the professional's concept of control and discipline. This not only affects the aims of appraisal, but who should carry it out. The traditional notion of the immediate boss being the appraiser is called into question. If that boss is a member of the same profession as the appraisee, there is a considerable chance of them colluding to make it a non-event if they do not feel downward appraisal to be appropriate. Or it may focus exclusively on professional content – the appraisal may be seen as an opportunity to discuss arcane technical issues and to review career development and may therefore neglect the less intrinsically interesting matter of meeting objectives. If the boss is not a fellow professional, then the situation may be even worse – the appraiser can be viewed by the appraisee as lacking the knowledge and skills to make a valid judgment about performance, as well as not being in a position to offer career development advice. An additional problem is that, in some organisations dominated by professional staff, there are very few, and often ill-defined, layers of authority. The consequence is that where line management responsibility can be defined, the number of appraisees to each appraiser may be rather high. So, the question of who the appraiser should be therefore requires careful consideration. There are several options:

1 Allow choice

The idea of people choosing their appraisers is found in both teacher and (some) university appraisal schemes. The virtue of letting people nominate their own appraisers is that they can pick those individuals who have most relevant knowledge of their work and their professional specialism, and whom they respect. There are certainly occasions where it can be appropriate to follow such a route –

- where there is no obvious immediate superior who is in a position to appraise
- where the person works in a very highly specialised field
- where the numbers of staff to be appraised would be too great for the appraiser and some way has to be found to spread the load.

Unfortunately, there are many potential problems that limit the value of taking this approach more generally. The main one is that appraisees may choose appraisers on less desirable grounds – personal friendship, or the knowledge that X is a 'soft touch' – which result in a less than thorough or constructive discussion. Even where they are chosen for more legitimate reasons, such appraisers may not be in a position to give the broader perspective and support necessary to help the appraisee. There are also administrative difficulties that arise if this choice process is allowed on a widespread basis. So, the principle of allowing choice of appraiser is useful in some special circumstances, but has to be carefully controlled – the choice needs to be sanctioned by whoever has responsibility for the appraisal process.

2 Multi-level, multi-source appraisal

Some general points on multiple appraisal were discussed in Chapters 6 and 7; most of these apply in appraising professionals. Again, this approach has been used in various forms in teaching and university appraisal, and now increasingly with doctors, as indicated in Box 11.1. The attraction of multiple appraisal to professional staff rests mainly on self- and peer-review, both of which fit the professional ethos much better than appraisal by superiors. In universities and in the scientific community, the peer review process has long been established and accepted as the best way of judging the merit of individual pieces of work and of assessing the suitability of people for promotion. However, it has to be noted that, in this context, the word 'peers' is often used to refer to members of the same professional group and specialism rather than necessarily to imply people of the same rank or level. Input to appraisal from colleagues working in the same professional field is acceptable because they are knowledgeable about that field and the individual's contribution to it, and not because they are in some sense senior or in a position of authority – their authority comes from expert power, not rank.

But the concept of multiple appraisal has wider implications for some professionals than it generally does for managers. It can include input from patients about the way they are dealt with by health care professionals, from students on the way they are taught by lecturers, and so on (there are limits to this – criminals' views on their arresting officers may be a touch biased). Where such sources of information are mooted, they are sometimes questioned on their capacity to offer objective or useful evidence. However, to take the case of lecturers as an example, the evidence shows that student ratings of their teachers are sufficiently reliable and valid (for example, they correlate quite highly with ratings of teaching ability made by superiors, peers and classroom observers) to use in feedback aimed at performance improvement and in personnel decision-making (Rushton and Murray, 1985).

If the author may be permitted to indulge in a little personal, anecdotal evidence, I have, when heading up a university department, used student feedback in the 12 to 18 performance reviews (really far too many – five or six is optimum) that I held each year. Almost invariably, the student evaluations are fair, perceptive, and consistent. The students are well able to differentiate between their personal liking – or lack of it – for an individual lecturer and the quality of his or her teaching. And (contrary to what some academics would like to believe) they are able to separate the intrinsic level of interest of the subject matter from the way it is delivered; in other words, lecturers teaching them about the physiology of the inner ear are not automatically rated less favourably than those teaching them a course on sex and violence.

The problem with appraisal input from consumers of professional services is that getting it is usually time-consuming and sometimes costly. But with the growing focus on quality considerations, this is something that may well play a larger part in appraisal in the future, and not just with professionals. It is a hard one for some professionals to take, though. Again resorting to the anecdotal, I was giving a talk on 360-degree feedback at an event held at the Royal College of Physicians, and when it came to question time, a consultant physician leaned forward with a pained look and asked 'Professor Fletcher, do you really think that patients have anything to offer in the assessment of doctors?' I think most of us who have been patients at one time or another might answer affirmatively.

3 Split-role appraisal

Sometimes an alternative is to have a form of multiple appraisal but in separate sessions – which might be called split-role appraisal. This is useful in addressing the problem of the appraisee having dual responsibilities and roles. On the one hand there is the professional specialism and all that it entails, and on the other there is the administrative and managerial role the individual may fill in the organisation. It is quite possible to have different appraisers for each, a professional mentor for the professional role and a senior manager for the organisational role. There are some difficulties with this, mainly in connection with the areas of interface and overlap, and it is more costly in resource terms, but it can work well enough, provided that the appraisers consult where necessary before and after the session.

Box 11.2: Developing a performance management system for corporate lawyers

This case study relates to a request by the legal services division of a multinational oil company to help them develop a new performance management system. Some – but not all – of the most senior lawyers wanted a new form of appraisal that encouraged a more objectively based assessment of peformance and one that could be used to assist in development. A team of external and internal consultants was commissioned to carry out this task. The first step was to develop an agreed competency framework, which was done by using a mixture of job analysis techniques, and then feeding back drafts of the output to focus groups to check validity. At the same time, the focus groups, representing varying levels of legal staff and drawn from different operating companies and countries, were consulted about the existing appraisal arrangements and what they wanted from the new ones. This proved to be a long, slow process, as it takes time for such a diverse group of people to find something they can all agree on. It was of crucial importance to build the competency descriptions in the words and language that they could relate to – if there is any professional group likely to pour over the slightest ambiguity in meaning, it is lawyers!

Eventually, the competency descriptions were agreed, and after another round of focus groups held in two countries, so was the performance management framework. It consisted of a two-part process, with an assessment of performance that linked in with pay and – at a separate point in the year – a developmentally-oriented discussion based on the assessment. Training the senior lawyers in appraisal brought to light all the problems outlined in this chapter, and also some of the tensions within the managing group of lawyers themselves – some wanting the kind of system designed and some still hankering after something very much simpler; one said 'I only have 15 minutes to spend on performance management for each member of my staff!' The hope of some of his colleagues was that the new system would help drive a culture change that would make it difficult if not impossible for that kind of attitude to survive.

One point about this example, though, is that it relates to professionals who are deeply embedded in a competitive commercial environment, and who are thus more familiar with management concepts and control mechanisms than some of their professional colleagues who operate in private practice.

Appraisal training

The concept of training can receive a very mixed reception amongst professionals. Some see no difference in kind between attending an appraisal training course and the prolonged training they have already received for their professional career. Others see it as somewhat threatening. I well remember a college principal saying, when asked about the training to be given to appraisers in the institution: 'I do not like to use the word training. I prefer to think that we can deal with this through discussion meetings.' For some senior professionals, the idea of attending a skills-based appraisal course, with the attendant risk of being seen not to perform well (or, as they might think of it, of making a fool of themselves) in front of others may not be very appealing. In view of these mixed reactions, the first step in setting up appraisal training for professionals is to gauge their attitude to the idea, and to assess how much help – and in what form – the professionals concerned feel they need.

The briefing sessions that introduce the appraisal system can be used as a vehicle for assessing the demand for training. Such sessions may also have the function of examining some of the professional–organisational ethos differences, if these have not been brought out in a prior consultation process. While it might be rather late in the day to bring these up, it is better that they are made explicit and thought about rather than simply ignored. The briefing sessions can be extended to have a more direct training function by going over guidance notes on how to handle the interview, discussing ways of dealing with problem performers and so on. This in itself can be used to raise awareness of the need for training, and to demonstrate its potential value. There is little point in forcing people to undergo training that they do not want, so being able to offer training to those that would like it, without it being mandatory (at least, initially), is a reasonable approach. In addition, the use of e-learning is often especially appealing to professionals; they have become used to studying alone at their computers, and so software based training packages of the sort mentioned in Chapter 8 are highly relevant for this group. For some professionals, after doing appraisals for the first time their attitudes can change and any resistance to the idea of attending a skills training course may decrease or disappear.

The actual content of appraisal training, where professional staff are involved, does not usually need to be any different from normal. However, there are some points to be aware of, and these are relevant to the briefing sessions, too. HR staff who have been involved in appraisal training in organisations with large numbers of scientific staff will tell you that the latter tend to apply their normal perspective on the world to appraisal as well: they will want some evidence that what is being presented to them works. This evidence can take the form of examples of how the same approach is used successfully elsewhere, in similar organisations of sufficient status for them to respect, and/or it can be in the form of academic research demonstrating that the principles embedded in the appraisal scheme are effective in achieving the desired ends (in this context, see the research cited in the final section of Chapter 13). Any figures or statistics delivered in the course of this will be subject to careful scrutiny and evaluation. Concepts and assumptions will be examined in detail. All of which can make the delivery of appraisal training to groups of this kind fairly demanding for the trainers. They will need to be prepared to deal with questions of a rather different kind from scientific and professional staff, who are more inclined to focus on underlying principles than is the average manager.

There is also a need for trainers to be sensitive to likely differences between professional groups in how they react to the subject of appraisal. Typically, the more technically based professionals are prone to emphasising content and procedural issues. They often feel quite happy and comfortable with rating scales and quantitative measures, with appraisal that revolves around clear procedures and the completion of report forms. In contrast, experience suggests that the 'soft' professions and disciplines, those that deal with human and social issues in the main, are much more likely to react negatively to the quantitative aspects of appraisal and assessment. Instead, they direct their attention to the process aspects of appraisal, and show more concern about handling the interaction with the appraisee in a sensitive and conflict-free manner. Both groups and perspectives have their strengths and weaknesses. It is the task of the trainer to organise the appraisal training to cater for these. Two basic approaches are possible. One is to make sure that on any course, the participants are from a mixed group; the idea here is that they act as corrective influences on each other. The alternative is to try to make the course membership group-specific and to gently shape the training in such a way as to counterbalance the biases of that particular group.

Appraising promotion potential among professional staff

There are, broadly speaking, two different pathways open to professionals: one is to make progress in their own specialism and reach positions of responsibility within the profession, while the other is to branch out into more generalist roles, where their training may still play a part in their work, albeit a steadily diminishing one. In the early career stage, the promotability of an individual will often be based on both professional competence and development, and on effectiveness in their organisational role. It is usually important for both these to be assessed and taken account of in the promotion decision. Sometimes they go hand-in-hand, and there is no great problem. It is not always the case, though, and many organisations – for example, those operating in the advanced technology field – find that some of their staff are so good technically that they have to be given career advancement on this basis alone (if the company is to keep them), even if their more general personal skills are seriously deficient. For other individuals, the balance tilts in the opposite direction. If this is the situation, then the appraisal process has some role in identifying both to the individual and to the organisation what the future career pattern is likely to be, so that everyone concerned knows where they stand. It seems essential here that the appraisal does include inputs from both professional and organisational perspectives.

In some settings, the relationship between the professional and the organisational aspects of performance can become distorted by the reward system. A classic example of this is to be found in research-led universities, where young academic staff quickly learn that their promotion will very largely be determined by their personal research output and their capacity for winning external funding – with the result that many of them will seek to minimise their teaching hours and their share of administrative duties, though these are vital to the organisation and to their 'customers'.

As with other staff groups, appraisal does not itself offer a very satisfactory mechanism for making decisions on longer-term promotion potential. The alternative methods, reviewed in Chapter 10, can all be applied with professional groups. Of these, though, the assessment (or development) centre is perhaps the most appropriate. Its flexibility makes it possible to devise AC exercises that are designed to assess potential for managing professionals or exercises that are designed to assess potential for generalist management. The latter can be quite useful in acting as a realistic job preview, giving candidates a taste of what such work might be like and allowing them to decide whether they would want to go down this route.

In summary

The context in which performance appraisal operates is rather different in public sector organisations, which can serve to make it a more challenging process to introduce and run. In particular, such organisations often have a high proportion of technical, scientific or professional staff, and the attitudes and ethos of these groups can sometimes work against the management aims of the organisation – not least because they may take a more independent viewpoint and not identify with some of the organisation's aims or policies. The design of an appraisal system for professional staff needs to address this, and in particular to encourage participation in the development of the process and to place emphasis on developmental aspects. Other features of the scheme – for example, in terms of who actually conducts the appraisal – may also need some tailoring. Finally, there are implications for how training is delivered to such groups and for the way promotability and potential are assessed.

Discussion points and questions

What are the main challenges to devising and implementing performance appraisal in the public sector?

How are professionals likely to differ from general administrative or managerial staff in their attitude to appraisal, and why?

Select one of the following: Police Officers, Teachers, GPs (Doctors). How would you assess their performance – what do you think would be most relevant criteria to judge them on?

Key references

Department for Education and Skills (2006) *Education (School Teacher Performance Management) (England) Regulations 2006*. DFES: London.

Department for Education and Skills, Rewards and Incentive Group (2007) *Teachers' and Head Teachers Performance Management*. DFES: London.

Department of Health (2006) *Good Doctors, Safer Patients*. DH: London.

Department of Health (2007) *Trust, Assurance and Safety: The Regulation of Health Professionals*. DH White Paper, The Stationery Office: London.

Simmons, J. and Iles, P. (2001) Performance appraisals in knowledge-based organisations: Implications for management education. *International Journal of Management Education*, 2, pp. 3–18.

Chapter 12

Cultural challenges in applying performance appraisal

Although numerous changes in appraisal have been charted and described elsewhere in this book – principally, the rise of 360-degree feedback and the increasing application of appraisal to professional groups – there is another development that has not yet been fully considered (only briefly mentioned in Chapter 7) but which will be addressed here. This is the impact of culture in the context of appraisal. With increasing freedom of movement of labour within the EU, and the growing internationalisation of business, the question arises as to the applicability of management concepts and approaches developed in one culture to people coming from another, different one. How well do our ideas on how to structure and carry out performance appraisal travel?

The vast majority of published research on performance management emanates from the developed countries of the West – in fact most of it comes from the US, with some additional input from Western Europe. Since workers in the UK have been found to react differently to feedback to those in the US (Early and Stubblebine, 1989), a reasonably similar culture, it seems likely that generalising from the existing research base to other cultures, especially those in developing countries, is unsafe.

Indeed, research has found systematic differences in work-related values across countries (e.g. Elenkov, 1998; Fernandez *et al.*, 1997; Smith *et al.*, 1996). Thus, the question arises as to whether established appraisal methods, in so far as they do largely come from western advanced economies, are appropriate or effective in other cultural settings? Addressing this issue is becoming more urgent because of the increasingly international nature of business referred to above. However, it is not simply a question of whether imposing western appraisal philosophies on other countries will prove effective; it also relates to differences within countries. Kikoski (1999, page 301), talking in an American context, observes that – 'the problems of face-to-face communication in an essentially monocultural work force may be insignificant compared to the interpersonal communication difficulties which may accompany the more culturally diverse work force that is forecast'. Whilst Kikoski is referring to the growing proportion of US workers from Hispanic, Asian or African backgrounds, cultural diversity may be equally marked in the European Union, with its freedom of movement of labour.

To illustrate some of the potential problems that might be encountered, we can turn to the work of Hofstede (1980, 2001), whose research is the most frequently cited on the relationship between national culture and work-related values (Fernandez *et al.*, 1997). Hofstede identified a number of dimensions of cultural difference; these are described in Box 12.1. Here, we will focus on just two of them – Power Distance and Individualism/Collectivism – as there is more evidence in relation to these in the context of appraisal. Readers interested in a fuller treatment are referred to Bailey and Fletcher (2007) and to Fletcher and Perry (2001).

Box 12.1: Hofstede's dimensions for describing cultural differences

Hofstede (1980, 2001), working largely in the context of the multinational IBM, identified four major dimensions of cultural value difference. His model is used by the vast majority of theoretical and empirical investigations in this area, and it describes national cultures in terms of their position along these dimensions: Power Distance, Uncertainty Avoidance, Masculinity/Femininity and Individualism/Collectivism. Although all four are described below, more attention will be given to the first two as they generally are seen to be the most relevant in this context.

Power Distance (PD) concerns how less powerful organisational members accept and expect that power is distributed unequally. In *high PD* cultures there is acceptance of unequal distribution of power within a culture. Supervisors and subordinates consider themselves unequal and subordinates are more dependent on their supervisors – they may be afraid to express disagreements with their supervisors, whilst the latter tend to have an autocratic or paternalistic management style. High PD is also associated with greater centralisation of power in the organization.

In *low PD* cultures, relationships between individuals across hierarchical levels are closer and less formal in nature. They are marked by more limited dependence of subordinates on their supervisors and the use of and preference for a consultative or participatory style of management. In addition, when power distance is low, so too is emotional distance – resulting in subordinates' possibly showing more willingness to approach and even contradict their supervisors.

Individualism/Collectivism (I/C) reflects the extent to which the interests of the individual prevail over the interests of the group. *Individualistic* cultures value personal identity and choice – people act in their own interest and the relationship between the employee and employer is conceived of as a business relationship. Emphasis is often placed on personal freedom of choice, and individual initiative – and companies are not expected to get involved in the personal lives of their employees.

Collectivist cultures emphasise group values over individual goals, and the welfare of the group over individual needs. Thus, the interests of the group prevail over the interests of the individual. Emphasis is given to reducing differences between members of the collective and to maintaining group harmony, loyalty, and pre-serving relationships and 'face'. Collectivist societies tend to be hierarchical and to value seniority. The relationship between the employer and employee typically involves protection in exchange for loyalty (rather akin to the 'old' psychological contract – see page 131).

Uncertainty Avoidance (UA): The degree to which people in a country prefer structured over unstructured situations. Low UA cultures are more risk-taking, and tolerant of organisational ambiguity and change than High UA cultures.

Masculinity/Femininity (M/F): Masculine cultures are associated with values like assertiveness, performance, success and competition (associated with the male role in almost all societies). Female cultures are associated with values like quality of life, maintaining warm personal relationships, service, and care for the weak.

There is some evidence that power distance and individualism are in fact cor-related (Hofstede, 1980). But Hofstede's model has been hugely influential in our thinking on cultural differences and has been well supported. The individualism/ collectivism dimension is increasingly being used as an explanatory concept in cross-cultural psychology (Kagitcibasi and Berry, 1989), and the power distance dimension has been found to correlate with theoretically similar factors in other studies of cross-cultural values (Smith *et al.*, 1996).

To give some geography to Hofstede's descriptions – high Power Dis-tance countries include France, Malaysia and Mexico; low Power Distance include the US, UK and (to a lesser extent) Germany. High Collectivist cultures can be found, for example, in Japan, Thailand and Singapore, while countries high on Individualism include the US, Chile, France and Australia. It is not difficult to see how the differences outlined in this theory are likely to have an impact on appraisal schemes. According to Hofstede, western cultures are high in individualism, medium in levels of power distance and uncertainty avoidance and are masculine more than feminine. Within the appraisal setting, this manifests itself as a need for individual achievement and recognition, with individuals being encouraged to express assertive, challenging behaviours and to be personally ambitious at the cost of group-oriented actions and nurturing behaviours. Subsequently, appraisal systems are generally focused upon the individual (not the group) and have emphasised stereotypically masculine values over feminine ones. As a result, the appraisal system can be viewed as an opportunity for negotiation between the individual and the organisation.

Things look very different elsewhere, though. Asian organisations, Schneider and Barsoux (1997) suggest, emphasise what the employee 'is', with greater concern for employees' personality and other characteristics, in comparison to most western organisations where the focus of the appraisal is on what the employee 'does'. Snape *et al.* (1998) observe that in societies such as China, with a strong collectivist orientation, a sense of hierarchy and acceptance of authority, the focus of 'western' PA practices on individual performance, accountability and open confrontation are unlikely to be seen as appropriate. That is supported by Huo and Von Glinow (1995), who found that Chinese managers were reluctant to engage in two-way communication or provide counselling in the performance appraisal process, because of the high PD values of Chinese culture. Thus, employees' participation in appraisal was low in comparison to Western countries, and peer evaluation was seldom encountered – because of the high Power Distance, only the immediate manager is regarded as sufficiently qualified to appraise subordinates' performance (but see below in relation to multi-source feedback).

It looks much the same if one examines the literature on Russian attitudes and values. In terms of leadership style, Koopman *et al.* (1999) found that managers from central and eastern Europe had significantly less negative attitudes toward autocratic behaviour and valued diplomacy as a managerial behaviour significantly more than western managers. This is supported by Elenkov (1998) in a study which compared Russian and American perceptions of performance feedback. He found that direct feedback between managers and employees was perceived as undesirable, and concluded that this was a result of the collectivist value orientation which regards such feedback as harmful to group harmony, the employee's self-image and loyalty to the organisation. As a result, he suggests that appraisals that focused on group rather than individual achievements were likely to be more acceptable.

Whilst there is some research on value differences in other countries, overall the evidence is somewhat thin. But what there is, however, makes it seem doubtful that much of the appraisal research (with its western orientation) can be generalised and applied successfully to Chinese or Russian organisations – and if that is the case, the same may well be true in relation to many other countries also.

Cultural differences in the context of multi-source feedback

Multi-source feedback in particular, with its capacity to deliver critical assessments across hierarchical boundaries, may be susceptible to widely varying reactions according to the cultural background of the participants. Shipper *et al.* (2002) assessed the effectiveness of a 360 feedback process implemented within a large multinational organisation. Their study found varying levels of effectiveness across five different countries; for example, 360 was related to declines in performance in Malaysia but improvements in Ireland! The authors argued that the application of multi-source feedback in cultures whose values are inconsistent with those inherent in the process may be detrimental. Somewhat similarly, study of upward feedback ratings carried out in a multinational across ten countries it operated in did show some variations in rating characteristics (Adsit *et al.*, 1997). These international differences are further reflected in a study which looked at the characteristics of such systems as they operated across six countries (Brutus *et al.*, 2006). To pick out just some of their findings:

- Argentina – had a high proportion of non-voluntary participation (80 per cent) and developmental use (90 per cent)
- China – had the highest input to appraisal (78 per cent), highest mandatory participation (89 per cent), raters were often chosen by third party (67 per cent), and supervisors had access to the feedback report in 100 per cent of the cases encountered in the study
- Slovakia – mostly developmental use and voluntary participation in all (100 per cent) cases
- Spain – line manager chose the focal managers' raters in two-thirds of cases
- UK – more likely (86 per cent of cases) that raters will be chosen by focal manager than in any of the other countries covered in the study

There are some interesting variations here, but it comes as no surprise to find the rather top down, somewhat hierarchical approach taken in China. Nonetheless, the fact that such systems are operating at all there perhaps indicates a significant shift – and it should be noted that they have only a very recent history of using them compared to the US and Europe. The pattern in Argentina is also unusual; mainly a developmental focus, but with a hint of authoritarianism thrown in – you will be developed whether you like it or not! Despite the variations noted, Brutus *et al.* (2006) report that the suggested solutions to the problems and challenges posed in implementing multi-source feedback were surprisingly consistent across the countries sampled. For example, pre and post communication were seen as key to success. HR professionals and others responsible for introducing such processes in these countries commented at length on their communication efforts, prior to implementation, to attain required levels of trust and support from users. They also discussed the need for follow-up efforts in order for feedback to have an impact.

Cultural variation within organisations

Problems of cultural differences can, of course, also arise within a single organisation, when the feedback provider and feedback recipient are from different national cultures – a situation that is becoming increasingly common. Triandis and Brislin (1984) noted that when a supervisor from one culture appraises the performance of a subordinate from another, the accuracy of appraisal is likely to be lower, in part due to the fact that the appraiser is not aware of the norms in the other culture that govern certain behaviours. So let us look at how differences in Power Distance and in Individualism/Collectivism might impact an appraisal session at an individual level; two examples will serve to illustrate some of the possible difficulties –

Situation 1: An appraiser from a culture lower on Power Distance than an appraisee seeks the latter's self-assessments and their views on how to solve job problems. The appraisee may feel reluctant to participate in the performance appraisal process in this manner and feel it is not their place to do so – they feel it is their superior's job to propose solutions. Indeed, the appraisee may also view the appraiser's request for input of this kind as a sign of weakness. The appraiser, on the other hand, may be disappointed by the response and judge the appraisee as being uncooperative or simply devoid of ideas on how to deal with the problems identified.

Situation 2: The appraiser is from a culture higher on individualism than the appraisee, and focuses on the personal contribution of the individual, paying less attention to team issues. The appraisee, in contrast, wants to emphasize their role in the team and in consequence fails to highlight their personal achievements, leading to the appraiser assessing them less positively.

Clearly, there is scope for a host of problems and variations in such cross cultural interactions, and in an organisation where this may be an issue, it will be important – ideally – to take some account of it in designing the system, but more especially in the training delivered both to appraisers and appraisees (see Chapter 8, pages 111–112). But the difficulties can also be over-played. The influence of organisational culture should not be underestimated. Multinational companies tend to build up a strong, identifiable and pervasive culture of their own, and this can to some extent ameliorate the impact of differences in the national cultures of their work-force over time. Because there is a set way of doing things in the organisa-tion, it can become the accepted norm for everyone when they have become fully socialised into the organisation. Resorting to anecdotal evidence again, when the author was addressing a group from the Employers' Or-ganisation of Portugal on the subject of multi-source feedback, some in the audience felt that their national culture was not ready for such initiatives – but a representative of an international hotel chain operating there spoke up to point out that, in fact, they used 360-degree feedback and had experi-enced no problems at all, with staff being enthusiastic about it.

What should we conclude?

That differences in cultural values exist and that these can and do impact on appraisal and other HR practices is well supported in general terms (Harris, 2007). However, although there has been quite a lot written about the effects of culture on appraisal, the amount of empirical work is still small, and more is needed to test out to more precisely how and to what extent these influences impact on appraisal in the actual workplace. There are also two other significant factors that have to be taken into account. The first is that cultural and economic conditions change; the emergence of multi-source feedback in the 1990s is an example of a phenomenon that was not widely acceptable prior to that in the UK cul-ture – so we are looking at a dynamic situation where conclusions drawn at one time point may be invalid a decade later (Fletcher, 2001). Another example of this is that some countries have been shown to have shifted their position on the Hofstede dimensions from the time of his original observations (Fernandez et al., 1997). As noted earlier, the 'melting pot' of international business, not to mention the influence of the internet, prob-ably serves to reduce (but not eliminate) differences in approach and expectations over time.

The second factor comes down to the individual – someone who is never very far away in appraisal. Within any culture, there are always individual differences, and these may have an effect that swamps even that of the broader culture in which a person was raised. Indeed, there is an interplay between the culture and the individual's own disposition. Research on this intersection between culture and self has focused almost exclusively on variations in how individuals are 'tuned in, sensitive to, oriented toward, focused on, or concerned with others' (Erez and Earley, 1993, p. 25). Such a perspective, has given rise to the notion of self-construal, which defines the Self along two broad types: an independent or individualistic self and an interdependent or collectivistic self (Earley and Gibson, 1998). Variations in self-construal are reflected in people's belief about their relationships between them and others and, more precisely, the extent to which they see themselves separate from others versus connected with others. Independent self-construal is characterised by the extent to which individuals construe an inherent separateness between themselves and others. In contrast, those high on interdependence or collectivism strive for connectedness; for these individuals, the imperative is to maintain one's position as a member of a larger social unit. In many respects, then, self construal is a personality variable akin to the cultural dimension of individualism–collectivism. Brutus, et al. (2007) found that this was related to attitudes to appraisal. As expected, people who think of themselves as independent of others were much more comfortable in making or communicating appraisal ratings, handling the discussion and so on – they had higher self-efficacy in relation to appraisal in general.

This may be one particularly influential personality variable, but there are likely to be a whole host of other cognitive, personality and group differences, and that one cannot assume a blanket effect of culture on an individual's reaction to appraisal – it is likely to result from a complex interaction between the nature of the scheme, the organisational context, the relationship with the appraiser, culture and individual differences. All of which points to the importance of making line managers aware, in their training, of the kinds of influences at work. At the end of the day, much depends on the sensitivity of the appraiser in understanding and taking account of these, and showing skill in conducting the appraisal interaction accordingly.

The present chapter has only signalled some of the kinds of cultural difference that may influence appraisal interaction and attitudes – there are certainly others (see for example, Trompernaars, 1993). Organisations – particularly those operating across national and cultural boundaries – would be well advised to (a) read the literature available on this topic (b) seek guidance from those external or internal to the organisation who have expertise and experience in dealing with cross cultural issues (c) consult the different cultural groups involved about their expectations in relation to appraisal processes – and then to build the results into both the design of their appraisal systems and the training they offer. One size will NOT fit all.

In summary

With the internationalisation of business, it becomes more important to understand how culture may influence responses to appraisal. Assumptions about performance appraisal based on experience and research in predominantly western countries may not hold good when transferred to other cultures. For example, individuals from cultures high on individualism and low on Power Distance (which typify the US and some European states) may have a very different attitude to appraisal to people who have been raised in collectivist and high Power Distance cultures; such differences can impact on an individual's willingness to give feedback, to question feedback, to claim achievements for themselves rather than the team, and so on. This is at least equally relevant for the use of multi-source feedback, and should thus be taken into account when devising systems – they need to be consistent with the cultural values in which they will be embedded. However, with an increasingly multinational workforce, there may be a wide range of cultural backgrounds represented within a single organisation, and both appraisers and appraisees need to be sensitised about some of the possible differences and resulting outcomes in appraisal training. That said, it is important not to make assumptions too quickly on the basis of national cultures, as individual differences and organisational culture may be equally influential in determining how any given individual responds in the appraisal situation.

Discussion points and questions

What might be the problems or issues in an appraisal discussion being held between a line manager who is from a culture that (in Hofstede's terms) is Masculine and marked by low Uncertainty Avoidance and an appraisee who is from a more Feminine culture and one that is high on Uncertainty Avoidance?

Other than the ones already mentioned in this chapter, what other countries would you think were (a) high on Individualism (b) high on Collectivism (c) high on Power Distance (d) low on Power Distance?

What sort of elements would you include in appraisal training if there was likely to be a range of different cultural backgrounds represented in both the appraisers and the appraisees in your organisation?

Key references

Bailey, C. and Fletcher, C. (2007) Performance management and appraisal – an international perspective. In M. M. Harris (ed.) *The Handbook of Research in International Human Resource Management*. Organization Management Series, Lawrence Erlbaum: Mahwah, NJ (and indeed the whole book!).

Fletcher, C. and Perry, E. (2001) Performance appraisal and feedback: A consideration of national culture and a review of contemporary trends. In N. Anderson, D. Ones, H. Sinangil and C. Viswesvaran (eds) *International Handbook of Industrial, Work and Organizational Psychology*. Sage: Thousand Oaks, CA.

Hofstede, G. (1980) *Cultures' Consequences: International Differences in Work-related Values*. Sage: Beverley Hills, CA.

Chapter 13

Appraisal: The way ahead

Throughout the preceding 12 chapters, I have discussed numerous changes – in social and economic circumstances, government policies and in management thinking – in terms of their impact on organisations and their consequences for performance appraisal. Today, many organisations are structured very differently from the way they would have been ten to fifteen years ago, or in some cases even two years ago. The implication of this is that performance appraisal *cannot* stay the same and still claim to be relevant. The traditional model of a centrally devised and run appraisal system, with an emphasis on assessment and overall ratings of performance, applied to all staff in the same manner, is no longer appropriate to a high proportion of advanced companies, and is likely to be decreasingly suitable for many more in the next few years. The fact that it is no longer clear in many organisations as to who is the most appropriate person to be the appraiser for an individual is enough in itself to indicate how things have changed.

As we have seen, many organisations have responded dynamically to the challenge by, for example, adopting multi-source feedback systems and increasing the use of IT based appraisal platforms of the sort exemplified by the UBS example cited in Chapter 5. The pace of change is likely only to increase in the years ahead, though, and especially in terms of the internationalisation of business, dealt with in the previous chapter. All this suggests that it is more than time to deconstruct the traditional approach to appraisal. Quite apart from anything else, it has consistently been found to fail to deliver on almost every count – it satisfies the needs of neither the organisations nor the participants (Industrial Society, 2001; Hirsh, 2006). The only way for practice in this field to make any sense is to break the domain and purposes of performance appraisal down into a series of linked processes, the main ones being:

1   *A performance planning session* that involves reviewing achievement of objectives over the period in question and setting objectives for the

period ahead. If PRP has to come into the picture – and this writer believes that, in the case of merit pay, it would be better if it did not – this is what it is related to.

2   A *development review*, probably based on competencies or skill dimensions, that looks at the training and development needs of the individual, and which can feed into the assessment of potential (where the latter is done by other, more effective, methods). If a competency approach has been used, then those competencies can be reflected in selection, appraisal, training and in assessing potential

For an example of splitting the main functions of appraisal into two processes, see Box 13.1; this organisation adopts a slightly different approach to spreading the appraisal load across different sessions, and perhaps in contrast to some companies prefers to use the word 'development' in reference to the session built around objective setting and review, whilst the word 'performance' relates to the session on assessment against competencies. However, this simply illustrates how organisations may find their own solutions and terminology to meet their own requirements whilst still following the general principle of separating out different functions of appraisal. This view of how appraisal should operate is not new; in various and sometimes rather different forms, it has been around since Meyer and his colleagues (Meyer *et al.*, 1965) called for split roles in performance appraisal as a result of their work in the American company GEC in the 1960s. But it is far more relevant now than at any previous time. Organisations are increasingly knowledge based, and are focusing to a greater extent on training managers in learning techniques to help them become more flexible and adaptable. This, along with the flatter and more flexible management structures, and the need for greater self-reliance and autonomy in career planning, is beginning to produce the kind of situation and employee attitudes that have hitherto only been found in organisations characterised by a high proportion of professional staff amongst their workforce. In other words, some of the conflicts of ethos that were described in Chapter 11 in relation to professional staff in the public sector are likely to become more relevant to general management staff in the private sector, too. Trying to persist with traditional appraisal approaches in these circumstances seems doomed to failure.

In addition to the elements of appraisal described in 1 and 2 above, other elements may be added:

3   *Multi-source feedback*, which should feed into the developmental session, but which could nonetheless be an element of the on-going appraisal of the individual, focused on some (not all) of the key competencies

4   *Use of Assessment and Development Centres, and possibly Psychometrics* in the assessment of potential.

Both of these are already widespread in their application, and are only likely to become more so. The important thing is to make sure that they are properly integrated with performance and development reviews rather than happening as potentially confusing parallel processes. What one calls this overall approach is another issue. Referring to it as 'appraisal' does it less than justice, and even the overall term of 'Performance Management' smacks of being overly organisation-centred in perspective. Perhaps something along the lines of 'Feedback and Development Process' would be more appropriate, but organisations will find their own language for it.

Box 13.1: an example of a multi-process performance appraisal and management system at BSI

This system was built around the BSI Core Success Factors which were developed through a process that included consultation and discussion with all divisions of the organisation. These factors are:

- Delivery
- Customer focus
- Teamwork
- Self-management
- Adaptability
- Ownership

BSI's annual performance review process is called 'Focus on Performance'. The manager and the person reviewed independently complete a draft copy of the review form. Performance is reviewed against a four-point rating, from 'Consistently exceeds the expectations of the job role' to 'Consistently fails to meet the expectations of the job role'. An interesting feature of the BSI system is that the form records *both* the manager's ratings *and* the appraisee's self-assessed rating. Also notable is the way it is kept simple – a single page – allowing both parties to focus on content rather than procedure. The form is reviewed by a more senior manager subsequently.

The second element in the BSI review process is called 'Developing Success' and is an annual performance objective setting and development planning session. It is carried out separately from the Focus on Performance session, though it obviously links in with it, and has a strong forward-looking emphasis. The Manager and the person reviewed together agree performance objectives for the next six to twelve months, and record these, together with a reference to the wider relevant business objectives they relate to. They then go on to assess the areas where some development activity is necessary to achieve the objectives. These are framed in terms of the Core Success Factors. Following this, both parties consider the reviewee's development successes attained over the last review period, and also discuss career aspirations. On the basis of all of this, a Development Plan is recorded on the form. Again, the paperwork is kept as brief and simple as possible, with the Developing Success Form running to just two pages.

Performance appraisal centred on performance improvement and development, and wider, more objective evidence, along the lines of the linked processes described above, is likely to be more successful – and perhaps even essential for organisational growth. In recent years the emphasis on bottom-line considerations has been so strong, and the changes in organisations so great, that an atmosphere of considerable uncertainty and a focus on short-term objectives has prevailed. These are conditions that erode the psychological security necessary for individuals to be willing to take the risks involved in innovation (King and Anderson, 2002). Yet the need for organisations to foster innovation has never been stronger and is recognised right up to government levels. A more developmentally and future-focused appraisal system can contribute to creating the right conditions for innovation.

Although some of these ideas about splitting the functions of appraisal have been around for a while and have been put into practice by a number of organisations, stand-alone, monolithic appraisal system is still with us, especially – and perhaps not surprisingly – in some traditional British manufacturing companies. How can these and other companies be persuaded that they are wasting their time and resources in following an approach that has repeatedly been shown to be bankrupt? It is usually down to the HR department, and/or external consultants, to bring the message home. There are a number of strategies that can be used, individually or in concert, to effect change in this area:

- The use of questionnaire surveys of attitudes to management, to communications, to reward systems and to the current appraisal arrangements is often a powerful way of highlighting problems and the need to take action.

- The use of external examples is something that tends to hold senior management attention. Knowing what other, high-performing and respected companies are doing can have a salutary effect. No board of directors likes to feel that the company is looking dated and backward in its approach, and that (in particular) the competition is stealing a march on them. The HR department can be judicious in picking its examples for comparison.

- Using research findings (see below) on appraisal from studies done elsewhere can be quite useful in presenting a case in the more science and technology based companies. This can be done through written briefings, but is usually more effective if embedded within a presentation by consultants and outside experts. Such people can make board-room presentations about what is going on in appraisal and what the latest thinking is. They will often, and probably quite unjustifiably, be more listened to than would the organisation's own HR staff.

- Running a pilot study of a new appraisal scheme in one department can be an effective way of demonstrating the value of the approach and the principles it embodies. Having been shown it can work within the organisation is reassuring and persuasive to senior management.

- Getting senior management to participate in any kind of strategic analysis of where the organisation is going, what it will look like in a few years' time, what sort of staff it will need, and so on, should inevitably lead to a re-consideration of how people are selected, appraised and developed. This kind of exercise may be facilitated by the HR department, with or without external consultants, and can be presented as part of organisational development as a whole (which it is) rather than as simply a mechanism for reviewing appraisal.

- The adoption of performance management within the organisation can act as a vehicle for the review of appraisal arrangements – indeed, it has to, as appraisal in one form or another is the pivotal mechanism of performance management.

The HR professionals are always the key facilitators in bringing about changes in appraisal. Making appraisal a line-led activity actually strengthens their hand. They are in the position to guide and support, rather than being in the invidious role of demanding and enforcing. They will have access to much wider knowledge and expertise in the area than will the line managers, and they can use this to great effect in shaping what is set up and how it runs. By involving the line in setting the agenda for appraisal and in determining how it will run, the HR department is able to work alongside them in a more cooperative and positive relationship than is the case where appraisal is seen as an activity imposed by HR and for HR.

Evidence that appraisal can work – and what we have to do to make it work better

Performance appraisal can make a big difference to attitudes. Fletcher and Williams (1996) found that better performance management practices related to job satisfaction and organisational commitment in both public and private sector organisation. Looking beyond attitudes to the bottom line, it has been demonstrated (e.g. by Patterson *et al.*, 1998) that good HR practices, and especially effective implementation of appraisal, show a close association with organisational performance indicators – though the relationship is complex (Guest *et al.*, 2003). Perhaps the most striking example of this is the study by West and Johnson (2002) which looked at the relationship of HR practices and procedures to various performance indicators across 61 hospitals in the UK Health Service. Amongst the findings, the strongest correlation to emerge was between the quality of appraisals and patient mortality rates, with the former accounting for 25 per cent of the variance in the latter – even after many other factors such as doctor/patient ratios and size of hospital were controlled for. The researchers concluded that a significant number of lives could be saved by better HR systems, and in particular better appraisal. So, it seems that appraisal is not just important, in some settings it is a life-and-death matter. It *can* be successful, but only if it is applied in a coherent and evidence-based way. Appraisal can contribute more when integrated into the framework of a performance management system, and in these circumstances looks likely to achieve more from the organisation's point of view than it ever would by itself.

Yet despite becoming a little more sophisticated, too often performance appraisal remains fairly crude. Part of the problem is that the level of understanding of what motivates people at work is not all that it might be. I greatly enjoyed the contribution from the floor at the end of a paper given at the Chartered Institute for Personnel and Development National Conference; the speaker rose and said, with complete confidence, that there are only two things that motivate people: fear and greed. The thinking behind some appraisal systems is obviously based on a similar premise. However, until we can do somewhat better than at present in our analysis, it is going to remain difficult to make appraisal fully effective as a motivating force. Giving greater emphasis to understanding motivation in appraisal training will help, but more research is also needed to improve our basic knowledge. Part of that effort needs to be directed at the appraisal interview itself. We are closer to getting the processes and procedures right, but in doing so have perhaps lost sight of making them user-friendly and relevant to the participants and their needs, as was noted in Chapter 2. A deeper understanding of the dynamics of the appraisal interview, and how to conduct it on both sides so as to make it a more motivating and satisfying experience – and putting this across in training – would be a big step forward.

The lessening of central control in organisations and the empowerment of employees places more responsibility than ever on the shoulders of the individual. There is a danger here that the pressures can get out of proportion, and it is no coincidence that all the social and organisational changes referred to in this book have been accompanied by a burgeoning concern – backed up by evidence – about the levels of work stress. Better performance does not come from simply setting goals, giving a small amount of extra financial reward and exhorting people to go for improved quality and customer care. It comes from a better and more even relationship, or contract, between organisations and individuals, one that recognises individual differences in needs and capacities, and which accepts that, beyond certain levels, asking more of people is actually counter-productive. So, alongside the performance culture and the learning organisation, we have to put something else – the caring organisation (Newell, 2002). Only within that kind of environment will appraisal realise its full potential for offering routes to improved performance.

Discussion points and questions

How would you apply appraisal as a set of linked processes in your organisation? What would you have to change to bring this about and make it work?

How would you 'sell' the need for this new approach to top management and others in your organisation?

Key references

Newell, S. (2002) *Creating The Healthy Organisation: Well being, Diversity and Ethics at Work*. Thomson Learning (Psychology@Work Series): London.

Patterson, M., West, M., Lawthom, R. and Nickell, S. (1998) *Issues in People Management*. IPD Report No 22. Institute for Personnel and Development: London (now CIPD, London).

West, M. and Johnson, R. (2002) A matter of life and death. *People Management*, 21 February.

Appendix A
Example of appraisal scheme documentation

The appraisal documentation presented here, and the scheme it describes, is not in any sense supposed to be a 'model' for others to follow. It simply provides an example of a fairly basic and straightforward approach to appraisal and incorporates a fair amount of involvement and self-appraisal on the part of the appraisee. It contains an element of objective-setting, but avoids the use of rating scales and does not seek to come up with some overall performance measure. The amount of paperwork is kept to a minimum. Variations of it have been used successfully in both the private and public sectors in past years, but it does represent a rather minimal approach in the sense that it stands alone and is not closely linked with other HR procedures or with business planning as a whole.

This example also provides an illustration of some of the more detailed guidance that may be given to appraisers about how to handle the appraisal interview. Normally, one would hope that this simply summarises what would have been put over in proper appraisal training.

Anyco Ltd
Performance appraisal scheme.
Appraisers' notes for guidance.

Aim of the appraisal scheme

The purpose of the company appraisal scheme is to make the most effective use of its staff resources by developing them in a systematic way, in the interests both of the company and of the individuals being appraised. It provides those appraised with a formal opportunity to present what they feel to be their main achievements over the last year, to discuss their performance in general and to make plans for the year ahead. The scheme is a highly participative one, with a great deal of emphasis on self-appraisal, ensuring that staff have a major role in determining their own development.

It is also very much future-oriented, being chiefly concerned with setting objectives and with improving performance.

One of the most frequent problems that arises with appraisals is that they become too closely identified with pay and promotion. Inevitably, there is a link between appraisal and rewards, but it is by no means a direct one. In terms of merit pay, appraisal is but one input to the decision – several other factors are taken into account. In the case of promotion, this is based on performance over a number of years, not just one. It is therefore of prime importance that the appraisal session is conducted in such a way that it emphasises (a) the development of the individual in the more immediate future, rather than the longer-term issue of promotion (b) the establishment of priorities and achievement of aims that reflect not only the needs of the individual, but also the wider needs of the company.

What follows is a guide to the appraisal process, and should be looked at in conjunction with the appraisal forms.

Procedure

- Hand the appraisee the self-appraisal form and agree a date for the actual appraisal discussion, preferably in about a week's time. Check that the individual concerned has got a copy of the guidance notes for appraisees.
- The appraisal discussion takes place, centred on the headings of the self-appraisal form.
- On the basis of this discussion, the agreed main action points and objectives for the year ahead are subsequently noted on the appraisal review form by the appraiser.
- Return the completed appraisal review form to the appraisee for signature as a correct record of the action points, aims and priorities.
- Give a copy of the appraisal review form to the appraisee, keep a copy for yourself, and send one to HR.

Preparing the appraisal session

Your starting-point will be the headings of the different sections of the self-appraisal form – you may not have the appraisee's completed form in advance of the meeting, but you need to look at the headings and think about what may come up, what you would expect to come up and what you would *want* to come up under each one:

In section 1, the appraisees are being asked to list their main responsibilities as they see them. It is always worth starting an appraisal discussion by checking that you and the appraisee have the same picture of what the job actually entails at the present time; it is very easy for it to have changed (particularly in a period of rapid development) without one or both parties fully appreciating the fact. *What do you expect to see written here?*

The objectives set in the previous appraisal need to be reviewed, and the appraisees have been asked to look back at these under section 2 of the self-appraisal form. *In preparing, you need to assess the objectives in terms of the extent to which they have been met, exceeded or not achieved.* What evidence are your assessments based on?

Sections 3 and 4 ask the appraisees to look back and identify the strengths they have demonstrated and the areas where they feel they could improve. It is important here to recognise that the appraisees are being invited to assess themselves by their own standards, not to compare themselves with other people. In other words, an individual may feel that he/she could have done certain things better, but that does not necessarily mean they have done them any less well than anyone else would have. Correspondingly, because someone has identified what they feel to be a strength does not of itself mean they have performed better in that respect than have their peers. *You will wish to give some thought to what you see as the more and less positive aspects of the individual's performance in the period under review.*

Under section 5, the appraisee is asked to suggest how performance might be improved in the year ahead. What do you think he/she should do – *and what can you do to help them where you feel they need to improve?* In section 6, the appraisees have been invited to think about their main objectives for the year ahead. Taking account of the Business Plan and the departmental objectives, *what do you feel should be the key objectives for each appraisee?*

The appraisal interview

The appraisal interview will take the headings of the self-appraisal form as its starting point, so the person appraised has a major responsibility for making the discussion a fruitful and constructive one. However, the more effort both parties have put in to preparing the interview, the more they will get out of it. There is no one correct way to handle an appraisal interview, but there are some general guidelines that can be given; if followed, they will help you carry out an effective interview and to avoid some of the most common pitfalls.

- Clear an adequate period of time for the discussion (better to err on the side of too long than too short, so two hours would not be inappropriate). Make sure that you will not be interrupted during the interview.

- Start by reminding the appraisee of the purpose of the appraisal and of the interview; make clear that you consider this as an important review process.

- Use the self-appraisal form as an agenda, and work through its headings. You may find it best to take them in the sequence printed, but there is no need to stick to this rigidly. There is no requirement for the appraisee to actually show you what he/she has written on the form.

- Throughout the interview, put the onus on the appraisee to make the running. Ask the individual to expand on his/her own comments under each section of the form as you deal with them. When the appraisee has had the opportunity to say his/her own piece, add your own comments and discuss the issues generally.

- Do the achievements and the areas where the person feels he/she has done less well coincide with your own perceptions of their performance? If there are any significant discrepancies, they will have to be discussed. *Make sure you are considering the whole period under review – and not just what has happened recently.*

- Be sure to give full recognition to the appraisee's achievements and strengths; note specific examples of good work. It is particularly helpful to express appreciation of tasks which have not come easily and which have called for real effort or persistence on the individual's part.

- When tackling performance weaknesses (remember that there may be aspects of the person's performance that are only weak in comparison with that individual's overall performance, and not weak in comparison with other people), commend appraisees for their frankness where they have identified real shortcomings. Discuss them firmly but constructively, as ever trying as far as possible to get the appraisees to produce their own ideas and plans for overcoming the problems. There may be cases where the weaknesses mentioned by the appraisee on the self-appraisal form do not reflect the deficiencies in performance that you have identified. In such instances, you will need to address the difference of views in the appraisal discussion. Where an individual has identified an aspect of performance that has fallen short of their own standards but which you perceive as being perfectly satisfactory, little more than some reassurance may be needed. Potentially the most difficult disagreement is where you perceive weakness and the appraisee does not. In dealing with a situation of this kind:

  - be specific; make sure you have evidence to back up your comments
  - do not make vague and unsupported assertions

- try to be firm but positive, keeping the emphasis on what constructive action can be taken; the aim is to improve performance, not to demotivate the individual
- do not tackle more than two areas of weakness in any depth; this is as much as most people can take without becoming defensive
- confine your comments to remediable weaknesses; there is little point in commenting on aspects of the individual which are not amenable to change. The emphasis is on appraising job performance, not the appraisee's personality.

In identifying what action could be taken to improve performance (Section 5 of the form), you need to assess, and perhaps discuss, whether the individual has made suggestions that are realistic and practical. To what extent has he/she taken responsibility for the action needed as opposed to projecting it on to others?

Section 6 asks for suggestions on the objectives for the year ahead. You will want to evaluate and (through discussion) possibly modify these suggested objectives in terms of:

- how demanding they are
- how they relate to the individual's personal development
- how they relate to the wider picture of the department's and the company's objectives and priorities, and any anticipated developments in the near future
- how their achievement can be measured, where appropriate in terms of both *time* and *end results*.

Where there are some changes to the individual's responsibilities being suggested, be sure to put them in the wider context of the needs of both department and the company.

When discussing training and development needs, look back at what has been identified as being the individual's relative strengths and weaknesses; how can the former be capitalised on, and how can the latter be improved through formal training, changes in duties, etc? Amongst other things, you should also consider the likely work demands in the period ahead and reflect on whether these will call for updating existing skills or knowledge or the development of new capabilities on the appraisee's part. Be careful not to make promises on development issues that cannot be fulfilled.

At the end of the interview, summarise the main points of the discussion: in particular, each party should summarise what action they have agreed to take and what should be entered on the appraisal review form. Make sure that the appraisee has nothing further to raise.

The appraisal review form may be completed in the interview itself, or very shortly thereafter (in which case, return it to the individual quickly for signature, while the discussion is still fresh in mind). Both parties sign the form and keep copies.

Self-appraisal form section headings

1   Briefly list the main responsibilities of your job, and roughly what percentage of your time is spent on each.
2   Looking back to the objectives agreed at the last appraisal, which ones have been (a) exceeded, (b) met, (c) not achieved? What evidence have you to base these assessments on?
3   What do you feel you have done particularly well *by your own standards* over the last 12 months?
4   What do you feel you have done least well *by your own standards* over the past 12 months?
5   To help improve your performance in the job still further, what additional steps could be taken by:

(a)   you
(b)   your boss
(c)   others in the company?

6   What are your principal objectives for the year ahead? List four or five.
7   What changes, if any, in your responsibilities would you like to see in the near future?
8   What training and other steps could be taken to further your career development?
9   Is there anything else you wish to raise in the appraisal?

Appraisal review form headings

1   Review of past objectives:

Objectives   Extent Achieved   Measures/Evidence

2   Action to be taken by:

(a)   The appraisee
(b)   The appraiser
(c)   Others in the company

3   Objectives for the coming year:

Objective   *Priority*   *Form of Measurement*
1
2
3
4
5

Signed as an agreed record:
Appraisee
Appraiser
Date

Anyco Ltd
Performance appraisal scheme.
Appraisees' notes for guidance.

Aim of the appraisal scheme

The purpose of the company appraisal scheme is to make the most effective use of its staff resources by developing them in a systematic way, in the interests both of the company and of the individuals being appraised. It provides you with a formal opportunity to present what you feel to be your main achievements over the last year, to discuss your performance in general and to make plans for the year ahead. The scheme is a highly participative one, with a great deal of emphasis on self-appraisal, ensuring that you have a major role in determining your own development. It is also very much future-oriented, being chiefly concerned with setting objectives and with improving performance.

What follows is a guide to the appraisal process, and should be looked at in conjunction with the appraisal forms.

Procedure

1   You and the appraiser agree a date for the appraisal discussion, preferably in about a week's time. The appraiser will give you a copy of the self-appraisal form.
2   You complete the self-appraisal form.
3   The appraisal discussion takes place, centred on the headings of the self-appraisal form. You do not need to give the form itself to the appraiser.

4   On the basis of this discussion, the agreed main action points and objectives for the year ahead are subsequently noted on the Appraisal Review Form by the appraiser, who returns it to you for signature as a correct record. Both of you keep copies.

Completing the self-appraisal form

The headings are straightforward enough, but there are some additional points that need to be made by way of guidance:

- In section 1, you are being asked to list your main responsibilities as you see them, and to give a rough estimate of the percentage of time you spend on them. It is always worth starting an appraisal discussion by checking that you and the appraiser have the same picture of what the job actually entails at present; it is very easy for it to have changed (particularly in a period of rapid development) without one or both parties fully appreciating the fact.
- You need to look back at last year's appraisal form and confirm the objectives agreed. The extent to which these objectives have been achieved will be discussed, along with the circumstances that have had an impact on your performance, under the second section heading.
- Sections 3 and 4 ask you to identify what you have done best during the period under review and the areas where you feel you could have done better. It is important here to recognise that you are being invited to assess yourself by your own standards, not to compare yourself with other people. In other words, you may feel that you could have done certain things better (nobody is perfect.), but that does not necessarily mean you have done them less well than anyone else would have. Try to pick out the two or three most important things under each heading. Be *realistic* in your self-appraisal – it will impress nobody if you try to make out that you have done everything brilliantly and have no scope for improvement.
- In completing section 5, make your suggestions as realistic and practical as possible; resist the temptation to suggest the complete reorganisation of the company or changing government policy!
- When listing your main objectives for the period ahead under section 6, consider how you would like to measure your success in achieving them; they will be reviewed again at the next appraisal, where appropriate (in some instances, circumstances may have changed in such a way as to make the objectives less relevant). The objectives set should reflect priorities for performance development rather than simply

routine work. In framing them, consider the wider perspective of the needs of your department and of the company as a whole.

- The question of what changes you would like to see in your responsibilities in the future must, again, be tempered by realism (section 7). The appraiser may of course have some suggestions to make in this context.
- Section 8 deals with training and development. In thinking about your needs in this area, look back at what you identified as being the strengths you identified in section 3 – how can these be capitalised on? How can the less successful aspects of your performance you mentioned be tackled through changes in job content, through training or by other means? Will any changes in the demands made on you in the near future require that some steps be taken now to equip you to deal with them?

The appraisal interview

The agenda for appraisal interview will be based on the headings of the self-appraisal form, so the starting point for the whole discussion will be *your* ideas and perceptions (though the appraiser will obviously contribute his or her views too). This means that the major responsibility for making the appraisal interview a successful and effective vehicle for constructive action will be *yours*. The more thought and preparation you have done for it beforehand, the more you and the company as a whole will get out of it.

There may be some occasions where you and the person doing the appraisal do not have the same view – and this can be especially sensitive where it concerns how well you have performed in some respect. Try not to respond to suggestions that there may be areas where you could do better as if they reflected a personal criticism – they are about doing the job. Listen, and be as objective as possible. You and the appraiser should as far as possible focus on the *evidence*, rather than unsupported opinion or feelings, and discuss it calmly and carefully.

Appendix B

Attitude measures

There are a number of questionnaire measures that are both relevant to assessing broad employee attitudes and motivation, and are readily available. These include:

- The Organisational Commitment Scale produced by Cook and Wall (1980). This breaks down into three components: organisational loyalty, organisational identification and organisational involvement.
- The Job Satisfaction Scale (Warr *et al.*, 1979). This taps satisfaction with 15 different aspects of work, broadly grouped into intrinsic and extrinsic job satisfaction.

Both of the above, and several others (covering factors such as goal clarity), were used in Part 2 of the (former) IPM report on performance management, and the reader can find the questionnaire items and various other details given there by Fletcher and Williams (IPM, 1992). The report data, about a number of private and public sector organisations, should facilitate making comparisons for other companies using the scales. There are, however, other measures, such as:

- Job Involvement (Lodahl and Kejner, 1965). This measures the extent to which a person identifies psychologically with work and the importance of work in their self-image.
- Organisational Commitment – another measure of this construct, provided by Mowday *et al.* (1979) and consisting of 15 items.

References

Adsit, D. J., London, M., Crom, S. and Jones, D. (1997) Cross-cultural differences in upward ratings in a multinational company. *The International Journal of Human Resource Management*, 8, pp. 385–401.

Alimo-Metcalfe, B. and Alban-Metcalfe, Juliette (2003) It don't matter if you're Black or White: Not according to 360-feedback. *Proceedings of the BPS Annual Occupational Psychology Conference*, Brighton, 8–10 January, pp. 63–66.

Antonioni, D. and Park, H. (2001) The relationship between rater affect and three sources of 360 degree feedback ratings. *Journal of Management*, 27, pp. 479–495.

Archer, J. C., Norcini, J. and Davies, H. A. (2005) Use of SPRAT for peer review of paediatricians in training. *British Medical Journal*, 330(7502), pp. 1251–1253.

Arnold, J. and Schoonman, W. (2002) Maintaining and enhancing motivation as a contribution to organizational effectiveness. In I. T. Robertson, M. Callinan and D. Bartram (eds) *Organizational Effectiveness: The Role of Psychology*. Wiley: Chichester.

Arthur, W., Day, E. A., McNelly, T. L. and Edens, P. S. (2003) A meta-analysis of the criterion-related validity of assessment centre dimensions. *Personnel Psychology*, 56, pp. 125–154.

Arvey, R. D. and Murphy, K. R. (1998) Performance evaluation in work settings. *Annual Review of Psychology*, 49, pp. 141–168.

Atchley, S., Coomber, J. and Goodge, P. (2001) Guidelines for using 360 degree software. *Selection & Development Review*, 17, pp. 7–9.

Atwater, L., Ostroff, C, Waldman, D., Robie, C. and Johnson, K. M. (2005) Self-other agreement: Comparing its relationship with performance in the US and Europe. *International Journal of Selection and Assessment*, 13, pp. 25–40.

Atwater, L. and Brett, J. (2006) Feedback format: Does it influence manager's reactions to feedback? *Journal of Occupational and Organizational Psychology*, 79, pp. 517–532.

Audit Commission (1995a) *Paying the Piper: People and Pay Management in Local Government*. HMSO: London.

Audit Commission (1995b) *Calling the Tune: Performance Management in Local Government*. HMSO: London.

Audit Commission (1995c) *Management Handbook: Paying the Piper and Calling the Tune*. HMSO: London.

Bailey, C. and Fletcher, C. (2002a) When do other people's opinions matter? The credibility of feedback from co-workers. BPS Occupational Psychology Conference, Blackpool, January.

Bailey, C. and Fletcher, C. (2002b) The impact of multiple source feedback on management development: Findings from a longitudinal study. *Journal of Organizational Behaviour*, 23, pp. 853–867.

Bailey, C. and Austin, M. (2006) 360 degree feedback and development outcomes: The role of feedback characteristics, self-efficacy, and importance of feedback dimensions to focal managers' current role. *International Journal of Selection and Assessment*, 14, pp. 51–66.

Bailey, C. and Fletcher, C. (2007) Performance management and appraisal – an international perspective. In M. M. Harris (ed.) *The Handbook of Research in International Human Resource Management*. Organization Management Series, Lawrence Erlbaum: Mahwah, NJ.

Bartram, D. (2007) Work profiling and job analysis. In N. Chmiel (ed.) *Introduction to Work and Organizational Psychology: A European Perspective*. 2nd edn. Blackwell: Oxford.

Beehr, T. A., Ivanitskaya, A, L., Hansen, C. P., Erofeev, D. and Gudanowski, D. M. (2001) Evaluation of 360 degree feedback ratings: Relationships with each other and with performance and selection predictors. *Journal of Organizational Behaviour*, 22, pp. 775–788.

Bertua, C., Anderson, N. and Salgado, J. F. (2005) The predictive validity of cognitive ability tests: A UK meta-anlaysis. *Journal of Occupational and Organizational Psychology*, 78, pp. 387–410.

Bevan, S. and Thompson, M. (1991) Performance Management at the Crossroads. *Personnel Management*, November, pp. 36–39.

Bevan, S. and Thompson, M. (1992) *Performance Management in the UK: An Analysis of the Issues*. Institute of Personnel Management: London (now CIPD, London).

Bono, J. E. and Colbert, A. E. (2005) Understanding responses to multi-source feedback: The role of core self-evaluations. *Personnel Psychology*, 58, pp. 171–203.

Boyatzis, R. (1982) *The Competent Manager*. Wiley: New York.

Brannick, M. T., Levine, E. L. and Morqueson, F. P. (2007) *Job and Work Analysis*. Sage: Thousand Oaks, CA.

Brett, J. F. and Atwater, L. E. (2001) 360 degree feedback: Accuracy, reactions and perceptions of usefulness. *Journal of Applied Psychology*, 86, pp. 930–942.

Briscoe, J. P. and Hall, D. T. (1999) Grooming and picking leaders using competency frameworks: Do they work? An alternative approach and new guidelines for practice. *Organizational Dynamics*, Autumn, p. 37.

Brutus, S., Derayeh, M., Fletcher, C., Bailey, C., Velazquez, P., Shi, K., Simon, C. and Labath, V. (2006) Multisource feedback systems: A six-country comparative analysis. *International Journal of Human Resource Management*, 17, pp. 1888–1906.

Brutus, S., Fletcher, C. and Bailey, C. (2007) The influence of independent self-construal on rater self-efficacy in performance appraisal. Academy of Management Annual Conference, Philadelphia, July.

Carrick, P. and Williams, R. (1999) Development centres: A review of assumptions. *Human Resource Management Journal*, 9, pp. 77–92.

Catano, V. M., Darr, W. and Campbell, C. A. (2007) Performance appraisal of behavior-based competencies: A reliable and valid procedure. *Personnel Psychology*, 60, pp. 201–230.

CIPD (2003) *Reward Management 2003: Survey Report*. Chartered Institute of Personnel and Development: London.

Cleveland, J. N. and Murphy, K. R. (1992) Analyzing performance appraisal as goal-directed behavior. *Research in Personnel and Human Resources Management*, 10, pp. 121–185.

Clifford, C. L. and Bennett, H. (1997) Best Practice in 360-Degree Feedback. *Selection and Development Review*, 13(2), pp. 6–9.

Conway, J. M., Lombardo, K. and Sanders, K. C. (2001) A meta-analysis of incremental validity and nomological networks for subordinate and peer ratings. *Human Performance*, 14, pp. 267–303.

Conway, N. and Briner, R. B. (2005) *Understanding Psychological Contracts at Work: A Critical Evaluation of Theory and Research*. Oxford University Press: Oxford.

Cook, J. D. and Wall, T. D. (1980) New work attitude measures of trust, organisational commitment, and personal need non-fulfilment. *Journal of Occupational Psychology*, 53, pp. 39–52.

Cook, J. D., Hepworth, S. J., Wall, T. D. and Warr, P. B. (1981) *The Experience of Work*. Academic Press: London.

Currall, S. C., Towler, A. J., Judge, T. A. and Kohn, L. (2005) Pay satisfaction and organizational outcomes. *Personnel Psychology*, 58, pp. 613–640.

Day, A. L. and Carroll, S. A. (2003) Situational and patterned behaviour description interviews: A comparison of their validity, correlates and perceived fairness. *Human Performance*, 16, pp. 25–47.

DeNisi, A. S. (1996) *Cognitive Approach to Performance Appraisal: A Programme of Research*. Routledge: London.

Department for Education and Skills (2006) *Education (School Teacher Performance Management) (England) Regulations 2006*. DfES: London.

Department for Education and Skills: Rewards and Incentive Group (2007) *Teachers' and Head Teachers Performance Management*. DfES: London.

Department of Health (2006) *Good Doctors, Safer Patients: Proposals to Strengthen the System to Assure and Improve the Performance of Doctors and to Protect the Safety of Patients*, DH: London.

Department of Health (2007) *Trust, Assurance and Safety: The Regulation of Health Professionals*. DH White Paper, The Stationery Office: London.

Donovan, J. J. (2001) Work motivation. In N. Anderson, D. Ones, H. Sinangil and C. Viswesvaran (eds) *International Handbook of Industrial, Work and Organizational Psychology*. Sage: London.

Dulewicz, S. V. and Herbert, P. (1992) Personality, competences leadership style and managerial effectiveness. *Henley Management College Working Paper Series*, HWP 14/92.

Dulewicz, S. V. and Herbert, P. (1996) General management competences and personality: A 7-year follow-up. *Henley Management College Working Paper Series*, HWP 96/21.

Dunnette, M. D., Campbell, J. P. and Hellervik, L. W. (1968) *Job Behaviour Scales for Penney Co. Department Managers*. Personnel Decisions: Minneapolis, MN.

Early, P. C. and Gibson, C. B. (1998) Taking stock in our progress on individualism-collectivism: 100 years of solidarity and community. *Journal of Management*, 24, pp. 265–304.

Early, P. C. and Stubblebine, P. (1989) Intercultural assessment of performance feedback. *Group & Organization Studies*, 14, pp. 161–181.

Eder, R. W. and Harris, M. M. (1999) *The Employment Interview Handbook*. Sage: Thousand Oaks, CA.

Egan, G. (2001) *The Skilled Helper: A Systematic Approach to Effective Helping*. 7th edn. Counselling series. Brooks/Cole: Pacific Grove, CA.

Elenkov, S. E. (1998) Can American management concepts work in Russia? A cross-cultural comparative study. *California Management Review*, 40, pp. 133–156.

Erdogan, B., Kraimer, M. L. and Liden, R. C. (2001) Procedural justice as a two-dimensional construct: An examination in the performance appraisal context, *Journal of Applied Behavioural Science*, 37, pp. 205–222.

Erez. M. and Earley, P. C. (1993) *Culture, Self-Identity, and Work*. Oxford University Press: Oxford.

Erikson, A. and Allen, T. (2003) Linking 360 feedback to business outcome measures. Paper presented at the 18th SIOP Conference, Orlando, Florida.

Fernandez, D. R., Carlson, D. S., Stepina, L. P. and Nicholson, J. D. (1997) Hofstede's country classification 25 years later. *The Journal of Social Psychology*, 137, pp. 43–54.

Fletcher, C. (1978) Manager–subordinate communication and leadership style: A field study of their relationship to perceived outcomes of appraisal interviews. *Personnel Review*, 7, pp. 59–62.

Fletcher, C. (1991) Candidates' reactions to assessment centres and their outcomes: A longitudinal study. *Journal of Occupational Psychology*, 64, pp. 117–127.

Fletcher, C. (1997) Self-awareness – a neglected attribute in selection and assessment. *International Journal of Selection and Assessment*, 5, pp. 183–187.

Fletcher, C. (1999) The implications of research on gender differences in self assessments and 360 degree appraisal. *Human Resource Management Journal*, 9, pp. 39–46.

Fletcher, C. (2001) Performance appraisal and performance management: The developing research agenda. *Journal of Occupational and Organizational Psychology*, 74, pp. 473–487.

Fletcher, C. (2002) Appraisal – an individual psychological analysis. In S. Sonnentag (ed.) *The Psychological Management of Individual Performance: A Handbook in the Psychology of Management in Organisations*. Wiley: Chichester.

Fletcher, C. (2006) Where the assessment centre may not reach: Assessing candidates for the top levels in a UK Government context. 33rd International Congress on the Assessment Centre Method, London, September.

Fletcher, C. and Williams, R. (1992a) *Performance Management in the UK: An Analysis of the Issues*. Institute of Personnel Management: London (now CIPD, London).

Fletcher, C. and Williams, R. (1992b) *Performance Appraisal and Career Development*. 2nd edn. Stanley Thornes: London.

Fletcher, C. and Williams, R. (1996) Performance management, job satisfaction and organisational commitment. *British Journal of Management*, 7, pp. 169–179.

Fletcher, C. and Anderson, N. (1998) A superficial assessment. *People Management*, 4(10), pp. 44–46.

Fletcher, C. and Baldry, C. (1999) Multi-source feedback systems: A research perspective. In C. L. Cooper and I. T. Robertson (eds) *International Review of Industrial and Organizational Psychology Vol 14*. Wiley: New York/London.

Fletcher, C. and Perry, E. (2001) Performance appraisal and feedback: A consideration of national culture and a review of contemporary trends. In N. Anderson, D. Ones, H. Sinangil and C. Viswesvaran (eds) *International Handbook of Industrial, Work and Organizational Psychology*. Sage: Thousand Oaks, CA.

Fletcher, C. and Bailey, C. (2003) Assessing self awareness; some issues and methods. *Journal of Managerial Psychology*, 18, pp. 395–404.

Fletcher, C., Lovatt, C. and Baldry, C. (1997) A study of state, trait and test anxiety and their relationship to assessment centre performance. *Journal of Social Behaviour and Personality*, 12, pp. 205–214.

Fletcher, C., Baldry, C. and Cunningham-Snell, N. (1998) The psychometric properties of 360-degree feedback: An empirical study and a cautionary tale. *International Journal of Selection and Assessment*, 6, pp. 19–34.

Fullerton, J. and Kandola, R. (1998) *Diversity in Action*. Institute of Personnel and Development: London (now CIPD, London).

Garland, H. and Price, K. H. (1977) Attitudes towards women in management, and attributions of their success and failure in managerial positions. *Journal of Applied Psychology*, 62, pp. 29–33.

Gaugler, B. Rosenthal, D. Thornton and Bentson (1987) Meta analysis of assessment centre validity. *Journal of Applied Psychology*, 72(3).

Gillen, T. (1998) *Handling the Appraisal Discussion* (Management Shapers). Institute of Personnel and Development: London (now CIPD, London).

Gioia, D. A. and Longenecker, C. O. (1994). Delving into the dark side: The politics of executive appraisal. *Organizational Dynamics*, 22, pp. 47–58.

Glaze, T. (1989) Cadbury's Dictionary of Competence. *Personnel Management*, July, pp. 44–48.

Greatrex, J. and Phillips, P. (1989) Oiling the wheels of competence. *Personnel Management*, August, pp. 36–39.

Greguras, G. J., Robie, C., Schleicher, D. J. and Goff, M. (2003) A field study of the effects of rating purpose on the quality of multisource ratings. *Personnel Psychology*, 56, pp. 1–21.

Guest, D. E., Michie, J., Conway, N. and Sheehan, M. (2003) Human resource management and corporate performance in the UK. *British Journal of Industrial Relations*, 41, pp. 291–314.

Hall, D. T. and Moss, J. (1998) The new protean career contract: Helping organizations and employees adapt. *Organizational Dynamics*, Winter, pp. 22–37.

Halman, F. and Fletcher, C. (2000) The impact of development center participation and the role of individual differences in changing self assessments. *Journal of Occupational and Organizational Psychology*, 73, pp. 423–442.

Handy, L., Devine, M. and Heath, L. (1996) *Feedback: Unguided Missile or Powerful Weapon?* Report published by the Ashridge Management Research Group, Ashridge Management College.

Harris, M. M. (1989) Reconsidering the employment interview: A review of recent literature and suggestions for future research. *Personnel Psychology*, 42, pp. 691–726.

Harris M. M. (ed.) (2007) *The Handbook of Research in International Human Resource Management*. Organization Management Series. Lawrence Erlbaum: Mahwah, NJ.

Higgs, D. (2003) *Review of the Role and Effectiveness of the Non-executive Director.* Department of Trade and Industry: London.

Higgs, M. and Dulewicz, V. (1999) *Making Sense of Emotional Intelligence.* NFER-Nelson: Windsor.

Hirsh, W. (2006) *Improving Performance Through Appraisal Dialogues.* Corporate Research Forum: London.

Hofstede, G. (1980) *Culture's Consequences: International Differences in Work-related Values.* Sage: Beverly Hills, CA.

Hofstede, G. (2001) *Cultures' Consequences: Comparing Values, Behaviors, Institutions and Organizations Across Nations.* Sage: Thousand Oaks, CA.

Holdsworth, R. (1991) Appraisal. In F. Neale (ed.) *The Handbook of Performance Management.* Institute of Personnel Management: London (now CIPD, London).

Hollyford, S. and Whiddett, S. (2002) *The Competencies Handbook. 2nd edn.* Chartered Institute of Personnel and Development: London.

Huo, Y. P. and Von Glinow, M. A. (1995) On transplanting human resource practices to China: A culture driven approach. *International Journal of Manpower*, 16, pp. 3–15.

Industrial Society (2001) *No 86 Managing Performance.* Managing Best Practice series, The Industrial Society: London.

IPM (1992) *Performance Management in the UK: An Analysis of the Issues.* Institute of Personnel Management: London (now CIPD, London).

Jacobs, R., Kafry, D. and Zedeck, S. (1980) Expectations of behaviourally anchored rating scales. *Personnel Psychology*, 33, pp. 595–640.

Jackson, D. and Rothstein, M. (1993) 'Evaluating personality testing in personnel selection'. *The Psychologist*, 6, pp. 8–11.

Jones, L. and Fletcher, C. (2002) Self assessment in a selection situation: An evaluation of different measurement approaches. *Journal of Occupational and Organizational Psychology*, 75, pp. 145–161.

Jones, L. and Fletcher, C. (2004) The impact of measurement conditions on the validity of self-assessment in a selection setting. *European Journal of Work and Organizational Psychology*, 13, pp. 101–111.

Kagitcibasi, C. and Berry, J. W. (1989) Cross-cultural psychology: Current research and trends. *Annual Review Psychology*, 40, pp. 493–531.

Kandola, R. and Galpin, M. (2000) 360 degree feedback goes under the microscope. *Insights*, Volume 1, pp. 6–7. Pearn Kandola: Oxford.

Kanji, G. K. and Asher, M. (1996) *100 Methods for Total Quality Management.* Sage: London.

Kikoski, J. F. (1999) Effective communication in the performance appraisal interview: Face-to-face communication for public managers in the culturally diverse workplace. *Public Personnel Management*, 28, pp. 301–323.

King, N. and Anderson, N. (2002) *Managing Innovation and Change; A Critical Guide for Organisations.* Thomson Learning (Psychology@Work Series): London.

Kluger, A. N. and DeNisi, A. (1996) The effects of feedback interventions on performance: A historical review, a meta-analysis, and a preliminary feedback intervention theory. *Psychological Bulletin*, 119, pp. 254–284.

Koopman, P., Den Hartog, D. and Konrad, E. (1999) National culture and leadership profiles in Europe: Some results from the GLOBE study. *European Journal of Work and Organizational Psychology*, 8(4), pp. 503–520.

Krajewski, H. T., Goffin, R. D., McCarthy, J. M., Rothstein, M. G. and Johnston, N. (2006) Comparing the validity of structured interviews for managerial level employees: Should we look to the past or focus on the future? *Journal of Occupational and Organizational Psychology*, 79, pp. 411–432.

Krause, D. E., Kersting, M., Heggestad, E. D. and Thornton, G. C. (2006) Incremental validity of assessment centre ratings over cognitive ability tests: A study at executive management level. *International Journal of Selection and Assessment*, 14, pp. 360–371.

Kudisch, J. D., Ladd, R. T. and Dobbins, G. H. (1997) New evidence on the construct validity of diagnostic assessment centres: The findings may not be so troubling after all. *Journal of Social Behaviour and Personality (special issue on assessment centres)*, 12, pp. 129–144.

Latham, G. P. (1989) The reliability, validity, and practicality of the situational interview. In R. W. Eder and G. R. Ferris (eds) *The Employment Interview*. Sage: Beverly Hills, CA.

Latham, G. P. and Saari, L. M. (1984) Do people do what they say? Further studies on the situational interview. *Journal of Applied Psychology*, 69, pp. 569–573.

Latham, G. P. and Sue-Chan, C. (1996) A legally defensible interview for selecting the best. In R. S. Barrett (ed.) *Fair Employment Strategies in Human Resource Management*. Quorum Books/Greenwood Publishing: Westport, CT.

Latham, G. P., Saari, L. M., Pursell, E. D. and Campion, M. A. (1980) The situational interview. *Journal of Applied Psychology*, 65, pp. 422–427.

Lefkowitz, J. (2000) The role of interpersonal affective regard in supervisory performance ratings: A literature review and proposed causal model. *Journal of Occupational and Organizational Pyschology*, 73, pp. 67–85.

Lievens, F. (2001) Assessors and the use of assessment centre dimensions: A fresh look at a troubling issue. *Journal of Organizational Behavior*, 22, pp. 203–221.

Locke, E. A. and Latham, G. P. (1990) *A Theory of Goal Setting and Task Performance*. Prentice Hall: Englewood Cliffs, NJ.

Lodahl, T. M. and Kejner, M. (1965) The definition and measurement of job involvement. *Journal of Applied Psychology*, 49, pp. 24–33.

London, M. and Smither, J. W. (1995) Can multi-source feedback change self awareness and behavior? Theory-based applications and directions for research. *Personnel Psychology*, 48, pp. 803–839.

Longenecker, C. O. and Gioia, D. A. (1988) Neglected at the top: Executives talk about executive appraisal. *Sloan Management Review*. Winter, pp. 41–47.

Lyons, N., Caesar, S. and McEwen, A. (2006) *The Appraiser's Handbook: A Guide for Doctors*. Radcliffe Publishing: Oxford.

Mabe, P. A. and West, S. G. (1982) Validity of self-evaluation of ability: A review and meta-analysis. *Journal of Applied Psychology*, 67, pp. 280–296.

McDowell, A. and Fletcher, C. (2004) Employee development – an Organizational Justice perspective. *Personnel Review*, 33, pp. 8–29.

McFarland, L. A., Yun, G., Harold, C. M., Viera, L. and Moore, L. G. (2005) An examination of impression management use and effectiveness across assessment center exercises: The role of competency demands. *Personnel Psychology*, 58, pp. 949–980.

Maier, N. R. F. (1958) Three types of appraisal interview. *Personnel*, March/April, pp. 27–40.

Meyer, H. H. (1980) Self-appraisal of job performance. *Personnel Psychology*, 33, pp. 291–295.

Meyer, H. H., Kay, E. and French, J. R. P. (1965) Split roles in performance appraisal. *Harvard Business Review*, 43, pp. 123–129.

Michaels, E., Handfield-Jones, H. and Axelrod, B. (2001) *The War for Talent*. Harvard Business School Publishing: Boston, MA.

Mowday, R. T., Steers, R. M. and Porter, L. W. (1979) The Measurement of Organisational Commitment. *Journal of Vocational Behaviour*, 14, pp. 224–247.

Nathan, B. R., Mohrman, A. M. and Milliman, J. (1991) Interpersonal relations as a context for the effects of appraisal interviews on performance and satisfaction: A longitudinal study. *Academy of Management Journal*, 34, pp. 352–369.

Nealy, S. M. (1964) Determining worker preferences among employee benefit programs. *Journal of Applied Psychology*, 48, pp. 7–12.

Newell, S. (2002) *Creating the Healthy Organisation: Well being, Diversity and Ethics at Work*. Thomson Learning (Psychology@Work Series): London.

Ostroff, C., Atwater, L. E. and Feinberg, B. J. (2004) Understanding self–other agreement: A look at rater and ratee characteristics, context and outcomes. *Personnel Psychology*, 57, pp. 333–376.

Patterson, F., Lane, P., Ferguson, E. and Norfolk, T. (2001) Competency based selection system for general practitioner registrars. *BMJ Classfied*, 1st September, pp. 2–3.

Patterson, M., West, M., Lawthom, R. and Nickell, S. (1998) *Issues in People Management*. IPD Report No 22. Institute for Personnel and Development: London (now CIPD, London).

Peyton, J. W. R. (2000) *Appraisal and Assessment in Medical Practice*. Manticore Europe Ltd: Rickmansworth.

Pollack, D. M. and Pollack, L. J. (1996) Using 360 degree feedback in performance appraisal. *Public Personnel Management*, 25, pp. 507–528.

Randall, R., Davies, H., Farrell, K. and Patterson, F. (2006) Selecting doctors for postgraduate training in paediatrics using a competency-based assessment centre. *Arch Dis Child*, 91, pp. 444–448.

Redman, T. and Snape, E. (1992) 'Upward and onward: Can staff appraise their managers?' *Personnel Review*, 21, pp. 32–46.

Rodgers, R. and Hunter, J. E. (1991) Impact of management by objectives on organisational productivity. *Journal of Applied Psychology Monograph*, 76, pp. 322–335.

Rose, M. (2001) *Recognising Performance; Non-cash Awards*. Chartered Institute of Personnel and Development: London.

Rushton, J. P. and Murray, H. G. (1985) On the assessment of teaching effectiveness in British universities. *Bulletin of the British Psychological Society*, 38, pp. 361–365.

Rynes, S. L., Gerhart, B. and Parks, L. (2005) Performance evaluation and pay for performance. *Annual Review of Psychology*, 56, pp. 571–600.

Salgado, J. F., Viswesvaran, C. and Ones, D. S. (2001) Predictors in personnel selection: An overview of constructs, methods and techniques. In N. Anderson, D. Ones, H. Sinangil and C. Viswesvaran (eds) *International Handbook of Industrial, Work and Organizational Psychology*. Sage: London.

Schneider, S. and Barsoux, J. (1997) *Managing Across Cultures*. Prentice Hall Europe: Hemel Hempstead.

Scott, S. B. (1983) Evolution of an appraisal programme. *Personnel Management.* August, pp. 28–30.

Shackleton, V. J. and Newall, S. (1997) International selection and assessment. In N. Anderson and P. Herriot (eds) *International Handbook of Selection and Assessment.* Wiley: Chichester.

Shipper, F., Hoffman, R. C. and Rotundo, D. M. (2002) *Does the 360 feedback process create actionable knowledge equally across cultures?* Paper presented at the Academy of Management Annual Conference, New Orleans, LA.

Simmons, J. and Iles, P. (2001) Performance appraisals in knowledge-based organisations: Implications for management education. *International Journal of Management Education,* 2, pp. 3–18.

Smith, P. B., Dugan, S. and Trompenaars, F. (1996) National culture and the values of organizational employees: A dimensional analysis across 43 nations. *Journal of Cross-Cultural Psychology,* 27, pp. 231–264.

Smith, P. C. and Kendall, L. M. (1963) Retranslation of expectations. *Journal of Applied Psychology,* 47, pp. 149–155.

Smither, J. W., London, M., Flautt, R., Vargas, Y. and Kucine, I. (2002) Does discussing multisource feedback with raters enhance performance improvement? Paper presented to Seventeenth Annual Conference of the Society for Industrial and Organizational Psychology, Toronto, April.

Smither, J. W., London, M., Flautt, R., Vargas, Y. and Kucine, I. (2003) Can working with an executive coach improve multisource feedback ratings over time? A quasi-experimental field study. *Personnel Psychology,* 56, pp. 23–44.

Smither, J. W. and Walker, A. G. (2004) Are the characteristics of narrative comments related to improvement in multi-rater feedback ratings over time? *Journal of Applied Psychology,* 89, pp. 575–581.

Smither, J. W., London, M. and Reilly, R. R. (2005) Does performance improve following multi-source feedback? A theoretical model, meta-analysis, and review of empirical findings. *Personnel Psychology,* 58, pp. 33–66.

Snape, E., Thompson, D., Ka-ching Ya, F. and Redman, T. (1998) Performance appraisal and culture: practice and attitudes in Hong Kong and Great Britain. *International Journal of Human Resource Management,* 9(5), pp. 841–861.

Sparrow, P. (1996) Too good to be true? *People Management,* 5 December, pp. 22–29.

Sparrow, P. and Cooper, C. L. (2003) *The Employment Relationship: Key Challenges for HR.* Elsevier: London.

Spreitzer, G. M., McCall, M. and Mahoney, J. D. (1997) Early identification of international executive potential. *Journal of Applied Psychology,* 82, pp. 6–29.

Stanton, J. M. (2000) Reactions to employee performance monitoring: Framework, review and research directions. *Human Performance,* 13, pp. 85–113.

Stillman, J. A. and Jackson, D. J. R. (2005) A detection theory approach to the evaluation of assessors in assessment centres. *Journal of Occupational and Organizational Psychology,* 78, pp. 581–594.

Stinson, J. and Stokes, J. (1980) How to multi-appraise. *Management Today,* June, pp. 43–53.

Storr, F. (2000) This is not a circular. *People Management,* May, pp. 38–40.

Strebler, M., Robinson, D. and Bevan, S. (2001) *Performance Review: Balancing Objectives and Content.* Institute for Empoyment Studies: Sussex.

Sturges, J., Conway, N., Guest. D. and Liefooghe, A. (2005) Managing the career deal: The psychological contract as a framework for understanding career management, organizational commitment and work behaviour. *Journal of Organizational Behavior*, 26(7), pp. 821–838.

Summers, D. (1991) BP exploration staff to assess managers' work. *Financial Times*, 7 May, p. 10.

Taylor, M. S., Tracy, K. B., Renard, M. K. and Harrison. (1995) Due process in performance appraisal: A quasi-experiment in procedural justice. *Administrative Science Quarterly*, 40, pp. 495–523.

Taylor, P. J. and Pierce, J. L. (1999) Effects of introducing a performance management system on employees' subsequent attitudes and effort. *Public Personnel Management*, 28, pp. 423–451.

Taylor, P. J. and Small, B. (2002) Asking applicants what they would do versus what they did do: A meta-analytic comparison of situational vesus past-behavior employment interview questions. *Journal of Occupational and Organizational Psychology*, 75, pp. 277–294.

Toplis, J., Dulewicz, S. V. and Fletcher, C. (2004) *Psychological Testing: A Manager's Guide*. 4th edn. Chartered Institute of Personnel and Development: London.

Triandis, H. C. and Brislin, R. W. (1984) Cross-cultural psychology. *American Psychologist*, 39, pp. 1006–1017.

Trompernaars, F. (1993) *Riding the Waves of Culture: Understanding Cultural Diversity in Business*. Economist Books: London.

Tyson, S. and Ward, P. (2004) The use of 360 degree feedback technique in the evaluation of management learning. *Management Learning*, 35(2), pp. 205–223.

Van Hooft, E. A. J., van der Flier, H. and Minne, M. R. (2006) Construct validity of multi-source performance ratings: An examination of the relationship of self-, supervisor- and peer-ratings with cognitive and personality measures. *International Journal of Selection and Assessment*, 14, pp. 67–81.

Walker, A. G. and Smither, J. W. (1999) A five year study of upward feedback: What managers do with their results matters. *Personnel Psychology*, 52, pp. 393–423.

Warr, P. B., Cook, J. and Wall, T. D. (1979) Scales for the measurement of some work attitudes and aspects of psychological well-being. *Journal of Occupational Psychology*, 52, pp. 129–148.

Weisband, S. and Atwater, L. (1999) Evaluating self and others in electronic and face-to-face groups. *Journal of Applied Psychology*, 84, pp. 632–639.

Weisner, W. H. and Cronshaw, S. F. (1988) A meta-analytic investigation of the impact of interview format and degree of structure on the validity of the employment interview. *Journal of Occupational Psychology*, 84, pp. 275–290.

Wensing, M. and Elwyn, G. (2003) Methods for incorporating patients' views in health care. *BMJ*, 326, pp. 877–879.

West, M. and Johnson, R. (2002) A matter of life and death. *People Management*, 21 February.

Wilkinson, S., Sanger, J. and Matheson, K. (2002) *The Use of Evidence in the Appraisal of Doctors*. Earlybrave Publications Ltd: Brentwood.

Williams, R. (1989) Alternative Raters and Methods. In P. Herriot (ed.) *Assessment and Selection in Organizations*. Wiley: Chichester.

Williams, R. (2002) *Managing Employee Performance: Design and Implementation in Organizations*. Thomson Learning (Psychology@Work Series): London.

Wolf, A. and Jenkins, A. (2006) Explaining greater test use for selection: The role of HR professionals in a world of expanding regulation. *Human Resource Management Journal*, 16, pp. 193–213.

Woodruffe, C. (2007) *Development and Assessment Centres: Identifying and Developing Competence*. Human Assets Ltd: London.

Wright, P. M., Lichtenfels, P. A. and Pursell, E. D. (1989) The Structured Interview: Additional studies and a meta-analysis. *Journal of Occupational Psychology*, 62, pp. 191–199.

Wright, V. (1991) Performance-related pay. In F. Neale (ed.) *The Handbook of Performance Management*. Institute of Personnel Management: London (now CIPD, London).

Zedeck, S. and Baker, H. T. (1972) Nursing performance as measured by behavioural expectation scales: A multitrait-multirater analysis. *Organisational Behaviour and Human Performance*, 7, pp. 457–466.

Index

Lightning Source UK Ltd.
Milton Keynes UK
UKOW050340031112

201620UK00003B/34/P